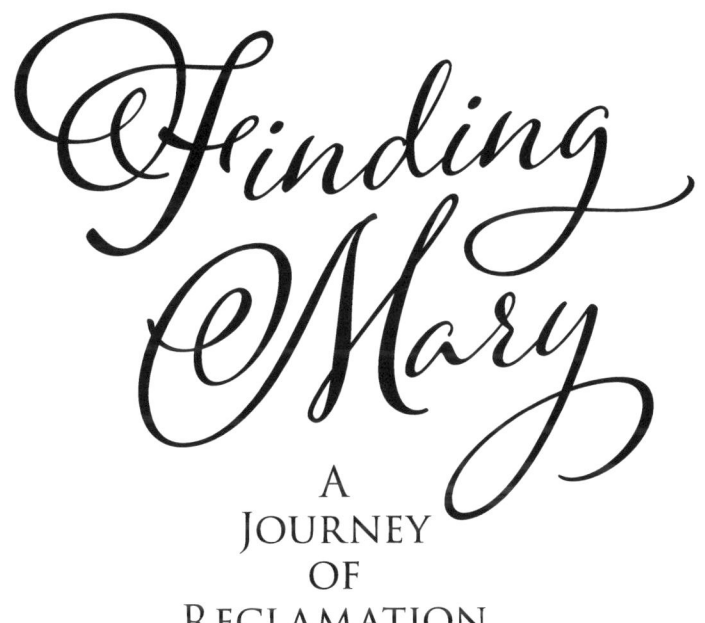

Finding Mary

A
Journey
of
Reclamation

Julie Rumrill

Red Bird Press

WEST HAVEN

First edition, March 2021, is printed in hardback by special arrangement with Red Bird Publishers. RedBirdPublishers.com

Printed in the United States of America

Paperback ISBN: 978-1-09835-603-3
eISBN: 978-1-09835-604-0

Cover design by *Periwinkle Sky Artisans*. Cover image location, outside of Orr Cove, Quaddick Lake, Thompson, CT.

Author note: While this is a true story, some names and identifying information have been changed to protect the privacy of those who appear in the pages.

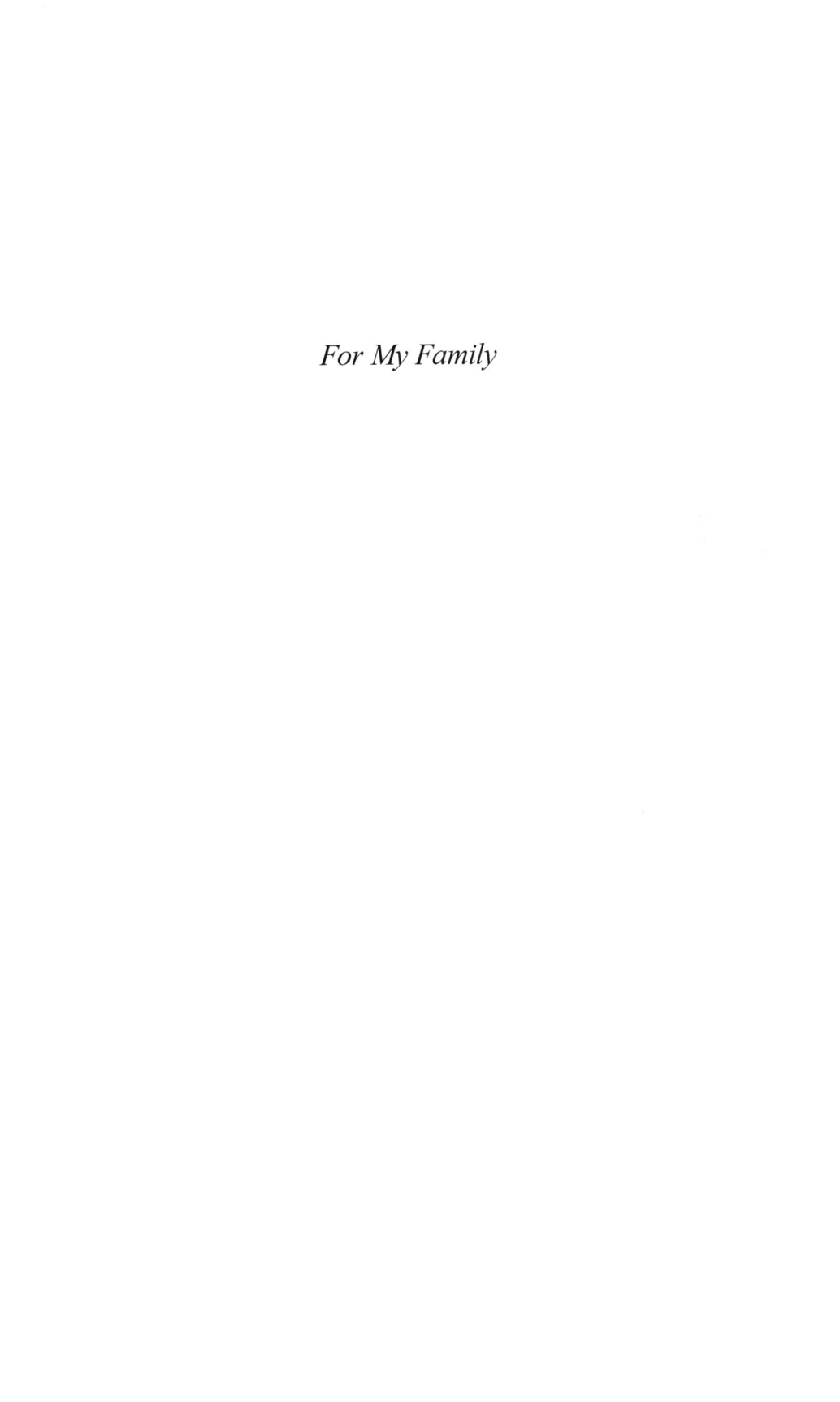

For My Family

CONTENTS

Introduction   3

PART ONE *Revenant*   5

PART TWO *Recollection*   47

PART THREE *Fractals*   111

PART FOUR *Charybdis*   201

PART FIVE *Transcendence*   305

Acknowledgments   341

Finding Mary

Introduction

We erased them from the family.

That was not our intention; it was survival.

We *had* to be strong. The 70's nearly broke us. After my sister Mary died in the summer of 1976, my older brother Kevin locked himself in his bedroom and blasted the song "Seasons in the Sun" by Terry Jacks, over and over on his turntable. I would knock on his door and ask him to play with me. The only response was the song itself. I would sit on the floor in the hallway, back against the door, knees pulled into my chest, listening to the somber lyrics. Lyrics about joy and laughter being brought to a shuddering halt.

It wasn't just Kevin; everyone in the family suffered in their own way, and none of us talked about it. We were still reeling from my sister Louise's murder three years earlier. I was 7 years old with endless questions and no answers. Questions made people sad. Questions made people angry.

Silence fed my deep-seated survivor's guilt, until it finally broke the surface four decades later.

* * *

Easter Sunday, April 5, 2015

The sun faded behind the trees as I drove home from dinner at my younger sister Nicole's house. I turned on the radio, set to a public broadcasting station out of New York. The host had just begun an interview with the parents of two children who were murdered in the Newtown massacre at Sandy Hook Elementary School. He explained that there is no word in the English language that refers to a bereaved parent, perhaps because no one should have to endure it.

I turned up the volume.

The host continued with a powerful statement: The surviving parents have one fear remaining—that the deceased children would be forgotten. I wiped my eyes, but truth kept refilling them.

Siblings fear this too.

When my older sisters, Louise and Mary, died over 40 years ago, their pictures came down, their belongings were packed away, and their names were not spoken. We lived with the unrelenting fear that in our silence, Louise and Mary would fade into obscurity, like colors exposed to the sun that were so vivid for a time.

I realized that I was the only one who could or would challenge the family contract of silence.

To know them again, to memorialize them, I have had to unearth the parts of me that could not be separated from my sisters; the parts I had buried with Louise and Mary in order to survive. This would come to involve reliving the experience of their loss. Pain that, being a child at the time, I had only felt the edges of. Pain that had so much to teach me about how impossible it was to shut off the past, shut down my emotions, and still try to connect with others.

At several points along the journey, fear and doubt nearly defeated me. I persevered; the timeless message carried along by the sound waves of that radio show ringing through my head.

They must not be forgotten.

PART ONE

Revenant

"One need not be a chamber to be haunted,
one need not to be a house. The brain has
corridors surpassing material place."

—Emily Dickinson.

Chapter 1:

Mary

Summer 1975 at Grandma's farm

We wriggled through the slats of the tractor gate and paused just long enough to fling off our sandals. The lane was paved with a shag carpet of emerald grass, cool and damp beneath our bare feet. Silky, honey-blonde hair swishing over her shoulders, Mary held the glass jar of milk with both hands as we hurried down the lane, past the umbrella-like shade of the mulberry tree.

She was seven years older than me, and her skinny legs had a stride twice as long as mine, but Mary kept a similar pace. Speeding up just made her cough and wheeze. We skipped past the garden with its neat rows of veggies, down the hill to the corner where our feet squished into the soil saturated by a spring and splotched with fresh cow manure, which made the grass taller but not us. We always stopped at this spot where just a few squeaky pumps of a long, rusty lever filled the cement trough, and cows could stop to dip their noses and slurp the cold groundwater.

Once a week we would navigate the entire length of the lane, more than a mile down and back, to bring milk to our bedridden Babcia, Polish for grandma. We knew her as Babcia even though she was our *great* grandma, because that's what Mom called her.

With pink cheeks and soggy hairlines, Mary and I finally reached the weathered grey, barn-board cabin with the oval, hand-braided rugs that looked like the inside of a kaleidoscope. The tiny cabin, warm and cozy, that always smelled like cloves, and where glittering streaks of sun filtered in through dusty panes and landed on Babcia just right so that she looked like one of the stained-glass angels in church.

We gave her the bottle of milk and lingering hugs and the energy of youth. If it was mid- to late-summer, the return trip up the lane to our Grandma's farm included a stop at the berry patch. We climbed up the stone wall and sat cross-legged, picking and eating high-bush blueberries until our fingers and tongues were stained with the sweetness of summer. The stone wall where yellow jackets built their papery nests and skittish garter snakes sunbathed. The stone wall built by hand by our Dziadzia, Polish for grandpa, pronounced Jah-joo. Piece by piece, he had assembled the sturdy boundary with rocks he cleared from the pastures several decades earlier. There Mary and I would sit, surrounded by an abundance of life: people, animal, vegetable and mineral, and enveloped by the scent of fresh-cut hay drying in the summer sun.

We filled re-purposed plastic containers from yogurt or sour cream, until berries tumbled over the rims, and then made-up rhymes or sang songs like "Row-row-row Your Boat," as we walked with the juicy cache back up the lane. Over the lush grass, we followed monarchs and periwinkle-blue butterflies, whistled to songbirds and mimicked the *whoo, whoo-whoo-whoo* of mourning doves.

Back at Grandma's house, we swept and washed and brought in wood, baked and cooked and kept Grandma company after Dziadzia died. When Mom brought Grandma to the Thrifty market, we pushed her cart and helped her grind fresh peanut butter and Eight O'Clock coffee. To show her appreciation, Grandma always let us pick out a candy bar. "Let's get the Caravelle," Mary would suggest. "It has two pieces, and we can share." That was Mary.

* * *

March 8, 1976

When the bedtime story ended and all was still right in my sleepy, almost 7-year-old world, Mary closed the Little Golden Book and set it on the narrow shelf between her diary and a Nancy Drew mystery she had borrowed from the library. She flipped off the light switch, climbed into bed, and pulled the covers up to our chins. I wrapped one arm around my favorite doll, Drowsy, and tugged at the retractable cord on her back. "I'm sleepy," she said. Mary and I giggled. The last thing Mary said to me was "goodnight." Drowsy and I curled up in the safety of our nest and drifted off to sleep, peaceful and safe under Mary's wing.

Panic disrupted our slumber sometime after midnight, as Mary was coughing and struggling to breathe. My older brother Shane rushed from his room, flipped on the hallway light, stuck his head into the doorway and then called downstairs to Mom. A glaring slice of light parted the darkness as I pushed the covers away and sat up next to her on our twin bed. She was almost 14, my big sister. Just half her age, I always looked to her for answers. I wasn't sure what to do.

Just a moment later, the old chestnut stair treads creaked under Mom's footsteps as she rushed up to our room. She flipped on the light and sat beside Mary, with one hand on her back and the other holding a Primatene inhaler to her mouth. I moved back and stayed out of the way. It was another asthma attack. She helped Mary down the stairs, and Dad carried her out to the car. I heard him shout to Mom, "Call the ER!"

Brake lights flashed on the gravel driveway just before the Malibu raced out of our yard, down the street, and out of sight.

The next morning, voices rose through the heat grate from the kitchen below. I slipped one arm out from the covers and reached over to wake Mary, but she wasn't there. The air in the room chilled my nose and with each breath formed wispy little clouds that disappeared almost as quickly as they arrived. I remembered the asthma attack. Mary was sick. She went to the hospital often. She'd be home later.

I glanced around at our wallpaper, covered with Shasta daisies in shades of watermelon, lemon, and lime. The small bookshelf packed with Little Golden books, the Magic 8-Ball, the conch shell, our pet rocks, birthstone jewelry, and Barbie Doll shoes. Frozen raindrops tapped against the window glass. I reached over and scratched at the paper-thin ice that coated the inside of the pane. Dark grey clouds blotted the sun. I heard Dad's voice, calling for me to come downstairs.

I peeled away the blankets, grabbed Drowsy, and hopped out of bed. The rough, hand-hewn floors of the 18th century cape chilled the soles of my feet. As I neared the middle of the staircase, I saw Dad.

I wondered why he had brought a chair from the kitchen table into the living room. He sat, bent forward with his forearms propped on his knees, hands together, and eyes down. When he noticed me, he pressed his back against the chair and opened his arms, as if to gather any bit of energy I had to offer.

I climbed up onto his lap, and he squeezed me tight. Daddy wasn't smiling or laughing. He didn't call me by my nickname, "Dodo Bird." He didn't start off our well-worn jingle: "My doh-da." To which I'd always reply: "My Dad-a." He would say: "My little pip squeak." And I would return the affectionate jab with: "My big fat tub-o-lard!" No. Today there was no banter.

He held my shoulders and faced me, his cheeks and eyes wet with tears.

"Your sister Mary died last night."

At once everything froze except my thoughts—racing with worry and confusion. What did that mean? I could hear Daddy breathing and crying. His words had tumbled out fast, almost as though if he said it quick enough, the truth would be gone and not return. But the words were as permanent as Mary's departure from this world.

Still gripping Drowsy by the arm, I held Daddy tightly, like he held me whenever I cried. "It's okay, Daddy." I couldn't focus on the words, his or mine. Holding onto him, I was desperately holding on to life. His world was my world—if he crumbled, so would I. The thought of not having control is terrifying. In that moment, I was as terrified as a person could be.

"But you won't ever be able to play with her again," he explained.

"That's okay, Daddy," I repeated. "It will be okay."

With my face buried in his shoulder, I squeezed my eyes shut and pulled Drowsy close to us.

It's okay, Daddy. It will be okay. But even though I had yet to reach 7, I had already learned that sometimes life was *not* okay. I knew that when my big sister Louise died three years earlier, she left and never came home. People left and didn't come home. Pets left and didn't come home. I didn't know where they went. Whenever I asked, Mom would get upset and say they were in Heaven, but I didn't know where that was. In the clouds? Which cloud? I didn't see them. I didn't ask anymore. They were just dead. I sometimes worried about who would be dead next.

Push it down. Hold it there. Be strong. Be happy. Don't look for attention. Don't ask questions. Clean up your toys. Help out. Be good. Be quiet. Behave.

You go to sleep with a big sister and wake up alone.

***

In total, Mom and Dad had thirteen children between them. Yet over the years, the number living at our little compound on Brandy Hill Road waxed and waned in a confounding mix of birth and death. When Mom and Dad had me, I joined the sibs I refer to as the *old family:* four children from Mom's first marriage--Louise, Tammy, Shane, and Mary; one child from Mom's second marriage—Kevin; and three boys from Dad's first marriage – Bobby, Dicky, and Harold – who lived at the house for short periods, but mostly visited on the weekends. Dad's boys were similar in ages to Louise, Tammy, and Shane, but their presence, particularly after Mary died, did not comfort Mom, and that was clear.

We had become a house of people anesthetized by loss. A house that hung suspended as time passed by. Each of us dormant within our own protective shell, having elected to isolate ourselves from the world outside, from our emotions, and from each other. As if punishing ourselves for being duped yet again. And we became strong. And we became insensitive. And we survived.

We turned into people who mocked the unfamiliar, who didn't try new things, didn't move too far because we were taught the excruciatingly painful lesson that the world is dangerous, unpredictable, and scary. It doesn't care what you want. It will crush you like an empty can. You'll be destined to crawl around for the rest of your life, flattened, mangled, never to be filled again. We secretly envied and resented those who were foolish enough to take risks, to push boundaries, to seek connection. Those who thought nothing of venturing outside of their small, known world with their suitcase full of sunshine and cluelessness. They weren't safe, and they didn't even realize it. But we did.

That cynical view of life, rooted in loss, was powerful and persistent. It ruled our home for decades and shaped my personality and the personalities of my four younger sisters, even though they were born after Louise's death and had no recollection of Mary at all.

Eventually, I found a comfortable niche where questions were welcomed, hypervigilance was a valued skill, and skepticism was appreciated—I became a scientist. But unchecked grief cannot be educated away or outflanked by a career change. It continued to unfurl its long, spindly fingers, reaching, clawing, and reminding—*watch out for me*. Grief cast aside never disappears.

It will eventually demand a reckoning.

Chapter 2:

The Embarkation

Quaddick Lake, Thompson, CT, early summer 2014

I wasn't thinking about Mary when the day began. I woke early, poured a cup of good, strong coffee, and ambled out to the deck. I sat on the lounger and watched as the sun stretched its arms wide, fingers of warmth reaching through the branches and over the tops of the white pines, oaks, and maples. A light breeze tickled the water and broke the surface of the lake into a trillion miniature suns.

It was so quiet I could hear the subtle wingbeats of Purple finches and Nuthatches nervously flitting as they approached the feeder. Summer at the lake was when I renewed, refreshed, and recharged from a busy semester of lecturing at the university. When I was teaching classes, I spent more time at our small home near the Long Island Sound in West Haven, Connecticut, and on semester breaks I spent more time at our Lake House in the quiet corner of Thompson. That summer was a time to continue my perennial deliberation of whether to embark on a PhD.

My husband, Eric, shook his head whenever I raised the subject. "It takes you forever to make a decision. Just do it." As a veteran police officer, he was trained that hesitation can be fatal, but I preferred a slow, methodical approach to decisions, and my science work in academia allowed me to isolate myself in a comfortable world with controlled variables and logical outcomes. I was hesitant to leave that zone of safety to be a full-time student again. I reclined in the lounger, pressed a pen to paper, and scratched out a list of pros and cons.

I valued progress, constant forward motion, and the mantra—*set goals, reach them, repeat.* Yet approaching midlife, this was increasingly difficult. It was as if I had reached the hypothetical point of zero acceleration. Like the classic example in physics where a ball is tossed into the air, reaches its maximum height, and pauses at the top of the arc before completing its journey to the ground. I was sensing a dramatic shift in viewpoint.

Why was it so hard to move forward? It felt like some critical piece of evidence, some necessary component, was missing. As was the case when making all big decisions in my life, I was missing Mary.

You go to sleep with a big sister and wake up alone.

Stop feeling sorry for yourself.

I continued working on my list. The cell phone rang. I glanced down at the screen. It was Dad.

"You wouldn't have time to follow me to the garage, would you? I need to drop off my car for service," he said.

"Sure. When do you want to leave?"

"Whenever you're ready."

"I'll be right over." Glad to escape my contemplative perch on the deck, I slid into some jeans and a hoodie, and gathered my hair into a messy knot on the top of my head. I glanced at myself in the mirror, doubtful for only a moment when I heard one of Dad's famous lines: *If they don't like it, they don't have to look.* Out the door, up the dirt road, past the O'Leary's dairy farm and the Thompson Rod and Gun club, I arrived at *The Compound*, Mom and Dad's house, about three miles away.

The Compound has changed little since my childhood. A small white cape surrounded by woods, wetlands, stone walls, and outbuildings, and occupied by chickens, a pony, several cats, and a dog. The most notable difference is sound. The clamor of children having been replaced by scampering chipmunks, swaying trees, and birdsong.

I followed Dad on the 20-minute drive to the Toyota dealer. We walked in together and he immediately asked a salesman if Rob was working. "Oh, I think he's around here somewhere," was the person's response.

Dad turned to me. "Rob sold me the Prius." That made sense. Dad bonds easily with people who are friendly toward him and tries to keep the connection, oblivious to whether the relationship was, in this case, motivated by a potential commission.

We kept walking, and Dad said hello to a few more people whom he remembered, but who clearly did not distinguish him from the scores of *buyers* who walk through the doors. I thought about how business probably used to be done when Dad was younger. He clearly saw things through that lens. It's one of the things I find endearing about him.

We reached the service department through a set of double-glass doors. The loud, bustling racket of pneumatic wrenches and air compressors echoed against the corrugated metal walls of the warehouse-sized garage. The stench of exhaust and solvents hung thick in the air. I stood at the counter, watching Dad's interaction with the thirty-something service advisor. Dad seemed to remember him by name too. "Hi Mike, I'm here to drop off my two-twelve Prius for service." Instead of the full year, Dad always abbreviates the year 2012 as "two-twelve." It is a quirk that would have annoyed me when I was a teenager, and I would have been quick to correct, but now it's just one of the things that makes him *Dad.*

The attendant typed in some info and asked how many miles were on the Prius. Dad responded first with a corny joke and then gave a number.

"Just an oil change and tire rotation. Should be 'bout a half hour," the attendant responded.

"Do you want to go for coffee while we wait?" I suggested.

Dad's face beamed. "Damn right. I'm buying."

I turned left out of the dealership, crossing two lanes of oncoming traffic, which has made me nervous since I began driving in 1986. I was a junior in high school, living at The Compound with my four younger sisters. I was the oldest of the kids at home, full of typical teenage angst and the belief that life hated my family. So I hated life right back. My driving habits had mirrored this anger and impatience, and I caused two accidents that year both due to "improper left turns." Mom's response was to worry about the cost of repairs and the insurance rates (understandable, in retrospect). Dad asked if I was okay and took me back out driving as soon as possible. I didn't want to get behind the wheel again. But he taught me that to overcome my fears, I had to face them.

I pulled into the parking lot of a Dunkin' Donuts a couple of blocks away. We ordered two cups of coffee at the counter and then found a place to sit near the TV. We glanced occasionally at the news and chatted. I was reminded what great company Dad is. Dad is an interesting and versatile conversationalist. A construction worker in his younger days, he has also worked in the fabric mills, and as a repair and maintenance specialist. He has the priceless gift of a mechanical mind. He can build or fix anything, and his contagious smile and prankster nature can lighten the gloomiest of moods. I thought about how as a child, I sometimes felt his presence was my lifeline.

After everyone else in the house had gone to bed, Drowsy and I would sit on the couch, battling to stay awake until Dad came home from his weekend gig in the band. I woke to the jingling sound of his keys in the lock. He wriggled through the self-closing screen door and into the house, barely visible, arms loaded with his guitar, microphone stand, two-liter bottle of soda, potato chips, and candy. After he hung up his jacket and put everything away, I raided his change purse and then we sat on the couch together and watched a Vincent Price or Boris Karloff thriller. More correctly, he would watch, and I would burrow into the space between his side and the back of the couch, curl up my knees to my chest, and peek through the slits between my fingers. If he was there,

I was safe. We were each other's solace. We were each other's strength. We still are.

"Dad, do you remember watching Boris Karloff?" I asked.

"Of course. Do you remember raiding my change?"

Just then an ad came on the Dunkin' Donuts TV for a new asthma inhaler. Our attention was drawn to the commercial. It was as if the TV was a time machine that dragged us back to 1976.

"They have so much more medicine now than they did then," Dad remarked.

I knew exactly the 'then' he was referring to. I nodded. The tag at the back of my neck began to itch. I shifted in my chair, eyes focused on the cup in my hands, but my mind was in the small bedroom with the daisy wallpaper and slanted ceiling. In our family, Mary was *never* discussed. Yet on that day, Dad began talking.

"I got up that night and got fully dressed. I don't know what made me do that. I guess something told me this was a bad one. Your mom went upstairs when she heard Mary coughing. She gave her the inhaler. It wasn't helping. I wanted your mother to come with me, but she didn't want to. I told her to call the ER. To let them know we were on our way. I drove as fast as I could. Had the flashers on and didn't stop for any red lights. Little Mary said, 'Daddy, please hurry.' That was the last thing she said."

I swallowed hard and fought the tears. I could imagine the blue Chevy Malibu racing through the streets of the sleepy town. Dad's left hand gripping the wheel, his right-hand holding Mary's frail body on the seat as momentum pulled her away.

It is seven miles from our house in Thompson to the hospital in Putnam—about a 14-minute drive. Dad got there in about ten minutes that night. He pulled up to the emergency room doors and rushed inside with Mary, who was unconscious and not breathing. He pleaded for a miracle but had to take the longest, loneliest drive of his life back to The Compound.

Dad stared into his coffee cup; tears slid down his cheeks. I offered him a napkin, but he shook his head. He was 40 years removed, holding Mary in his arms. I leaned forward and rested a hand on his shoulder. He seemed ashamed, embarrassed, and guilt-ridden. Maybe he was uncomfortable showing emotion in public; maybe he believed men of his generation were supposed to be too strong to cry; or maybe he felt awkward crying about a loss that was still so raw after four decades; maybe he felt he should have driven faster.

He turned toward the window, eyes searching the clouds. "If I had known CPR, things might have been different."

So *that* was where the guilt originated.

"Dad, it was asthma. It wouldn't have mattered. You shouldn't blame yourself."

The truth was I didn't know if CPR could have saved her. I just hated to see him cry. I was instantly 6-years-old and helpless, the day he told me that Mary died. *It's okay, Daddy*, was the only thing I could think of. But clearly both our lives had changed forever.

Once again, nearly 40 years later here in this coffee shop, Dad was crying for Mary. Once again, I sat with him, unsure of what to do. I began to stand up, but then sat back down. I moved my chair closer to his and held his strong hand, which could lift any weight yet was no match for the heaviness of loss.

The raw pain of grief smothered our conversation. Grief locked away, grief with no relief valve.

The TV continued to rattle off news somewhere in the background. Then Dad mentioned something about the Prius being done soon. I nodded. As I took the last few sips of my coffee, he scrubbed at stains on the tabletop with his paper napkin. If we were outside, he would have started clipping his fingernails.

Push it down. Hold it there.

But I didn't want him to push this away again. "I'd like to visit her grave sometime if you want to go with me," I said, almost without realizing I'd spoken out loud. "I've never gone there."

Dad met my glance, cleared his throat, and straightened up in his chair. "Yes. I want to go. I kept asking your mother every time we were in Webster, but she never wanted to stop."

"One day this summer," I offered, taken aback that the subject had even come up.

* * *

The exchange with Dad forced me to look directly at an old promise I made after Mary died: that I would give *anything*, including my own happiness, to lessen my parents' pain. A large part of that promise included upholding the family contract of silence, which I obeyed for years. Yet as I sat in the coffee shop with Dad, far from the days of being a frightened 6-year-old, still mired in unresolved grief, I realized the futility of that contract.

I felt our solid bedrock of denial shift along one of its few lines of weakness, a fault named Mary. It was as if speaking her name released some mysterious energy. For Dad, and apparently me as well, the contract was being questioned and opportunity fluttered in the newly created space; a kaleidoscope of butterflies circling, hovering, and invoking action. I knew the conversation at the coffee shop was only the beginning. I needed to talk with *both* of my parents about this difficult time in our lives. This might sound relatively easy to you.

But that's because you haven't met Mom.

Chapter 3:

Irritable heart

At The Compound, 2010

I knew the gun shot was coming, but I still flinched. I understood why she did it, but the second shot was still unsettling. She tossed the feline carcass over the stone wall and hurried toward my car. She carefully placed the 22-rifle on the floor in the back and straightened up for inspection. "Do I have any blood on me?" she asked.

"I don't see any."

She gave an affirming nod, sat down in the passenger seat and buckled her seat belt. "Okay. Let's go."

I hesitated to put the car in gear. "Do you want to wash your hands?"

"I don't want to be late for church. Let's go."

I had picked her up that morning and was pulling out of the driveway when she noticed the cat. It had been hit by a car and lay growling in pain, among the leaves and mud on the side of the road, its two hind legs flattened. Mom had recognized it as one of the neighborhood strays she often fed. "Oh— how awful. Go back to the house," she had said. "I have to get my gun."

And there I was, driving her to church with the gun in the back seat, still processing what had just happened. This woman bakes cookies with her grandchildren. This woman saves vegetable peels and cooks them for her chickens. This woman didn't hesitate to aim her 22-rifle in the face of suffering and squeeze the trigger.

Where the hell did I come from?

"Are you traumatized?" she asked, half joking, perhaps trying to lighten my mood.

"No. I get it. The cat was suffering."

"Yes. You should never let something suffer. That's cruel."

I could have suggested taking the cat to a vet, maybe having it put to sleep, but I knew better. I could write an infinite list of things that would make me look like a jackass to my mother. Unnecessary displays of emotion are near the top.

My relationship with Mom has often been difficult. She's a tough lady. She's into her 70s and hasn't slowed down much. She still cuts down trees with Dad, has a bigger garden than ever, and takes care of a coop full of chickens, a dog, several feral cats, and a 30-year-old pony. During her years working as a clerk at the local convenience store, she was held up at knifepoint twice and both times returned to work the next day. One spring, while prepping the soil in her garden, her hand got pulled into the belt of the rototiller and it cut the end of her middle finger off. One of the first comments she made was that God was punishing her for using that finger too often.

Despite how it may seem, she does care about appearances. When I was 14, I got a sewing machine needle stuck in my finger, and she took me to the emergency room. After I put some decent clothes on.

But maybe I should ease you into things.

* * *

I was born into a patchwork family of assorted half-siblings, where people argued over whose turn it was to spoil me. Mom was no exception. My earliest memory of us bonding as mother and daughter was the first time she introduced me to the sea. Surrounded by our family at Quonochontaug Beach in Rhode Island (locals call it "Quonnie"), Mom was 31, and I was a little more than a year old. A photo shows us surrounded by her brood, five of my half-sibs, two boys, and three girls ranging in age from 5 to 13 years. A caption scrawled in Mom's handwriting neatly summarized the splendid moment in our lives—"everybody at the ocean." *Everybody indeed.* Well, except for Dad's three boys, my older half-brothers, Bobby, Dicky, and Harold. Our family was so big and so blended, it made the Brady Bunch seem ridiculously simple.

My outfit was sparse, a sagging cloth diaper with silver safety pins, and a floppy, cotton sunhat. Mom held my right hand; my sister Louise held my left. The other kids gathered around us as Dad took the photo. As a family, we were like the beach sand, an interesting collection of sediments with different origins. Louise, Tammy, Shane, and Mary are my half-siblings from Mom's first marriage; Kevin is my half-brother from Mom's second marriage; and lastly, Dad and I are the newcomers to the family.

We walked in the chilly Atlantic, gentle waves nudging quartz grains at our feet. Breakers crashed on rock jetties in the distance, smashing the smooth ocean surface and spraying a beaded curtain of saltwater into the breeze. Seagulls circled above the rocks, awaiting a meal of fresh crabs and mussels at low tide.

Everyone had homemade bathing suits stitched on Mom's Singer sewing machine. Louise, Tammy, and Mary wore matching bikinis in a celery-green fabric printed with white flowers. Mom wore a black bikini with a vertical row of white buttons on each piece. Shane and Kevin wore simple black swim trunks.

I sat on the shore surrounded by my family and, while 'helping' them build a shimmering castle, stuffed a fistful of sand in my mouth. The day imprinted me with the salty, gritty taste of sand, and the energy of the shore as a place of restoration and true solace. It was a time when Mom's affection was a tender gathering point.

The sun warmed us, the sea entertained us, and Mom held me close on that carefree summer afternoon. It seemed like nothing could go wrong. We were all together, building castles, holding hands, and eating sand.

* * *

Mom was glamorous. She looked like Jackie Kennedy-Onassis in her large dark sunglasses and sheer scarf, knotted at the nape of her neck to gather her sleek, dark chocolate ponytail. Her lips shimmered in trendy, shell-pink lipstick, and her deep-set, brown eyes needed barely a sweep of dark liner, mascara, and frosted eyeshadow. She wore tasteful slacks and blouses, perfectly tailored at home on her Singer machine.

"She was the most beautiful thing I ever saw." Dad has recalled about the time they met. "I used to make excuses to go into the spinning room at work, just so I could see her."

Mom was petite and thin, even after five children. She was able to conceal me from Grandma throughout her pregnancy. She already had four children with her first husband, and one child with the second. She did not want to have to explain a baby out of wedlock to a Polish-Catholic woman from the old country. Mom's trick was to wear baggy clothes and not visit often, although it certainly helped that Grandma was not very observant of fashion or weight. After she retired from the mill, housework was Grandma's life. If you couldn't sweep it, wash it, cook it, or burn it, generally it wasn't worth her time.

My relationship with Mom was rocky from the start. After I was born, Mom took me and the other kids over to the farm to visit Grandma and Dziadzia. Mom claimed that I was the child of a friend whom Louise and Tammy were babysitting. I don't know how long it was before Grandma figured it out. Perhaps she was never fooled to begin with.

Mom has always told the truth when she saw fit and lied the rest of the time; a behavior she modeled after Grandma. Grandma was from a long line of fearless women and wasn't shy about letting that be known. On more than one occasion, she banged her fist on the table and exclaimed, "*My* mother wasn't afraid of anybody; *her* mother wasn't afraid of anybody; and *I'm* not afraid of anybody."

Grandma smoked Cuba berries from a corncob pipe, helped her brother make and sell moonshine during the prohibition, and owned several real-estate properties before she was married. Although, if you'd asked her, she'd have stoically denied the smoking and the liquor.

Apparently, it wasn't just the Bardy *women* who were fearless. Grandma's six brothers were entrepreneurs, authors, professional boxers, bootleggers, fortune-tellers, and war heroes.

The Bardys were *all* fearless, except for Uncle Joe. He had a nervous breakdown after he returned from the war and had to spend time in what Grandma referred to as 'the nut house'. He had a condition called "irritable heart," which is now known as Post Traumatic Stress Disorder (PTSD). The family didn't talk about it. Weakness was shameful. Going to the nut house was shameful. It was nobody's business.

Mom agreed.

* * *

If Mom's tenacity sounds extreme, consider the summer of 1973. When I pushed open the screen door and ran like the wind, as fast as my 4-year-old legs would carry me, toward Mom and Dad who stood at the edge of the driveway. They didn't see me at first. They were talking to the policeman. Mom snapped at Shane to take me in the house. I squirmed and whined. I wanted to be outside with them, Dad was upset, something was wrong. I wanted to see the policeman. I wanted to ask him to please bring Louise home.

Mom had spent nearly 17 years raising Louise, stitching matching outfits for her and Tammy, packing school lunches in brown paper bags, hanging her artwork on the fridge, watching her build relationships with siblings and friends, helping her grow into a young woman with her own beliefs, dreams, and personality. And then one night Louise didn't come home. Mom told me she was riding her bicycle and was hit by a car. I was in my early teens before I finally learned the truth.

Louise was murdered.

Three days after Louise went missing, she was found. The police called Mom to identify her first-born child at the morgue.

What does *that* do to a person?

* * *

There was no time for grief. Life moves on and death chooses another. Two years later, Mom's dad--her ally in gardening and avoiding grandma's scorn--my dziadzia, got sick.

I could barely see him over the edge of the bed, but I knew it was Dziadzia because of his hand. His hands with creased skin, puffed veins, fingers with leathery pads, strong fingers for gripping farm tools, lifting hay bales, and tying rope. His hands that helped me tie my shoes and showed me how to pluck Japanese beetles form the cornstalks. The same hands that cradled Mom when she was a baby, that later taught her how to grasp weeds by their stems and pull them out by the root, how to milk the Holsteins without getting kicked, and how to turn a cardboard box into a cozy shelter for a litter of barn kittens.

I thought of the way he ate dinner with the wooden-handled fork with the long tines, which was my favorite—for eating, and for untying knots in my shoelaces. At the time I didn't know he was dying. I just knew Dziadzia was very sick. He had tubes, machines, and wires connected to his arms and face and plastic bags filled with liquid hanging near his bed. I wanted to climb up and hug him, but then Mom saw me. "You shouldn't be in here," she snapped—and whisked me out. I wanted to stay with Dziadzia. I loved him too. That was the last time I saw him.

* * *

Not everyone is built to be a Bardy. I certainly didn't seem to inherit the fearless gene. After Mary died, I felt alone and afraid. At times I made the mistake of showing it. That's when Mom and I truly diverged.

Darkness terrified me. At 7 years old, I hated sleeping alone. Mom seemed to think she could *tough* it out of me, or perhaps she just knew that there were far worse things than the dark.

Kevin, my older half-brother by four years, showed no empathy either. "Ghosts? You don't know shit from Shinola." In retrospect, he was probably suffering too, but he never seemed to show it.

In my eyes, Kevin was a fearless predator. He hunted small animals with his 22 rifle. The mention of a woodchuck in the garden delighted him. It was an excuse to kill. Despite his violent nature, I gravitated to him. After Mary died, life was nebulous, and I desperately needed to feel grounded. I wanted an older sibling to look up to. He was my hero-by-default.

Despite Kevin's status, I tried not to rely on him. Most nights, I just sobbed under a twisted heap of blankets until I was exhausted and fell asleep, but when Dad was home, he rescued me.

One such time, the old wooden stair treads creaked under the weight of footsteps. I waited, curled up stiff and silent, clutching Drowsy.

"Where are you?" Dad asked, peeling away layer upon layer of blankets and stuffed toys. "And why is this bed such a mess?"

I dug my way out, sat on his lap, and held him and Drowsy tightly. "I heard a noise. It was a ghost. Or a monster."

"That was me. No monsters or ghosts in *this* house. I don't let them in," Dad explained, rubbing my back, trying to calm me down.

But I knew better. There *were* ghosts in the house. And there were probably monsters too. Like the ones I had seen on television. I had heard them move around at night. We *ALL* lived in the house. They were real to me.

Dad pushed the wet strands of hair from my face. "Come on, let's fix this bed. You can't sleep like this."

I climbed down from his lap, and together, we slid the entire mountain of pillows, blankets, and little stuffed soldiers onto the floor and untangled the heap, bit by bit. We reassembled the bed into an orderly nest. I worked slowly, trying to delay the inevitable. Drowsy and I were the last additions as Dad turned down one corner of the newly rebuilt and fortified bunker. He tucked the blankets up under my chin, and gave me a hug and a kiss goodnight.

I hated to see him go. I wanted to crawl into bed with him and Mom. But Mom said I was too old for that. They only had a full-size bed. I didn't want to make them argue.

"Please—can you leave the stairway light on?" I begged.

"I will," he promised. *Creak. Creak. Creak.* As he made his way down the stairs, farther and farther away from me.

I lay there frozen, eyes darting, searching, studying every twitch of a shadow, analyzing every sound. Then I heard footsteps at the bottom of the stairs. I always knew when Dad fell asleep. Mom promptly shut off the light.

Months after the bunker-building episode, as my fear of the dark lingered, I became increasingly anxious and aware that it caused arguments between Mom and Dad.

"If you keep going up there, she'll never be able to fall asleep by herself," I overheard Mom lecture.

I hated to hear them argue more than I hated the dark. One night after a bad dream, fear made me desperate. I crawled out of bed, tiptoed down the hall, and knocked on Kevin's door.

"What do you want?" he barked without getting up.

I pressed my face to the door-jamb. "Can I sleep in your room?" I begged in a whisper.

"No. You have your own bed."

"Please. I'm scared. I hear the ghosts."

"You're such a baby." Kevin pulled the light chain and yanked open the door. "Get a blanket. You can sleep on the floor. Hurry up. And stop whining."

I ran to my room, grabbed a corner of the bedspread, and dragged it down the hall just inside the doorway of his room. I curled up with Drowsy on the wide plank floor, bundling up against the cold drafts, dust, and mice, but mostly the ghosts. "Please don't tell Mom."

He turned off the light.

The next morning, we went to the farm to help with the chores. Kevin and I shoveled cow manure into the wheelbarrow, and Mom set up the pail and sat down on the wooden stool to milk Bossy, the black and white Holstein. Kevin puffed out his chest and proudly announced the secret to Mom. "Julie's afraid of ghosts." He glanced toward me, to delight in my reaction, as he proceeded to tell the story.

That betrayal was the end of his reign as my hero-by-default.

Mom stopped milking and leaned out from around the back of the cow, eyes narrow and angry. "There's no such thing as ghosts. Sleep in your own room."

That was the last time I ever divulged my fears to anyone in my family.

* * *

Special traditions fell away as well. When Mary was alive, we used to celebrate Christmas with abandon. It had been her favorite holiday. Mom would tear out craft ideas from the latest issue of *Family Circle* and the three of us would create them. One of my favorites was the pinecone wreath. We trudged into the woods to gather pinecones and branches in a brown paper grocery bag. At the edge of the swamp, we clipped and gathered stalks of red berries. We carried our spoils back to the house, scrubbed the sap and dirt from our fingers, and warmed our hands over the woodstove.

Mom placed the pinecones on sheets of old newspaper and coated them with gold or silver spray paint. Mary and I fanned out the pine boughs so any ice would melt away and bent the arms of a wire coat hanger into a circle to make a base for the wreath. When everything was dry, we attached the newly gilded treasures to our wire base with bread ties. After the entire hanger was filled, we attached small fans of hunter green pine needles and a few twigs of red berries. Simple, fun, and festive.

After Mary's death, Mom and I didn't make Christmas crafts together. Holidays can be hell for the bereft. Memories seem almost unbearable, and the sense that people are missing is inescapable. She not only avoided fanfare, but suffered so greatly, the phrase "I hate Christmas" became the new holiday tradition.

* * *

As the years passed, Shane moved out, and Kevin got his license and was seldom around. At the age of 12, I was the oldest at home, and often put in charge of the *new family*—my four younger sisters—born after Louise's death. Renee was 8, Angela was 7, Robyn was 5, and Nicole was just a few months old. I hated the responsibility of babysitting, but I liked order and rules and kept a tally sheet on the fridge whenever someone disobeyed. They nicknamed me *The Sergeant*.

One of my self-appointed responsibilities included defending Mom's occasionally perplexing and frightening behavior. Every so often she would have an emotional meltdown at what seemed like a slight annoyance. To avoid this, when approaching her with a question, we learned to preface it with "Mom, don't yell..."

One summer afternoon, I was huddled upstairs on the floor with the new family, trying to convince them that Mom wasn't really going to kill herself.

A few minutes earlier, we had been playing outside as we normally did when it wasn't raining. My younger sisters, Renee, Angela, Robyn, and I were making mud pies and tuna surprise in our wooded fort across the road. We reached a critical amount of time together and started to argue. The details went something like this: Robyn was upset because she didn't want to have tuna surprise, made from punky wood which flaked exactly like tuna fish from a can; Renee was mad because Angela stole the pan she was using; and I was just tired of watching them because I really wanted to work on my BMX trail.

We ran into the house, pushing and squeezing through the door like subway riders during rush hour, each racing to be the first to tell our version of the story. Mom stood at the kitchen sink doing dishes, and she reluctantly turned to face the barrage of complaints running into the house at her.

After about 10 seconds of *Mom-she-did-this-she-did-that* tattling, Mom snapped back. "Don't you kids know I don't feel good?" Then she launched into a tirade. "Why can't you kids just play? Why do you have to get me upset? Nobody helps me! I wish I never had kids! Maybe I'll go into the woods and kill myself." She threw the sopping wet dish rag on the floor, stormed past us, flung the door open, and went outside.

Amidst their crying and sniffling, I marshaled my sisters up to the safety and comfort of that small room at the top of the stairs. The room that I had shared with Mary in what seemed like a separate lifetime—another family.

They huddled together on the floor. I sat cross-legged, twisting my ponytail, trying to think about what I should do. "She didn't mean what she said," was all I could muster. I was afraid too. At 12-years-old, I didn't know about PTSD or what depression was or anything at all about the grief loop or that the month of June was a trigger because that's when Louise was killed.

"I don't want her to die," Renee pleaded between sobs, trying to catch her breath.

"She's not going to. Everything will be okay."

They held each other as I stood up and went to the window. What part of this was my fault? I wasn't helping out. I needed to do better.

In that room, we waited. I prayed that nothing bad would happen. I tried to distract them. "Do you want to play Barbies in the attic?" They *always* went for that.

Sniffles and silence.

After a time, I noticed Mom returning from the path in the woods and thanked God. I heard her moving about in the kitchen below. She finished washing the dishes. We went back outside and across the street to our fort. I would try harder. I didn't want her to die. I didn't want her to go to the nut house.

* * *

It was *her* grief. It was *huge*. And nobody had ever dared to question it. Until me. Until now.

Yet I had no idea how to approach her for fear of setting her off. I couldn't imagine having a heartfelt conversation with her about Mary. Would Mom be angry at me for breaking the contract? Ashamed of me for still holding onto sadness all these years? For being weak? The more I thought about talking to Mom, the more anxious I became.

Push it down. Hold it there. Be strong.

For heaven's sake—act like a Bardy.

Chapter 4:

The Shell

Early January, 2015

In my home state of Connecticut and elsewhere, there is an aquatic invasive species called horse-chestnut. It is a vine-like, aquatic plant that spreads by germination of a thorny nut that anchors itself into the muddy lake bottom. If conditions are hostile, it can remain there, dormant for 10 years. My family could teach the horse-chestnut a thing or two. We could stay dormant for over four decades.

* * *

What I needed to do was simple. I had to approach Mom and address the hard, spiky casing of our dormant relationship. I had to be fearless.

Simple does not mean easy.

Seven months passed since my conversation with Dad at the coffee shop. We had seen each other several times, but neither of us brought up Mary. The end of the semester had kept me occupied with students scrambling to submit final projects and final exams. The work chaos transitioned to the Christmas rush without skipping a beat, but then--an abundance of quiet. One solitary afternoon, I stretched out on the sofa in the loft at The Lake House, Mary's conch shell pressed to my ear, pondering New Year's resolutions, and how one becomes fearless.

I set down the shell to search for a notebook when the cloth cover of an old journal caught my attention. It was from the summer of 2002 during fieldwork in Kenya. I leafed through pages where I had sketched local plants, translated Swahili words, recorded data on game counts, and kept notes on interviews with the Maasai. Tucked into the binding, I found a letter written by my nephew Michael, who was 7-years-old at the time.

I recalled the student affairs manager passing out mail one evening at dinner time, as the field study group gathered under the thatched roof of the *Chumba*, or community area. I eagerly tore open the envelope and, with one palm on my chest, read his words. In the letter Michael asked, "Why did you go so far away from me?"

Instantly, my heart was in a vice. Fellow students consoled me as I tucked the letter back in the envelope.

Thirteen years later, tears filled my eyes again.

Michael's words swirled in my brain. *Why did you go so far away from me?* I glanced at the conch shell and thought, *how many times have I asked Mary that same question?*

I recalled Mary's last letter to her pen pal, written on her stationery with the row of pastel flowers at the top. In her neatest, 13-year-old cursive, she wrote:

> *Dear Brian,*
> *How are you? I am not so good.*

That was the beginning and the end of the letter.

Desperately searching for traces of her, I had found it in her desk after she died. I held onto it for many years but eventually lost track of it. Maybe on purpose. Proof that she was here was also proof she was gone. And it was unbearable.

But as I reclined on the loveseat, I imagined Mary sitting at her desk writing in cursive—letters to Brian and to our cousins in New Haven. There was something very liberating about the memory of her pen moving across the stationary. We weren't the type of people who displayed our fears or weaknesses. We weren't the type of family who talked about our feelings. But we *were* the type of family who *wrote*. Mary had kept a diary, had pen pals who she shared troubles with. Dad and his mom wrote poetry and songs. The Bardy men had authored books on bootlegging and adventures in the circus. Mom had written recipes and short stories and submitted them to magazines.

Writing was acceptable.

Would that be my path to fearlessness? I took out my most recent journal, opened to a blank page, and started writing.

* * *

Although I was pre-occupied with a heavy spring course load and painting projects at The Lake House in Thompson, I continued to write about my family. Some memories were just fragmented snippets of time, the color of a room, the scent of fresh pine boughs. Other memories were complete events, full of rich detail. Still, they were just *my* recollections. I knew the power of memory to skew and distort the truth. Could my truth be validated by others? The more I wrote, the more I remembered, and the stronger my drive to understand and stitch my family memories back together.

* * *

Mourning doves called to one another, and the scent of Lilac hung in the air as I pulled into Mom and Dad's driveway for a quick visit. Dad's car was gone, but Mom's was there. Max, their black and white Lab-Pitbull mix, barked from inside the house. I glanced around the yard but didn't see Mom. Max greeted me at the back door, pawing my thigh. I put him out on his chain and returned inside.

"Mom?" I called. There was no response. I walked through the kitchen and toward the bedroom. Maybe she was taking a nap. I knocked lightly, stepped inside the door and glanced around. Stillness. The bed was made with a simple white cotton bedspread tucked under the front edge of the pillows, and a pile of clothes was neatly folded near the footboard.

I noticed Mom's night table with the lamp she'd bought at a yard sale, a couple of books, her reading glasses, *Mother Earth News*. On her bureau: a bottle of hand lotion, an antique dish with costume jewelry, a few cosmetics, and a hairbrush.

The television sat front and center on Dad's bureau because he can't fall asleep if it's too quiet. There were a few miscellaneous nails and screws, small hinges, and some coins. On his night table, Dad had pictures of me and the new family, an alarm clock, and his cell phone charger.

When I was a child, Mom and Dad's belongings fascinated me. Some helped me define myself, or provided a sense of comfort. Is that why I was here, roaming around inside our family shell?

I thought about the familiar sights, scents, and sounds from my childhood. Vitalis hair oil and spearmint certs had meant that Dad was leaving for the club. Mom's wig, Chanel No. 5, and the *clack-clack* of her high-heels meant she was probably going somewhere without me. I worried about everyone when they left.

Because there was always the possibility that they wouldn't come back.

Stillness. Their things were there, but they were not. I imagined that this was what it would be like when they were gone. I felt that gut punch of loss and shook it off.

I wandered further into the space that had been created by my conversation with Dad. I opened the door to the second-floor stairway; a flood of cool air rushed past me. Dad had replaced the stair treads years ago, but I imagined the old, cracked, creaking oak under my feet, and the battle between the stairway light and the darkness. I continued.

The second floor was the domain of ghosts. It always seemed as though I could feel them crawling on my skin—their cold breath on the back of my neck.

I took a few steps toward the small bedroom at the top of the stairs. The flowered wallpaper had long been torn away and the walls repainted, but nevertheless that is what I saw as I peered through the doorway. The trinket shelf, the window where we would listen to the birds call in the spring and hang paper snowflakes in the winter. I imagined the tiny writing desk where Mary would struggle to do her homework, where she would write to our cousins and to her pen pal.

The small door to the hall closet rattled and caught my attention. Just steps away from Mary's room, I reached out and turned the oval-shaped latch. I ducked inside the closet and tugged on the silver pull-chain that hung from a ceramic socket. A single incandescent bulb glowed inches from my face. Thick, black cobwebs clung to my hands and arms. As I swiped at them, the point of a rusty spike protruding from the sheathing boards sliced through the skin on my palm. I recoiled, clutched my hand, and continued to move deeper into the cramped recesses of *holding on*.

Mom had stacked cardboard boxes of clutter, two or three high, along each wall. The brown shag carpet was littered with mouse droppings. I turned sideways, navigating the narrow aisle between the boxes, and became aware of the faint smell of Cedar—a scent that had become synonymous with death. I spotted the orange-hued wood of the small chest against the wall at the back of the closet. I knelt and ran my hand across the lid thoughtfully, respectfully.

As a child, I had been desperately curious about this box, but the Cedar chest was off limits to me. It had held treasures that belonged to Dziadzia, Babcia, Louise, and Mary. It had contained clothes, nail polish, trinkets, and several old china dolls that resembled little flesh-eating demons with realistic, white ceramic teeth. Their hand-sewn torsos left a trail of sawdust from their stitches. The backs of their heads were intentionally cut off at an angle to accommodate the brunette or strawberry-blonde French curls, first sewn to cardboard then glued in place against the remaining two-thirds of their china skull. Some of the dolls had lost their hair, exposing empty, sawed-off skulls with expressionless faces and dilated pupils, labotomously staring into that same space where Mom occasionally goes.

When I was a child, the cedar chest used to be stored in the hallway. Mom had a habit of piling blankets, bags of old clothes, and bolts of cloth on top of it. Perhaps to deter me from going in—or memories from coming out.

But there was nothing piled on it now. Distracted by cedar-scented sadness, I slid the latch, but Max's sudden bark startled me. My heart raced as I listened for other noises. Nothing. *He probably just wanted to come back inside the house.* I raised the lid of the cedar chest and paused. I expected to find a cache of memories. It was nearly empty. I fished through some old newspapers, a couple of magazines, and two rolls of vinyl wallpaper. At the bottom of the chest were two framed photos; one of Mary, and one of Louise.

I sat back on my heels, staring at the frames in my lap. It was a life I had pushed down. A life that was now staring up at me. I had spent the first four years of my life as Louise's little sister. She taught me how to wash my face with Noxzema, and how to shave my legs with a Lego-block razor before settling in for a bedtime story. Louise dressed me in the latest hippie styles and took me for rides on the minibike with reckless abandon. She taught me to appreciate the glow of a flickering candle and the subtle, sweet scent of incense. Louise sparked my obsession with baseball and exemplified the strength and independence of flower power. When I was her little sister, anything was possible.

I also spent seven glorious years with Mary, who taught me to spell, to read, to tie my shoes, and to love the sea. Together we marveled at the spectacular ordinariness of life. We preserved the fiery splendor of fall leaves, pressing them between sheets of waxed paper with a warm iron. We made gods-eyes with yarn and Popsicle sticks, and knelt among the tall grass of the pasture, plucking tiny wild strawberries from the ground.

We skipped past the hay fields to bring milk to Babcia, our great-grandmother, who was bedridden and lived in a small cabin that smelled of nutmeg and cloves. Babcia, whose mother read tealeaves and who held our hands and smiled at us with her whole being, grateful for the milk, but mostly for the company. It was Mary who taught me to protect the young and respect the old. Mary, whose death put an end to both of our lives.

I sat sequestered in that tiny closet, holding pictures of my two sisters nearly 40 years after their deaths, overwhelmed with sadness. A jumble of questions flooded my mind. Max barked again, this time louder and more excited. A pair of car doors shut in succession. Mom and Dad were home.

I stuffed the photos in the messenger bag slung over my shoulder, tugged the light chain, and hurried downstairs. After a brief visit with Mom and Dad, I returned to the lake house with the framed pictures of my sisters and thought about what to do next.

As I wiped away a grey film of dust from the glass, familiar eyes stared back at me. *Why did you go so far away from me?*

Questions made people angry. But I was no longer a child. I shouldn't be so controlled by my fears. *She is my mother. I have spent 46 years with her.* My recon into the shell triggered a mind shift. Maybe I didn't need to be fearless. Maybe I just needed to act, despite my fear.

It was time to visit Mary's grave.

But first I needed to find out where she was buried.

Chapter 5:

Approaching Mom

Mid-June, 2015

Ask and run. Essentially that was the plan.

I would stop by The Compound for a quick visit, pose a simple question in a nonchalant manner, and change the subject. Not *quite* a fearless Bardy.

I pulled into the gravel driveway, near the stone wall where Mary and I had admired scarlet and lemon tulips in the spring, and, years later, where Kevin and I had hunkered down and pelted the mailman's car with black walnuts and acorns.

I just wanted to confirm the cemetery and the general location of Mary's grave, hoping it wouldn't make Mom sad or set her off. Hoping she wouldn't view it as an abhorrent invasion of privacy, like when I was a child and the Jehovah's Witnesses would knock on our door. Mom would answer it, listening only for a moment to what she viewed as an offensive spiel. Then she'd rid the porch of them in short order. "Who invited *you* here? I hate company. Get out." Even now I cringed as I recalled her anger.

Max barked from his chain in the backyard as I walked toward the front door. I patted the front pocket of my messenger bag and felt the outline of a photo I had found at The Lake House. My stomach churned with anxiety. Was I being selfish? I thought back to the exchange between Dad and me at the coffee shop a few months ago. *No. Dad wanted to reconnect with Mary too.*

Mom was seated on the sofa in the living room, reading a book when I arrived. Her feet were propped up on the coffee table, glasses resting on the end of her nose as she leaned forward and reached for her bookmark.

"It's nice and cool in here. It's really humid outside already," I said, closing the door behind me. "Are you working in the garden today?" I sat in Dad's chair across from the sofa.

She put down the book. "I weeded earlier this morning. I'll water later on, when it cools down."

My heart beat faster. *Be fearless.* "I was going through some old pictures and ran across one of me and Mary in Dziadzia's garden at the farm."

"Oh?" She sat up a little straighter.

I pulled the photo from my bag, leaned over, and handed it to her. As her attention was fixed on the photo, I asked the question. "Mary was buried in Saint Anthony's, right?" I leaned back and held my breath.

Her eyes studied the picture. "Yes. Next to Dziadzia." She furrowed her brow and continued. "When he died, instead of a single grave, Grandma bought a plot with four graves because it was cheaper." She glanced up after her hard emphasis on the word cheaper, as if to assess *my* reaction.

"Hmmph." I was glad she wasn't upset by the question. Her resentment appeared to be directed at Grandma, but the confirmation of the cemetery was enough detail. I felt like I was walking a knife edge. Time to move on.

"Dziadzia sure knew how to grow plants," I said, making it clear that I would not be asking anything further on the subject.

She handed the photo back to me. "He loved his garden."

"Speaking of gardens, how's yours? Can I get a quick tour?"

Mom never passes up the chance to strut the horticultural catwalk. I followed her into the backyard, along the meandering field-stone path, up three steps of banded metamorphic rocks, past the woodshed and the toolshed, and into her garden. Compacted paths of rich, brown earth separated parallel rows of vegetables and herbs, their fresh young shoots capturing energy from the sun. She is a masterful gardener, another skill I did not inherit. When Mom was a child, she and Dziadzia spent much of the spring and summer planting, weeding, watering, and harvesting food. It was also a peaceful place to seek refuge from Grandma's demands.

* * *

Saint Anthony is the patron saint of lost or stolen things. He would be the saint to pray to for help, but I had given up on prayer decades ago. I was on my own. With the sun high in the sky, I drove to Saint Anthony's Cemetery and walked through each row of gravestones. I viewed several hundred plots, under the blazing heat of the mid-day sun. I saw many names that looked Polish or Slovak, but I did not see a stone with Dziadzia's name 'Rzeszutko,' or Mary's last name 'Tefft' on it. The humid air hung on me. Salty beads of water slid down the sides of my nose and over my lip. I brushed wet strands of hair from my forehead and bloused the front of my damp t-shirt.

The only sounds were passing cars on the adjacent roadway. The only sign of life was one lone songbird, a tufted titmouse, perched like a hood ornament atop a gravestone in the first row of the Saint Peter's section. The bird peered at me, its regal crown tapered to a point, its eyes fixed on mine. I lumbered through Saint Peter's a second time, just to be sure. No luck.

I returned to the car and blasted the air conditioning. I sat there for a few minutes with the engine running, feeling defeated. *Why did she go so far away from me? Why had I not searched for her sooner? Why was this so difficult?*

Whatever the reason, it became clear that if I *was* going to find her, I couldn't do it alone.

* * *

The next day, I stopped at Mom and Dad's house, and this time they were both home.

Mom filled the tea kettle with water to make coffee. I placed the two framed photos I had gotten from the cedar chest a few weeks ago on the table. "I borrowed these. I cleaned the glass and the frames." I hoped she wouldn't be mad.

Mom shot me a suspicious glance. "Oh. I didn't know you had them."

Before I had a chance to respond, Dad chimed in quickly. "Where did you find those? I've been looking for them."

Mom turned away from us toward the stove.

"I found them in the cedar chest," I explained. "I'll put them back; I just wanted to make copies."

"Leave them out. They should be hung up," Dad said, looking over the photos. "I haven't seen these in a long time."

I cringed. *Why did he have to make a big deal out of it?* "Well, I'll put them back upstairs for now so they're not in the way. At least now you know where they are." I hoped that would be an acceptable compromise for now.

Mom poured, and the three of us sat down at the table. "Your mother said you asked about the cemetery yesterday. Did you go to the grave?" Dad asked.

My eyes darted to Mom and then to my coffee cup. "Yep, but I couldn't find Mary's stone. I couldn't even find Dziadzia's." I had to admit failure in front of Mom. Weakness. Again. I leaned on the table and rested my chin in my hands.

Mom went to the counter for muffins. "There is no stone."

I sat back and folded my arms. It never occurred to me that there wouldn't be a stone. How did she expect me to find an unmarked grave? Maybe she didn't.

She set the bowl of muffins on the table and continued. "But there is a plot marker."

Dad agreed and insisted he knew the location. "Mary is buried in the same plot with Dziadzia in that cemetery. I've asked your mother several times if she wanted to visit the grave when we were in town but—"

I cut him off. "Can you go with me some time to help me find it?"

"Of course. When do you want to go?"

Mom picked up the newspaper and scanned the headlines. I looked back toward Dad. "Maybe the next time I'm in Thompson for the weekend," I said. Immediately followed by—"How has the Prius been running?"

* * *

A couple of weeks after my visit with Mom and Dad, my younger sister Robyn called. "I think that you asking about Mary is upsetting Mom."

I slumped in my chair and twisted my ponytail through my fingers. I thought about last week when I had invited Dad to the lake house for dinner and a movie while Mom was at work. I knew that lately he and Mom were at odds. I was afraid that would happen.

I could hear Robyn washing dishes and clanging pans in the background. "Mom has been really depressed. She and Dad have been arguing. I don't think she wants the pictures up."

"I only asked her about Mary once—and I didn't put any pictures up."

"I know. Dad did. But she still has to look at them. It's bothering her."

"Okay. I'll talk to him about it," I promised.

I called him that evening while Mom was at work. We chatted about the news and weather for a few minutes before I brought it up. "Robyn said Mom has been upset lately." I paused. "Do you think it has to do with seeing Mary and Louise's pictures out?"

It was as if he'd only heard part of what I said. "I told your mother I want Mary's picture on the windowsill where I can see it from my chair."

It became clear the contract of silence could not be torn up by a simple conversation. The pictures of Mary and Louise buried at the bottom of the cedar chest should have been a sign. Mom wasn't ready.

"Your mother's been so miserable lately that I don't even want to be home anymore."

His refusal to acknowledge her feelings puzzled me. "Maybe she's cranky because having the pictures out upsets her."

"She hasn't said anything. She keeps putting Mary's picture away whenever I put it on the windowsill."

I paused and thought about how to reach him. "Well, isn't that sort of saying that she doesn't want to look at the photo?" I was answered by silence. It was as if Dad disappeared to another time and place. Was it a painfully familiar place where his feelings are less important? A place where his grief lives quietly in the shadows, unrecognized? Unresolved?

It made sense to me that the old pictures brought Mom to a place she had become a master at avoiding. Hell, the pictures made me sad too. I had confided to Dad that I had been journaling, and I thought I'd like to write a family history and include Louise and Mary. Now I wasn't so sure. I wanted him to feel better, but I didn't want to upset Mom. Maybe I was being selfish. Maybe Dad and I were treading disrespectfully on her grief. I started to think I should back away.

PART TWO

Recollection

"...But I have promises to keep, and miles to go before I sleep, and miles to go before I sleep..."

—Robert Frost.

Chapter 6:

The Vulnerable Halves

Late June, 2015

I glanced at my cell phone, Mom and Dad had reluctantly agreed to come to the lake for dinner. Now I needed to figure out what to cook. Not only did I have a black thumb when it came to growing plants, but my culinary skills ranked somewhere between remedial and pathetic. Mom has often recounted the time when I was 19 and asked my 6-year-old sister how to cook Kraft Mac & Cheese. Embarrassing. And yet, that night I had to cook. Mom was bringing a salad with lettuce and kale from her garden, but I would provide the rest. *Why did I offer?*

I roamed the produce aisle as the front wheel of my grocery cart rattled and flailed in a tremor of indecision. As I picked up four ears of sweet corn, a white, carrot-looking, root vegetable caught my eye. It was a parsnip. Mom liked parsnips. How did I know this? I wasn't sure. I put three parsnips in the cart.

I wandered for another minute and my husband Eric called on his way home from the police barracks. I answered my cell with one of Dad's quips. "Your dime. Your time."

We chatted for a moment, and he asked if I had plans for dinner.

"My parents are coming over. Any ideas for food?"

"Pick up some ground Bison and rolls. I'll make burgers on the grill."

What a life raft. Now I just had to worry about easing the tension I caused between Mom and Dad.

* * *

That evening, the four of us ate dinner on the deck overlooking the lake. As birds flitted past, snatching seeds from the feeder and hurrying off, the energy of their little wing beats swept away some of my angst. "I love watching the birds. It seems to run in the family, huh, Mom?"

"Oh, I forgot to fill my bird feeder today."

I poured her a glass of lemonade. "Dziadzia used to have pet pigeons, didn't he?"

"Yes. He did. Sometimes Grandma would cook a couple of them for dinner, but they were mostly pets."

"I remember reading somewhere that Hemmingway ate pigeons he caught in Luxembourg Park in Paris. What do they taste like?"

She chuckled as she picked up a handful of chips. "They were good actually. That reminds me of the time Auntie and I played hide-and-seek in the pigeon coop. We weren't supposed to. We left the door open and all the pigeons got out. That was the closest we ever got to *the strap*."

The strap had a reputation that spanned several generations. It was made of saddle-brown leather, about two feet long and six inches wide. It was meant to sharpen knives, but Grandma and Dziadzia also used it to discourage bad behavior. They never actually paddled anyone's backside with it, but just its existence was a powerful deterrent.

As Dad and Eric talked about the Red Sox, Mom and I talked a bit more about life at the farm, spreading wood ash on tomato leaves to keep the bugs away, and a polish recipe for blood sausage—not that I was going to make it anytime soon.

* * *

The pigeons turned out to be a powerful segue into Mom's child-hood. Soon, she was calling me whenever she remembered a story or vignette she had yet to share. They were funny or interesting, sweet, or loving—it was a side of her I had not seen since before Mary died; a side of her I had nearly forgotten.

Dziadzia was coming back to life. When she talked about him, she softened. She recalled the slightest details about what he wore, how he worked, and what he valued in life. I scribbled down every story and every detail. Despite our progress, I was still reticent to bring up Mary.

So far, only Eric and Dad knew of my idea to write about the family. But as I realized how much I either suppressed or didn't know, the need to widen my net became obvious.

I thought about reaching out to my older brothers Shane and Kevin and older sister Tammy. But even *that* was difficult. We were all parties to the contract, and this was hardly the type of research I was used to.

I decided to create a questionnaire that would capture some details from our sisters' lives. I planned to send a copy to each member of the old family. In hindsight, it was embarrassingly like a qualitative research study, where the study participants were my family members.

Before I mailed a copy to Tammy in Vermont, I called her to let her know my plan. She asked about the questions and gave some of her responses over the phone. With that momentum I found the confidence to reach out to my half-brother Kevin.

Our adult relationship was cordial but we never bridged the emotional distance we felt as children. We saw each other a few times a year, and the dynamic was always the same; he was aloof, and I strove in vain for his acceptance. My heartbeat quickened as I sent him a text message. "I'm writing a book to honor Louise and Mary, and I'd like to talk with you about it. Can I stop by?"

To my surprise, he responded within the hour.

"No, thanks."

Ah, there it was. The contract. The familiar brick wall.

There's no such thing as ghosts. Sleep in your own room. Push it down. Hold it there. Be quiet. Behave.

I paced and muttered expletives to myself for a few minutes and then went out for a walk in the woods. A spongy carpet of dry leaves crunched under my feet and, deeper still, I felt the unyielding strength of glacial boulders beneath my hiking boots. The solid monuments of rock remained as tributes to the ice sheet that once carved and sculpted the landscape. Monuments are important. They remind us of our connection to the past and give us a foothold in the present.

The noise of my cell phone interrupted the silence. It was the sci-fi ringtone of the compound. Dad's voice on the other end lightened my mood.

"I'm going to visit Dicky tomorrow. Do you want to go? He might be able to give you some answers for your book."

Dicky is one of my older half-brothers from Dad's first marriage. I hadn't thought about contacting him, but it made sense. "Sure. I haven't seen him in a long time. I'd love to go."

* * *

The next day, Dad picked me up at the lake and we went to visit Dicky at the trailer he was renting in Douglas, Massachusetts. For most of the half-hour drive, the conversation consisted of a monologue of excuses from Dad, preparing me for Dicky's unkempt appearance and home.

"Dad, he's my brother. I know he's messy. It doesn't bother me."

Of the three boys from his first marriage, Dicky resembles Dad the most. He has dark hair and eyes and olive tones to his skin, but he's 6'5" and weighs about 300 pounds: a taller, heavier, Harley-Davidson version of Dad. He wears a frayed, red bandana headband; his long black hair is streaked with wiry strands of grey, parted in the middle, and tied back in a ponytail. Born in 1959, Dicky was two years younger than Louise. He is Dad's middle son, Bobby was a year older and Harold one year younger.

Dicky is the only one still alive.

His deep voice greeted us as he opened the door. "Hey ol' man. Come on in." He slapped Dad on the back, bent down, and gave me a hug. "Hey sis, good to see ya."

He led us through a narrow hallway, clogged with boxes and miscellaneous spare parts stacked against the wood paneling, to the main room of the trailer. There was a kitchenette with a counter and small table straight ahead, a TV on the entertainment center along the wall to the left, and a full-size bed stacked with blankets and pillows to our right. Despite being a pack-rat like Dad, his home was pretty clean for a bachelor. Dicky motioned for us to sit. "The bedroom's filled with junk, so my bed's out here. No room for a couch. Just sit on the bed." He pulled up a kitchen chair for himself.

Dad got right down to business. "Where's my coffee?"

I rolled my eyes. "He's *your* father."

"Uh huh. I know." Dicky heated some water on the stove, got out a spoon and a jar of instant coffee. He chatted with Dad for a couple minutes about a car he was restoring, and then turned to me.

"Whatcha been up to, sis? Dad said you wanna ask me about your sisters?"

I nodded. I liked how he referred to me as 'sis.' There was genuine feeling behind it. Feeling I didn't have to *earn*. "Yep. I'm trying to put together a book for the family."

"Don't remember much. Didn't live there very long." He took three mismatched coffee cups down from a shelf above the sink. He gave himself the one with the broken handle.

Dicky and I batted questions and answers back and forth. He poured water into the mugs while Dad watched some of the news.

"What was it like at the house when you lived there?" I asked.

"Well, your mom didn't like me, so that was hard. I don't blame her. I was an asshole."

I shook my head. "She's a tough lady to impress."

Dicky handed a mug to me. "You want milk? 'Cuz I think I'm out."

"No. Black is fine."

"I was 13. Always skippin' school, gettin' into trouble."

I lifted my mug and blew across the surface of the coffee. "The house was so small. Which bedroom did you sleep in?"

"Louise's old room."

That hadn't occurred to me. "Ugh. That must have sucked."

"Yep. Kinda weird. Like it was still her room, but she was gone." He shrugged. "I got to paint it any color I wanted. So, I painted it purple."

"*You're* the one who painted it? I thought *Louise* chose that color. All these years I thought purple was her favorite." I hesitated, adjusting to this revelation. "What was it *like* in the house? You know…"

"Well, everybody was sad about Louise. It was hard. Like Shane was always tryin' to get me in trouble. That little shit. I wanted to beat his ass, but your mom woulda got pissed. He picked on Kevin too. But Tammy—she'd pretend to be someone called 'Auntie May.' She was crazy. She'd sneak up behind us and give us wedgies. Then she'd say we had skid marks."

I laughed. I hadn't heard the 'Auntie May' story before, but it was classic Tammy. "I wish you could have stayed at the house." I took another drink of coffee and set my cup down on the counter. "What do you remember about Mary?"

"Little Mary was always in the hospital. Always sick."

I nodded. Everyone in the old family, except for me, called her "Little Mary." I think Grandma started it to distinguish her from Mom, whose name is also Mary. It occurred to me that Dicky never spent much time with our sisters. Mary was often sick, and Louise and Tammy had their own circle of friends that didn't include their school-skipping, weekend-visiting step-brothers. It was a 'blended' family in name only. We rarely mixed.

Dicky offered more about his time at the compound. "Harold moved in for a little while. But we had to leave. Didn't want no rules."

Dad turned away from the news and piped in. "Yeah—I'd drop you off at the front of the school, and you'd run out the back."

Dicky gave a throaty, garbled laugh. One that would have irritated Mom.

I swirled my coffee. "Bobby never lived there?"

Dicky furrowed his brow and smirked. "Puh-leaze! He was a momma's boy."

He was right. Out of the three boys, I saw Bobby the least. His tall, thin, slumped posture and shifty eyes made it look like he was always trying to hide something. He had his mom's pale skin, rusty-blonde hair, sharp features, and her odd way of thinking about the world.

Dicky described her as a "simple" person who "wasn't *trying* to do the wrong things. She just didn't know any better."

Unfortunately, her moral deficiencies were passed on to her sons. Bobby spent the most time in jail out of the three of them. He always seemed to be tangled up with bad people or bad situations and never learned how to stay free for very long. He died of lung cancer in 2010 at age 53, one year after Harold.

Dicky digressed to his conviction for armed robbery and recapped some of the trouble he and his brothers had gotten into. I didn't interrupt his reverie. As he and Dad exchanged stories, laughs, jabs, and jokes, I thought about Dicky's losses juxtaposed with mine. I sat back on the bed-couch and considered the ways in which age, personality, and life circumstance affect our grief.

As Dad and Dicky's voices faded into the background, I thought about the last time I saw Harold. It was mid-February of 2009 when I had gotten the news that my half-brother was riddled with cancer, and only had about three months left on Earth. Dad and I visited Harold at his home in Webster, a few days later.

* * *

We had climbed the enclosed stairway to Harold's second-floor apartment, past dirty windows, spare boards, old coats, wads of cat hair, and a couple of pans crusted with food. It smelled like cat pee, dirt, and old wood. Harold's wife, Robin, greeted us at the door and let us in to the kitchen. "Hey, guys, don't mind the mess," Robin said.

I thought it odd that she'd be worried about the condition of her house considering the diagnosis. To put her mind at ease, I borrowed one of Dad's lines. "If we don't like it, we don't have to look, right?"

Dad chuckled. Robin smiled and touched me on the shoulder. "I'll put the coffee on. You want coffee, right, Bob?"

"Damn right."

I shook my head at Dad's predictable reply. "None for me, thanks."

Harold sat on the living room couch, smoking a cigarette. He crushed it out when he saw us. "Hey, ol' man. Hey, sis." Dad sat beside Harold and I got a chair from the kitchen. We listened to him talk about the progression of his illness, the initial treatments, and the doctor's diagnosis. "No sense quittin'," he said. "Can't get worse." He wasn't bitter, he was strangely accepting of it.

Dad seemed hopeful. "They have any other treatments or new medicine?"

Harold shook his head. "Nope. It spread too far."

Robin walked into the living room and held out a paper cup to Dad.

Dad looked up at her with an expression that's come to be known as *The Rumrill Eyebrow*. "What's this?"

Robin's cheeks flushed with pink as she glanced away. "All the dishes are dirty."

"Well, you've had other things to worry about," I said quickly.

Harold explained in detail about a motor he was taking apart and rebuilding. He thought of clever ways to fix the unfixable and make it useful again. Just like Dad. I was both happy and sad at the same time. I regretted that I hadn't spent more time with him.

After that visit, I called Robin every week to check on Harold. Sometimes I would hear his voice in the background, proudly asking "Is that my sister?" or "Tell Julie I said hello. Tell her to give herself a hug for me."

That's what it feels like to have brotherly love. Spectacular.

A couple of months after Harold's diagnosis, I had gotten a job as a field scientist at a wildlife sanctuary near Acadia National Park in Maine. Although I was thrilled to get the job, Acadia was a five and a half hour drive from my brother. The position entailed paddling the lakes and ponds of Mount Desert Island (MDI), and monitoring the behavior of the common loon population. Their summer home was a sensory feast of rolling granite hills, polished by the last ice sheet, draped with a thin layer of dark organic soil, and studded with fragrant blue spruce. Each year, loons return to spend the breeding season on the lakes and ponds that fill deep troughs in the landscape.

I had recorded the loon's nesting sites, successes, failures, and mates. I listened for their calls and observed their swimming, diving, flying, and violent territorial battles. I watched how they lived and, in a few sad cases, how they experienced loss.

That spring there had been an awful spell where a murderous rain pounded and soaked the ground for days. As lake levels rose, I worried. Through the spotting scope at the sanctuary on Somes Pond, I watched as a pair of adult loons swam anxiously back and forth in front of their camouflaged nest on the far shoreline. Over the past 25 days, I had observed the expecting parents as they took turns incubating one pastel-green egg with brown freckles and hoped it would hatch before the nest flooded. Hours passed, and the loon pair was still pacing. The eyes of the day clamped shut.

That night, there was no moon, no light on Somes Pond. The adult loons' wail was not a typical call, yet I instantly recognized the haunting tone of anguish and heartbreak. It echoed for hours as I lay, wide-eyed, tears on my cheeks and pillow, surrounded by the relentless pounding of the rain and the loons' repeated begging. *Why did you go so far away from me?* We struggled with the loss of a family member, and the inability to help. Nature can be cruel.

Even before I had paddled out to the island the next morning and gathered the dead loon chick from its mucky grave, I knew. I had recognized the futility, depth, and weight of their sadness. It mirrored what I felt for Harold, and perhaps what I had attempted to avoid feeling for decades.

* * *

The last time I saw Harold was on June 17, 2009. That day—June 17—was a familiar date. It was also the last day I saw Louise, in 1973. The chance to say 'goodbye' was important to me. I hadn't gotten that chance with Louise or Mary. I'm not sure exactly what I expected. Personal comfort? The clichéd 'closure?'

What I found was an abandoned connection from an old life that I had nearly forgotten. Half-sibs who bonded in childhood, Harold and I were connected through Dad, and I loved them both unconditionally. I tried to comfort him--a hand on the forearm, a kind word, a corny joke. I knew this would be the last time we would see each other.

I placed my hand on his back. I could feel his shoulder blade through tissue-paper skin, stretched loosely over his skeleton. I whispered in his ear, "I love you. I'm proud to have you as a brother. You have nothing to be afraid of. I'll see you again." I held his hand and searched his eyes. He was trying to talk, but the sounds wouldn't connect into words. Even breathing was painful for him. Yet as I was getting up to leave, he gave me two hugs, the second of which he raised both arms, a difficult and exhausting motion, wrapping their frail remnants around me. It was time for his morphine. Time for me to go.

Robin walked me to the door and gave me a hug. I glanced back at Harold once more; there was nothing else I could do. I closed the door behind me and hurried down the stairs sobbing. His neighbors, milling about in the yard, stared as I ran to my car, digging the keys out of my bag, hands trembling as I struggled to fit the key in the ignition. I drove away, close to hyperventilating.

I drove faster, trying to escape the sadness. I drove and cried until I was completely exhausted and could barely see. And then I pulled to one side of an I-95 off-ramp, reclined the seat, curled up and slept. When I woke it was dusk. I still had a couple hours to go before I got to the sanctuary. I needed to talk about Harold with someone who could empathize.

I called Dad.

I told him how unfair I thought it was. "Little Julie is going to have to grow up without a Dad." Harold's daughter, Julie, was only seven. The same age I was when Mary died. She folded her hands and knelt by her bed each night in prayer, trusting that God would heal her Dad. I blew my nose and searched the car for more tissues. "I don't understand this." Rekindled anger burned in my mind. "What kind of God would do this?" I took a deep breath and sadness dampened the flame. "He was so fragile, so weak. He couldn't even talk." I recounted my last words to Harold: that I loved him, and I was proud he was my brother.

Dad responded here and there with an occasional *mmh hmm*, but mostly just listened with his whole heart. He was letting me get the sadness out. I could tell he was crying too.

"This is so awful. I'm so sorry Dad."

I didn't realize it then, but we were validating each other's grief.

* * *

I was jolted back to my conversation with Dicky by his deep, raspy voice. "Hellooooo? Anybody home?" he asked, and I suddenly remembered that I was in his home talking with him about grief. He leaned in close and waved a hand in front of my face.

I felt my cheeks and earlobes warm. "Sorry about that. I was daydreaming."

"'Bout me outrunnin' the Webstuh cops?" Dicky joked.

I chuckled and sat up straight. I pushed myself back on the bed-couch, tucked another pillow behind me and leaned on the wall. "I miss Harold."

Dicky's face softened, and his broad shoulders raised and lowered with a deep breath. "Me too. It's just me now."

I nodded. I knew exactly how he felt. We were each other's thin thread to a world that wasn't there anymore.

* * *

Talking with Dicky was easy and natural, like my connection with Harold. It was cathartic to let my guard down; to be present with vulnerability—his, theirs, and mine. It also made me realize how formidable and significant that guard was, and how seldom it got lowered. It spoke volumes about what I held close, how tightly it was bound, and how little I was willing to reveal to others.

Dad and I hadn't discussed visiting Mary's grave since our conversation at The Compound, but I was far from abandoning the quest.

Something about the visit with Dicky bolstered my resolve.

Chapter 7:

Searching the Stones

Early July, 2015

I may not be fearless, but there was at least one Bardy trait that I *did* manage to acquire—persistence.

The following week, I called The Compound and Dad answered. "Your dime."

I shook my head and smiled. "Hey, are you going to be around on Saturday? I want to take a ride to the cemetery in Webster."

"Yes, but I don't think your mother will go."

I knew Mom's refusal to visit the grave was a point of contention between them. I convinced him to keep the trip between us. If Mom asked questions, we would explain it as a road trip to get coffee or a car part perhaps; something that she would not be interested in. I didn't want to cause another battle.

During the 15-minute drive from The Compound to St. Anthony's Cemetery, Dad and I talked about household projects and his recipe for 3,000-pound cement. The family script was powerfully engrained in us. In the few quiet moments that punctuated the comforting chatter, I wondered how I would feel standing at the grave, finally being near Mary for the first time in 40 years.

I knew there was a lot buried in that small casket. It had become clear that her grave was where my trust, confidence, and ability to connect deeply with others had been entombed. Our entire way of life, prior to March 8, 1976, had been sealed inside a concrete vault.

I pulled into the entrance, drove toward the back of the cemetery, and parked the car. Dad seemed confident he knew where the grave was. "In the back to the right. That's what your mother said."

We walked together toward the far corner, past American flags, several stone angels, and arrangements of fake flowers with wide yellow ribbons. The Tony Orlando song, *Tie a Yellow Ribbon*, played in my head. Some of the gravestones had ornate etchings or engravings, and some had clay pots overflowing with carefully tended blooms. All were tributes and memorials to the lives of loved ones, and their impact on others. I thought about the exchange with Mom last week in the kitchen. "There *is* no stone," she had said. There was no epitaph for Mary or Dziadzia. No place to leave flowers tied with a yellow ribbon. I wondered why.

I turned to Dad. "I'm not sure how they arrange the plots, but we need to find one that's wide enough for two or four graves."

He agreed.

We split up and sought conspicuously empty space. Stone monuments in rectangles, squares and hearts, speckled with black, pink and white crystals, stood close together in the back-right corner. We found a couple of possibilities, each time calling out to the other "Maybe this is it?" Probably not. We kept searching.

Clouds approached, low and dark. The wind whipped through the torsos of trees along the fringe of the cemetery, their branches swaying like giant arms. Were they beckoning us? Or shooing us away? It began to rain. My feet sunk into the spongy grass with each step. I didn't like walking over the graves. It felt disrespectful.

We searched through row after row of monuments as the rain fell steady and cold. We had traversed the entire cemetery and ended up very close to where we started, staring at a couple of square silver plates a few inches wide, mostly obscured by the grass.

I looked up at Dad through the rain. "Are those the plot markers Mom mentioned?"

"I'm not sure." Dad pulled the hood of his jacket over his head, knelt, and scraped the grass away from one of the metal squares. "I think it has a number on it. It's hard to read."

Even if it was legible, neither of us knew the plot number, and we weren't sure if this was the location Mom described. Not quite the yellow ribbon I had hoped for. "I don't think we're going to find it. We'll have to ask Mom," I said.

He stood up, wiped the mud from his hand onto his thigh, and rubbed the back of his neck. "I could have sworn she said it was around here."

As we walked toward the car, something about the way Dad spoke of the grave didn't make sense. I wondered why he was relying on Mom's directions. "Where did everyone gather at the burial?" I asked, trying to jog his memory.

He tugged at the hood on his jacket and shielded his eyes from the rain that was falling harder. "I don't know. I wasn't there," he said plainly, as if that was common knowledge.

In an instant, everything faded away except for Dad. I stopped walking and stared at him through the rain. "You didn't go to the burial?"

He glanced back at me and stopped a few steps from the car. "I went to the wake and the funeral service. Can you unlock the door?"

I shook my head and fumbled for my keys. "Oh. Sorry." He didn't go to the burial? There had to be a compelling reason, but he didn't elaborate. I couldn't bring myself to pull at that knot right now. I would sort it out later. I was overwhelmed, soggy, and frustrated by another failed attempt to find Mary.

On the drive back to The Compound, Dad took a pair of fingernail clippers from his front pocket and cleaned the mud from his nails while we talked about the rain, our search, and our possible next step.

Mom was doing laundry and came up from the basement when we arrived. Dad made coffee while I divulged our clandestine trip to Webster. Guilt washed over me like I had betrayed her.

At first, she seemed doubtful of our trek. "You were walking around in the rain?"

As she posed the question, I searched her face for micro-expressions of anger. Dad came to our defense. "Well, we're not made of sugar."

"We weren't there very long," I said, minimizing our search. But that was a lie. It seemed like hours.

"You couldn't find it?" she asked as she turned away from us and tidied up the counter. She never used the words grave, or gravestone, or cemetery.

"No. We searched the entire place. I think we found some plot markers, but there were no names, and I had no idea what number to look for." Part of me was hoping she would offer to show us. But she didn't.

"What's the plot number?" Dad asked.

Mom went to the fridge. "I don't know." She took out a bunch of carrots and started peeling them at the sink.

Persistence.

"Who is in charge of the cemetery?" I asked.

"St. Anthony's church in Dudley." She continued to peel.

I glanced at Dad. "Okay. I'll try to contact someone and see if there's a map."

I went back to the lake house and found the phone number for St. Anthony's Parish online. What would I say? What would they ask? Would they wonder why I waited so long?

My call was sent to voicemail. It was humiliating and shameful to admit that I didn't know where my sister was buried. There was no way to dress it up. I left the world's most awkward message, hung up, and then ran away for a few days.

* * *

I needed some distance, or a new perspective, or both. I headed up to New Hampshire on a solo hiking trip and rented a cottage in Weirs Beach, overlooking Lake Winnipesaukee.

The name of the lake means "smile of the great spirit" or "beautiful water in a high place." Prior to colonial times, the Pennacook Indians set up an important fishing village at the lake's outflow. It had a long history as a place of sustenance and recreation—a place to come and be recharged, physically or figuratively.

The lake has an unusual natural history in that the last glaciation reversed its flow. It once flowed southeast through an outlet in Alton Bay and eventually to the Atlantic Ocean, but when powerful forces acted in concert and blocked this route with glacial debris, the current shifted direction to the northwest and created a new outlet near Weirs Beach. This little bit of natural history gave me hope; if the third largest lake in New England can be persuaded to make adjustments in the face of adversity, it should be relatively easy for one small human to do the same.

* * *

The next morning, I left the cottage after sunrise to hike in nearby Franconia Notch State Park. I parked at the trailhead where several other people were donning gear and preparing for a day of solace. A round-trip loop across the ridgeline comprised of the spines of Mt. Haystack, Mt. Lincoln, and Mt. Lafayette, was about seven hours.

Less than two miles into the woods, the Falling Waters Trail became relentlessly steep and the number of people diminished. I traversed exposed tree roots, rock stairs, and endless river crossings via slick stepping stones or fallen tree trunks.

After about three miles, the towering forest thinned. Giants that previously looked down on me had transmuted to gnarled and knotted dwarfs that I met face-to-face. The periwinkle sky stretched wide overhead, as I ascended into the alpine zone.

Following the ridge at an elevation near 5,000 feet, I traversed a saw-tooth pattern of short but steep climbs; weaving in and out of the clouds. They were like the thoughts breathing in and out of my mind. Some sailed past, some enveloped me and lingered. Why did Dad not go to the burial?

I approached the peak of Mt. Lafayette, stopped near a shed-sized boulder, and bent down to investigate a familiar shape.

My fingers dug into the rubble of weathered bedrock and plucked out a Smokey Quartz crystal about the size of my thumb. I flipped the cap on my water bottle and rinsed a thin film of clay from the crystal surface. The water revealed a translucent, hexagonal column whose faces joined to form a pyramid at one end. Quartz, a residual of weathered granite, is so enduring that it remains long after all other minerals have been eroded or decomposed. I wondered how it got here, more than 5,200 feet in elevation, in the middle of my path.

I tucked the quartz crystal into my pocket and continued on the trail. A thin veil of clouds slowly parted as if they were curtains, revealing a striking stage set. A lush quilt of evergreens cascaded down to the valley floor where it was stitched to the other side of the valley by the paved seam of Route 3. The exposed bones of bare, rocky peaks revealed a deep, solid strength. A strength that comes not only from the tenacity of individual minerals, but the matrix that binds them.

Within this magnanimous perspective, I breathed in the cool cloud droplets and felt irrelevant. Like I had been whispered an eternal truth; a truth about how small we really are. I ran my fingertips across the smooth faces of the crystal in my pocket, and my boots sprang from rock to rock as I headed down to join my fellow little people again.

Back at my car, I changed into my Tevas and drove south on Route 3, toward the rental cottage. Cell service was terrible, so I was surprised when my phone rang.

"Hi, Julie. This is Valerie from St. Anthony's returning your call about your grandpa's and sister's graves."

"Yes. Hi, Valerie. Thanks for getting back to me." I pulled the car off to the shoulder.

"No problem. We have your grandpa, Louis, buried in grave number one, of plot 18-B, which is a four-grave plot. It is in the St. Peter's section of the cemetery in the second to the last row."

I recalled my first trip to the cemetery and the little grey songbird that had been perched on a headstone, staring at me. It was in the St. Peter's section.

She continued. "Paul, our caretaker, cleaned off the plot markers. Now you'll be able to see them with no trouble. Your family plot is near a headstone with the name Celko. As I said, your grandpa is in grave #1. The other three graves are vacant."

"Vacant? No. That can't be right. My sister Mary is supposed to have been buried there too. My Mom said my sister is buried with my grandfather."

"I'm sorry, but I checked the plot plan and our records carefully and there is no record of a 'Mary Tefft' burial."

I paused. "Is it possible she's in a different plot?"

Valerie's voice was soft and considerate. "We have no record of anyone with that name buried here. Let 's check the spelling, just to be sure."

There was no mistake. I realized I was not going to get the answer I wanted. "I'm in New Hampshire right now, but can I meet with you when I get back to look at the plot plan and see where my grandfather is buried?"

"Yes. Of course. Just call the parish when you return."

The call ended, and I sat there in the car for a few minutes, staring straight ahead, trying to make sense of this. How could she *not* be there? Where on Earth is she? They *have* to be wrong. Or—maybe Mom was lying.

* * *

Valerie welcomed me into the small office lined with gray metal filing cabinets. A large, dark-walnut desk filled the center of the room. She pulled out a chair and invited me to sit as she cleared the top of her desk and unrolled a blueprint of the cemetery.

Her dark brown hair was pinned up loosely, with a few wavy strands framing her face. She was about 10 years older than me, had a soft voice, and deep smile lines. Her smile reminded me of Dad's—it seemed to light the room and instantly put me at ease.

Valerie gestured to the map as she mentioned different landmarks. "This is Old Worcester Road, and this is the cemetery. It's divided into sections named for different saints. Your grandpa's in the St. Peter's section." She pointed toward the right-hand boundary of the cemetery. "He's in plot 18-B. Grave number one. Right...here."

I studied the plot plan. Like a geologic map, it included details hidden beneath the surface. I was desperately hoping to see something on the plot plan that Valerie didn't. I wanted so badly to be able to point to the map and say, *See? Here is Mary's grave.* But I couldn't.

Valerie continued. "It's a four-grave plot, and the other three graves are empty. If your sister was buried here, we would have a record of it."

Empty.

I looked up at Valerie on the verge of tears. "How can I find out where she is? I need to find her."

"You should call the funeral home that took care of the service. They will have a record of where she's buried."

Hesitantly I stood, gathered my jacket and purse, and watched her roll up the map. "Right. Okay. I'll call them. Thank you for your help."

I felt Valerie's palm gently rest on my back, as if she realized that the search went far beyond a grave. "You're welcome. I wish you good luck, Julie."

* * *

Mom had said that Mary's services were held at the Valade Funeral home. That made sense; it was the only funeral parlor in town. As soon as I arrived back at The Lake House, I called them. An overly cheerful voice answered on the second ring. He identified himself as 'Bob.' Dad's name. I asked about Mary's service.

"Oh. 1976? That was a long time ago."

I drummed my fingers on the kitchen counter and waited.

"Let me see, that would be in the old file." I heard him thumbing through paper records. "I don't see it here, but it could be misfiled. Oh, wait! We have a Louise Tefft in 1973. Could the name be wrong?"

"No. Louise was—is—my sister too." That was one of the things I always tripped up on. Is she not my sister anymore because she died? The other thing I dreaded was the *how-many-sisters-do-you-have* question. I always felt guilty leaving out Louise and Mary, but I hated explaining their deaths more.

Don't' talk about it. It's nobody else's business.

"Louise is my sister too," I repeated, trying to sound confident.

"Oh?" He paused as if waiting for me to add something. "How did *she* die?"

I felt cornered by this sudden intrusion and blurted out the truth. "She was murdered. Can you just—"

"How awful!" he interrupted, prying for more none-of-his-business info. "Did they catch the person?"

I felt his invasive questions crawling, burrowing, wet and slimy into my skin. "Yes. And you don't see a record for *Mary*?" I asked sharply, having run out of patience. "I called to ask about Mary."

"Um, no. But I will check more thoroughly and let you know what I find. Should I reach you at the number on the caller ID?"

"Yes."

I hung up the phone without even saying goodbye and then, with a shortstop windup, fired it across the room at the couch.

He had brought up Louise.

Talking about Louise makes people angry. Louise, my oldest sister, a year older than Tammy. Mom's first little girl, who died in 1973 when she was only 16. Three years before Mary. I paced and stomped and cursed at Bob from the Valade funeral home. I reacted as if subjected to the sideways glances and whispers of strangers, identifying us as the family of the murdered girl, and then judging us.

I reacted like Mom.

A small sliver of space opened in that moment. The same old feelings had been stirred, but my perspective was beginning to shift. I felt like I was observing my reaction from somewhere outside of my own head, trying to trace it back in time to its source.

I remembered our family prior to Father's Day of 1973, when we had been whole. Not perfect but together. At 4-years-old, I probably didn't pay attention to individual days passing. They probably seemed similar to me; each day was simply a question of playing with the Fisher Price Little People, going for a ride in Louise's car, or perhaps getting penny candy. But one day stood out among all others that spring.

It was the day the police came to our house.

Louise hasn't come home. Mommy doesn't know where she is. Daddy has been looking for her. I ask so many times that everyone gets mad at me. I ask Mary but she doesn't know either. I want Drowsy. I want my bottle. I want my bedtime story. I want Mary to cuddle me. I want Dad to take me for penny candy. I like the squirrels and the bit-o-honey. Mary likes them too.

* * *

Later that day, a less-cheerful Bob returned my call and told me they had no record of a service for Mary.

What the hell?

He asked if I was sure the service was at Valade.

"Yes," I replied. "That's what my mom said." But in truth, I wasn't sure of anything at this point.

He suggested I find the prayer card. It would list the funeral home on the back.

* * *

Exhausted, I collapsed on the bed to rest, feet hanging off the edge.

I fell asleep and dreamed I was at a large party with my four younger sisters. The event was held in an old stone castle, made of giant blocks of granite. Instead of grout, crammed in the joints of the stone were thousands of black spiders with intricate patterns on their backs.

As people began to disperse. I noticed my youngest sister, Nicole, was missing. I rushed from room to room searching for her. I leaned out a window and noticed a child with a dog running zig-zag across the dirt road below. A car sped over the gravel road toward them, swerved, and kicked up a cloud of dust.

Suddenly the walls of the castle seemed to expand and contract— like I was trapped inside of an accordion with less and less air available. A dark wave of spiders flooded from the joints in the stones and crawled up my arms and legs.

I woke terrified but relieved and took a deep breath. I had slept for almost two hours. I went into the kitchen and poured a glass of wine. The terror was real. It wouldn't dissipate over time like a morning fog. I was nearly 13-years-old when Nicole was born. As a young teen, I spent most evenings babysitting her and my other sisters while my parents worked. My relationship with the new family was a complex muddle of big sister/ mother. I was aware of the ineffective ways I had tried to shoulder the burden of that responsibility. And how my younger sisters still carried a tangle of expectations and hidden resentments. Although I love all of them deeply, I've often felt incongruous.

My sister Renee joined the family just six months after we had lost Louise. Just when I needed attention the most, it became increasingly divided. Mom had Angela a year after Renee, Robyn arrived 2 years later in 1977, and finally the baby of the family, Nicole, joined us five years later. As adults, we all share the bond of sisterhood, but not equally. Renee and Angela are only a year apart and have always been close. They both have bachelor's degrees and stable careers, and Angela went on to get many professional certifications as well.

In contrast, Robyn and Nicole's career paths have been rambling. Both unmarried when they began having children, I've often worried about their jobs, financial stability, and their happiness. At times, probably too much. Nicole, the once-spoiled baby of the family, has sometimes looked at life through a skewed lens of entitlement. Robyn is probably the one whose plight I most identify with. She is the middle child and has struggled at times to claim her place. She works endlessly, tends a garden, and keeps chickens. Of my younger sisters in the new family, she is the one most like Mom and Dad. Her willingness to help anyone, anytime reminds me of Mary.

I needed to continue the search. I crawled into the storage space behind the knee-wall in the loft, hoping to find a prayer card from Mary's service. In reality, I knew that if one existed, Mom would probably have it packed away in the attic at The Compound. But I was not about to ask her.

You're upsetting Mom.

I excavated several boxes of pictures, photo albums, and memorabilia. The enduring smoky quartz crystal sat on my desk as a solid reminder. Persistence.

Strength comes not only from individual crystals or people, but from the matrix that binds them into rock or community. What or who was my matrix?

Chapter 8:

Jammy

July, 2015

As the last ice age ended, meltwater from the glacier sorted sediments into layers and left them as a reminder of the glacier's power to transform the landscape. But where is the ice now? Unrecognizable, its molecules reside somewhere within the vast water cycle, perhaps in a lake, stream, cloud, or soil, able to change their state of matter, and as the 13th century Persian poet Rumi said, "…disappear into emptiness with a thousand new disguises."

That evening, I stayed up late, sitting on the floor in the living room, sorting the past into stacks arranged by time. Photos and evidence that Mary once shaped our lives. But where is she now? In the emptiness before me, what new disguises might she have taken?

There was no prayer card.

* * *

I woke without an alarm, slipped quietly out of the bedroom, and brewed a pot of coffee. I plucked a photo album from the strata of last night's investigation, sat on the loveseat, and opened the album across my lap. Faded pictures of me as a toddler stared ghostlike from the pages.

I focused on a family photo taken after Tammy's 8th grade graduation. The old family and I stood in front of the little white cape, side by side, in two rows of three. Bright pink peonies as big as feather dusters were in bloom to our right. In the photo I waved from the front row, mouth open in a wordy grin, probably shouting *cheese!* Tammy's hand rested on my shoulder. Kevin, Mary, and Louise were all looking at me. I had everyone's attention. I belonged.

The photo album had a few more pictures of the old family, and several of Mary and me together, spending time lavishly; feeding chickens at The Compound, picking wild strawberries in the first pasture, and wearing bikinis in the backyard at Grandma's house. That was the most recent picture I had of Mary. It was taken her last summer on earth, when she was 13.

I glanced out the window and studied a nuthatch as it pecked upside down at the feeder, its slender beak selecting and tossing seeds. I barely noticed my husband, Eric, walk into the room, until he stuck his face in front of mine.

"Did you make enough coffee for me? What are you looking at?" He had the habit of asking questions in rapid succession without waiting for answers in between.

I met his gaze, closed the album, and then looked back out over the lake. "No one knows where Mary is." I took a breath and turned back toward him. "How can *no one* know? That's fucked up."

He nodded. "You're right. But someone *has* to know. You'll find out." He walked over and poured a cup of coffee.

I scoffed at his optimism. He squeezed beside me on the loveseat as a few drops of coffee sloshed over the rim of the cup. He pretended not to notice. "Did you talk to your parents?"

"No, and I'm not going to."

"I'm sure they'd talk about it. And I hope you're writing all this down. It's *some* story."

I felt the muscles in my jaw tighten. *Some story?* Eric knew about loss – firsthand. His older brother PJ died in a gun accident when he was 19 and Eric was 13. His family seemed to be able to all talk about PJ. They reminisce fondly. They know where he is buried. They visit the grave. My family's reaction to loss was different. Eric didn't know Mom and Dad like I did. And the daily entries in my journal? They were *not* for the public. Mine and my family's hardships were not a story. They were not entertainment. And they were nobody else's business.

"Leave it alone," I said with the chill of a stoic Bardy.

"You should tell your parents she's not in St. Anthony's—that there are questions."

"I can't talk to them." Very *un*-Bardy-like, I feared crossing a boundary that would make Mom shut down. "I'll think of something else."

But I wasn't sure I *had* another option. I got up and gathered my things for The Ocean House. I had to get the mail and then head to the university to play in a faculty softball game that evening. The thought of softball made me feel grounded, and I needed that.

My love for the sport was rooted in games with Louise and Tammy and their friends, Sue and Barbara Gefvert, on the Gefvert's front lawn. I'm sure it was more watching than playing since I was only 4, but that early connection between baseball and community was a powerful one. I can't cook or grow plants, but I'm a gold-glove infielder. I have always felt confident when I stepped onto the diamond, swung a bat, and fielded grounders.

Yet when faced with trying to find Mary, I was lost. I didn't know who to ask or what to do next. There were no records. Why? It was possible that there *was* no service. That there *was* no burial. Maybe it was none of my business. Maybe she didn't *want* to be found. My thoughts grappled with each other for the entire trip to West Haven, until I pulled up to the driveway at The Ocean House and was surprised to see a cheerful, floral welcoming committee.

Eric and I had been talking about re-paving the crumbling driveway for years. Each summer I spent more time pulling and spraying weeds. Yet that year, instead of weeds, the worn pavement sprouted deep purple, fuchsia, and pastel pink petunias, crowded and bursting from every crack. Miniature trumpets of velvet and satin surrounded by the fluted edges of supple green leaves that giggled in the gusty breeze. I parked on the street so I wouldn't disturb anything. Solid patches of pavement served as stepping-stones as I navigated through the mysterious, magical garden of colorful blooms to the back door.

I turned to survey the garden with curiosity. In the five years I had lived there, I had *never* planted petunias on this property. Neither had my neighbors.

The first thought that came to mind was Mary. Was she sending her approval? Her encouragement? Was she exclaiming, *"It's about time you looked for me!"*?

I certainly had no evidence to support a ghostly planting, but that spontaneous flower garden comforted and reassured me. I believed it was Mary's way of letting me know that the matrix of support was strong, even though it's not always visible. The matrix itself could emerge in a thousand new disguises.

Still mulling the potential symbolism of the driveway garden, I grabbed my softball glove from the basement and closed the bulkhead. The whir of a neighbor's lawn mower, the smell of fresh cut grass, and the soft leather of my glove created a vivid picture in my mind—a picture of those old baseball games on the Gefvert's front lawn. In that moment I knew who I needed to talk to. I needed to call Tammy.

* * *

Although we only talk a couple of times a year, our sisterly bond is deep. We understand its worth; we know the anguish of losing it. Tammy has a directness that, in conversation, is either completely refreshing, or completely unsettling. You never know what she'll ask, but she has an uncanny skill of getting right to the heart of the matter. Knowing that both reassured and frightened me. We'd rarely spoken about Louise or Mary prior to that conversation, and we'd never spoken about their deaths.

I scrolled to Tammy's number on my phone. She answered on the third ring, voice raspy. She works for the postal service and was in the midst of taking a nap between her morning and afternoon mail deliveries. I thought it might be a bad time.

"Should I call back?"

"No, no. I have to get up anyway."

Her voice put me at ease. After a few minutes of small talk, I spilled everything that had been going on—the lost records, the undocumented burial, and the questions I had about what happened to Mary's body.

"No records? That is *so* strange," Tammy uttered in disbelief. "I haven't thought about the funeral in years." She paused and then added, "I've never gone to Mary's grave."

I began to wonder who *did* go to the burial, but I had to stay focused. One thing at a time.

"Do you think Mom's lying?" she asked.

Her candor, although typical, still caught me by surprise. "I don't know, but why would there be no record of the funeral? No record of the burial? It doesn't make sense."

"It *does* seem like she's hiding something." Tammy paused. "I'm going to think about this some more."

"Okay. I should go. I have a softball game tonight. Thanks for listening. Please call if you remember anything."

"I will. Love you."

* * *

The softball game was a welcomed distraction, and afterward, a bunch of us planned to meet for beer and wings at a local bar. As I drove, I thought about my conversation with Tammy. Her voice was a comfort—her willingness to help gave me strength.

Over the years at her farm in Vermont, she has raised cows, pigs, chickens, a deer named Blackberry, a bear, and a wolf. She raised three children from her first marriage, and decades before that, when she was a teenager living at The Compound, she helped take care of me.

Because we only had one bathroom in the small cape, sometimes my evening routine overlapped with Louise and Tammy's. As they washed their faces and brushed their teeth, I watched them with fascination and took every opportunity to join in.

I remember how Tammy unscrewed the cover of the blue glass jar of *Noxzema* and swept her fingers into the silky, white cream. She smeared a little on each of my cheeks, and then on hers. The crisp scent of menthol flooded my sinuses. Tammy gazed into the mirror of the medicine cabinet, and I looked up at her from my vantage point below the top of the sink. I swirled the cream on my face in circles, just like she did. I loved the tingly sensation on my skin after she hoisted me up to cup my little hands in the running water and rinse my face. Even though they were only 15 and 16, Tammy and Louise were *big* girls from my perspective. That's what I wanted to be. To wear fringy clothes, burn incense, and give peace signs.

In those days, The Compound was a hub of activity and community. In addition to my sisters and brothers, Tammy and Louise had a large network of friends who were my extended family. Life was filled with mini-bike rides, swimming at the towers, marshmallow roasting, a wardrobe of groovy 70's outfits, and endless volunteers for bedtime stories. One of my favorite storytellers was Debbie--one of Louise and Tammy's best friends--whom I referred to as "my *other* big sister".

I would choose a story, most often "The Shy Little Kitten," by Cathleen Schurr, and climb up, with Drowsy in tow, onto the teller's lap. Drowsy attended every reading with me. She had little flesh-colored hands that I loved to hold. We were inseparable, as I had thought Louise and Tammy were.

But then came the day that Louise went missing.

And our world shifted on its axis.

Amidst a chaotic stew of emptiness, fear, misplaced blame and guilt, Tammy moved out of the house on July 8, 1973, three weeks after Louise's death. Louise was gone. Tammy was gone. And with them, my extended family vanished like the rising smoke from the incense. There were only two girls left at the house, me, 4-years-old, and Mary, 10.

Tammy moved in with her new boyfriend, Leo, and his family at a dairy farm in the adjacent town of Woodstock. The farm was home to hundreds of cows, chickens, pigs, and other animals, as well as Mr. and Mrs. Butts and their 15 children. Mom let me visit Tammy at her new home a few times. It was a comforting, grand cacophony of distraction, the real-life version of the old woman in the shoe--so many kids, all so noisy, silly and messy, and smelled like cow manure. We would chase each other around the yard, splash through mud puddles, leap from the hayloft, and swing on a thick rope, like Tarzan, from one of the roof joists in the barn.

I smiled as I thought about the craziness of the Butts Farm. I could almost smell the hay bales and hear the pigs and kids squealing. My smile faded as I thought about the questions that swirled in my brain— *What could Mom be hiding? What would Tammy remember? Where is Mary now?*

* * *

My cell rang as I parked my car in the lot behind the New West Cafe for a post-game beer. It was Tammy, and she was a current of nervous energy.

"Julie, I just can't stop thinking about this. I remember the wake, not all of it, but bits and pieces. It was so sad. Mary's pediatric nurse was there. Mrs. LePearle. She was crying. I remember that, so I know there was a service. What do you think happened to her body?"

"I don't know," I said. "But I remember someone saying something about donating her eyes. It seems like a dream, but it has stuck in my head all these years. There must be a reason."

"Do you think Mom donated Mary's body to science? That might explain why there's no record of her burial."

I felt relieved that I wasn't the only one thinking this way. "Maybe. And maybe she's not telling the truth because she thinks people will be mad."

"Would *you* be mad if that's what happened?"

I thought about it for a moment. I felt strongly that it was Mom's decision. I just wanted to know the truth. "No. I wouldn't be mad. If there was a way to help someone by donating some or all of her body, that's what *Mary* would have wanted."

"I wonder if that's what Mom did."

"Well, if she did, I doubt she'll ever tell us." *And I'm certainly not asking her.* I told Tammy I had to go. I needed a cold beer. I promised to call her with any updates.

As I walked slowly toward the cafe, I took inventory of what I knew for sure. The facts surrounding Mary's burial? There were few. Tammy knew there was a service because she remembered being there. But the question remained: Where was Mary's body? Tammy had little more info than I did.

I walked in, dusty, sweaty, and emotionally wiped-out, and found a seat near my teammates. The beer was cold and refreshing, but my mind was far from the softball banter at the bar.

It was back in 1976, at a funeral service for Mary, struggling to recall the slightest detail.

None came to mind.

Chapter 9:

A Crack in the Armor

While I was attempting to resuscitate 40-year-old memories from the bottom of a beer glass, unbeknownst to me, Tammy was calling Mom and asking questions.

Her inquiry was followed up by my meddling but big-hearted husband who called me at The Ocean House later that evening to confess. "Don't be mad, but I talked to your parents. They're not upset at all. They want to help."

"Seriously?! Why'd you do that? I specifically asked you not to say anything."

Eric paused for a moment. "I think your sister Tammy called them too," he added.

Both of them? Behind my back? I felt betrayed. I had spoken to Tammy in confidence, and why did *he* talk to them? Mary is my sister. It was none of his business.

Instantly I recognized my reaction—anger toward a lack of control. I felt like Mom.

Eric explained, justified, and defended. His words were a muffled blur. "Are you mad?"

"Well, it's done. So it really doesn't matter how I feel."

I ended the call and curled up in bed, eyes wide open. Would Mom and Dad argue? Would *they* feel betrayed? Would Mom be angry?

* * *

The next morning, I made the two-hour drive back to The Lake House in Thompson. I was putting away groceries when my cell phone rang. It was a call from The Compound. I leaned on the counter and braced myself. Was Mom calling to blast me for not minding my own business?

With softness unfamiliar, she said, "You know, Julie, I can talk about Mary. It's okay."

Her reaction left me stupefied. I lowered myself into the nearest chair and sank into an emotional slurry—relief, sadness, gratitude, guilt for feeling relieved. I tried not to cry. "I don't want to bring up bad memories and hurt you guys all over again. You've been through enough." Tears polluted my words. Damn emotions. Showing weakness, again.

"It was a long time ago. I can talk about it."

* * *

Later that afternoon, we sat in the living room at The Compound, and I listened as Mom tried to answer some of my questions. She insisted that Mary was buried in St. Anthony's Cemetery near Dziadzia, she was sure of it. But she wasn't exactly sure where Dziadzia was buried. I wanted to believe her, but I needed this to make sense and it didn't. Why were there no records? Why didn't she know what plot they were in?

She flipped through the pages of a recipe book as I recounted my conversation with Bob from Valade's. We chatted for a few minutes; it was the most time we had ever spent talking about Mary. But somewhere beneath the welcomed kindness and soft tone lurked something vague, suspicious, and elusive. Then it became clear.

No one in the family went to Mary's burial; not a soul.

As I thought about her being lowered into the ground by strangers, with no one there to say goodbye, my heart ached. I felt ashamed.

I needed to know why my family seemed to have abandoned her.

Mom stood up, recipe book in hand, and walked into the kitchen. "I want to make orange pinwheel biscuits, but I don't know if I have enough cinnamon."

I followed her into the kitchen and sat at the table, pulling at a hangnail on my index finger and glancing up at Mom as she rummaged through the cabinets, gathering ingredients for the recipe. And then I summoned every Bardy atom I had in me and breeched the subject head-on.

"How come no one went to the burial?"

"Huh? Oh, I don't know. I don't really remember."

I waited. For once I refused to dismiss my need to know the truth about my sister.

"They couldn't bury her the day of the service," Mom finally said. "The weather. I think it may have been bad weather."

Persistence. "So why was no one there?"

She opened a cabinet and started shuffling things around. I couldn't see her face. "Can you reach the flour sifter? It's there on the top shelf."

"Sure." I went to the cabinet, grabbed the sifter, and handed it to her. "Tammy said that the burial would have been close to your birthday." I could not imagine burying a child. I know I could not do it within a few days of my own birthday—a date that would serve as an annual reminder that you lived another year and they didn't. "She said that Grandma didn't want the burial to be so close to your birthday."

"No. I think maybe the ground was still frozen. Or it was bad weather."

Perhaps. But why was she so focused on talking about the delay? I had wanted to know why she wasn't there. I watched as she scooped two cups of flour from the bag and emptied them into the sifter. She cranked the small wooden knob: processing, separating, and aerating the flour.

"The funeral home put her in a glossy white casket. The state wouldn't pay for it. Valade's told me I would have to pay the difference. But we couldn't afford it."

I could imagine the spicy exchange that followed. Was there a delay because the caskets had to be swapped before the burial? I didn't ask.

Sometime after the funeral, she didn't say how long, Mom got a phone call from the cemetery. They were ready to bury Mary.

"They asked me if the family could gather for the burial. I told them to just go ahead; I didn't need to be there."

Those words were difficult to hear, but I was beginning to understand. The delay *was* the reason she didn't go. That's why she was focused on it. In her mind she had already buried Mary and could not do it a second time. She didn't tell anyone else or feel the need for anyone's approval. Mary was her daughter. It was her grief, and it was big. No one questioned it.

Max barked, trotted to the door, jumped up, and pawed at the glass. Dad was home.

I worried that I was sitting in the middle of a potential battlefield. "Hi, Dad."

He set a small bag from the hardware store on the table. "I'm glad you're here. I want to get to the bottom of this."

I quickly glanced over at Mom with a sudden urge to say, *don't yell*. But she didn't even look up. She was snapping the beaters into the electric mixer. I held my breath.

"You should look in the attic first," she said to Dad.

What? Clearly there was a plan that I wasn't aware of.

Dad went into the living room, pulled down the folding stairs to the attic, and marched up in search of a prayer card from Mary's service. I followed him and waited on the top step as he went through dozens of old boxes filled with an assortment of dishes, toys, 8-tracks, 33 LPs, books, clothes, spare parts for outdated electronics. It was a dog's breakfast of life over the years: things that were perfectly good, but whose value was not appreciated in the present.

We brought down five boxes in all: three cardboard, one plastic, and one metal. The containers were stuffed full of school papers with kids' scrawled handwriting, artwork, report cards, greeting cards, receipts, pay stubs, and thousands of family photos loosely mixed in among the contents. Unpacking the boxes was like thawing a life that had been frozen in time for 40 years; releasing clasts of my childhood before age 7.

I reached into one of the bins and picked up a photo of Mary at about 11-years-old. We were in the kitchen, pea green walls at our backs. We sat on a round, multi-colored, braided rug, woven from scraps of old clothes. The rug insulated us from the chilly, beige-colored linoleum, embossed with a pattern of various sized rectangles. Old linoleum with curled edges where the dirt, spare change, and Barbie doll shoes would collect, curled edges that would rip holes in our socks as we ran across the kitchen and skidded down the sloped floor. Rough corners that Dad tried to staple down, to no avail.

In the photo, Mary was behind me, sitting on her shins, knees snug against my back. I sat crossed-legged holding our black dust mop of a mini-terrier, Skippy, in my lap, little fingers laced into his shaggy coat. Kevin was kneeling to my left a foot or so away, his arms crossed, and body turned slightly away from us. A section of our Fisher-Price Little People Village was set up nearby.

The original Little People townsfolk were made of wood with similar painted smiling expressions and diverse skin tones, hair color, and occupations. Their bodies were hollow with a hole at the base to set them on pegs in various locations such as desks or seats in vehicles. We carefully arranged the downtown area with the police station, dentist, fire station, and store, into two city blocks. Our favorite building was the school.

We would lift the hinged flap of the roof, and one entire wall would lower like a drawbridge so we could configure the classroom. Inside, we would set up a green desk for the teacher and five yellow desks for the students. Sometimes Mary wore her blonde hair in a ponytail, which reminded me of the Little People teacher, and I was always learning from her. In the photo, colorful, plastic letters with little magnets on the back were arranged to spell out "Julie is my sister" on the white roof of the school house; my spelling lesson on that particular day.

Studying the details in the photo, I noticed a peculiar expression on my face. It was not a smile, not the joyful grin of a carefree 5-year-old, but rather the wide-eyed concern of a child who was fearful—even then—before Mary had left us. I have come to recognize that expression. It is known as anticipatory grief. Mary had been getting worse. In less than two years from when this photo was taken, there would never be another spelling lesson. Did I overhear the doctor, on one of Mary's many trips to the hospital, say to Mom, "You know, there will be a day when you won't be able to get her here in time?"

There was also something eerily familiar about the photo. It was as if I had modeled part of my life after it. Perhaps my career as a geology professor is rooted in those early lessons at the Little People schoolhouse and my perpetual reaching out for solid ground.

I ran my fingers across the photo and set it down. After going through only half of one bin, I was completely exhausted. The past pummeled me with a barrage of what-if questions. What would Louise and Mary be doing now? Would they be married? Would they have children?

Would I have had children if I wasn't so terrified of having to endure what my parents did?

After almost an hour, I finally found a prayer card with Mary's death announcement. The small words printed on the back, at the very bottom, read "Valade funeral home, Inc. North Grosvenordale, CONN."

Relieved, I held up the card. "I've got it. And it says Valade on the bottom." I handed the card to Dad, and he and Mom glanced quickly at the back.

The search was a success in Dad's eyes, and he got up and went into his office to pack for his part-time DJ job. Mom went into their bedroom to get changed for work. They left me in the living room surrounded by ghosts; decades of memories that I desperately wanted to process. A life that I had completely disconnected myself from but was now fanned out before me in all its black and white truth.

I knew I was going to cry, and I didn't want to cry in front of them. "Can I take these boxes home? I'll be careful and make sure I bring everything back."

"Yes. That's fine," Mom said, quicker than I expected. She seemed eager for me to take them.

What had Tammy and Eric said to her?

* * *

That evening in the privacy of the loft at The Lake House, I sifted through one of the boxes. Mixed in with family photos, I found several articles. One was titled "Mothers, Daughters, Sisters," written by Carol Saline and published in the November 1998 issue of *Ladies' Home Journal*. It described the powerful emotional connections between mothers and daughters. Saline wrote: "Nobody can love you more than a mother, daughter, or sister, and nobody can hurt you more. Our mothers are our memory banks, the repository of family history. We share a special bond that is unique and unbreakable...someone fashioned in our image, someone we can understand and identify with."

It was interesting to think about mother-daughter relationships in this way. Clearly Mom had valued the ideas in the piece, but she seemed more like a maximum-security prison for memories than a repository. I certainly didn't feel like I was fashioned in her image. Had she been reflecting on her bond with Grandma? With Louise? With Mary? Could that "unbreakable" mother-daughter bond be broken by death?

From the same box, I dug out a newspaper clipping about a 5-year-old boy named Andy who disappeared in September of 1978 and was never found. The article was written ten years later and recounts the day Andy went missing.

I had asked Mom about the article when we were in her kitchen the previous day. "I remember that little boy. Yes. He lived close—in Webster. The kids were excused from school to help search. That was terrible. They never found him." She was staring straight ahead as she spoke. I wondered if she was thinking of the high school students who searched for Louise.

Mom had always been keenly aware of news reports of children who were abducted or went missing, or of women who were murdered. She followed cases like Martha Moxley, Mrs. Riley in Canaan, Chappaquiddick, and victims of the serial killer named Ross. Because of Louise's murder, we felt a deep personal connection to those events and people. Because of the alienating whispers of small-town gossip, and the emotional isolation of tragedy, it was a connection that we did not experience with the community at large.

* * *

The next morning, I woke early, climbed the stairs to the loft and continued sorting photos, organizing them by decade into manila folders. I ran across a picture of Mom when she was about 8 years-old with Aunt Helen and Grandma, standing side by side in front of a Christmas tree. On the tree were lovely handmade decorations, including a red and green construction paper chain and a tin-foil star. I instantly recognized them. They were the same decorations that Mary and I would make each year.

It never occurred to me that the tradition was rooted in Mom's own childhood. Mom had described Grandma as a strict and intolerant mother. She had a wall around her heart as well; a trait shared by fearless

Bardy women. When I spoke to Mom about Mary, I had asked her about Grandma's first child, Mom's older sister who died at birth.

She had seemed surprised. "How did you know about that?"

"I remember hearing about the baby's death a long time ago. I don't remember who told me, but Tammy brought it up again the other day. I bet Grandma must have been traumatized. I'm sure she probably never got over it."

Mom had nodded slowly, staring into the abyss. "She told your aunt Helen and me about it once. But she never took us to the baby's grave. I don't even know where she is buried."

Suddenly, Grandma's controlling personality and intolerant behavior made sense. I thought back to the article about mothers and daughters. The boxes in front of me held much more than old photos and newspaper clippings. They contained skeleton keys to locks that I hadn't been aware of; keys to understanding the complex relationships that existed among the Bardy women, including me.

We shared much more than I had previously realized.

I thought about how difficult it is to be a woman in our family—the heartache caused by the emotional need for connection that we simultaneously reach toward and push away. I rubbed my stinging eyes and felt the tension of the past pulling at my heart and mind.

I was being drawn into the depths of a dark world that I wondered if I'd have the strength to return from. Yet I needed to spend time in that place.

When the pile of crumpled tissues on the floor reached a critical angle of repose, I decided to step away from the photos and take a break.

I called the Valade funeral home to let them know I had found the funeral card. The bookkeeper, Wendy, promised to do a complete search of their records and get back to me.

* * *

The call from Wendy came a few days later. "I looked through all of the records from the 70s. There is nothing for Mary Tefft. I found a Louise Tefft..."

I quickly cut her off. "I know. She's also my sister." I gave an exaggerated exhale, anticipating more questions.

But Wendy's voice softened as she explained, "The funeral home has changed hands four times since the seventies. During the time of your sister Mary's death, the owner, Joe Valade, was not well. He was getting very...ill. I'm sorry. Can you hold on a minute?"

"Sure." I could hear her talking with someone in the background.

Getting very ill. What did that mean? Physically sick? Mentally sick? Did he not bury my sister? Did he sell her body? Throw her out back in the river? In the pause, manic thoughts rapidly filled in the unknowns.

"Okay Julie. Sorry for the interruption. The records were poorly kept during the time of your sister's service. Just to be sure, I looked through online records of other funeral homes in the area as well—I couldn't find any record of the service or burial."

None of this made sense. "This is so frustrating. Thank you for checking."

"I'm really sorry I couldn't do more." Wendy added one last suggestion. "Do you have a copy of the death certificate? That would have the name of the cemetery listed on it."

Do families usually have death certificates for loved ones? I didn't know. "My parents probably have one. I'll check with them. Thank you again for everything." I set down the phone and rested my elbows on the table, forehead heavy in my hands.

I felt a ripple of suspicion in my stomach. It appeared Mom was finally opening up, but questions remained about the location of Mary's body. And my wild imagination was indulging every possibility.

* * *

I called Mom the next day with another difficult question. "Do you have a death certificate for Mary?"

"I don't think so," Mom said. "But I found a few more boxes we can look through."

We waded through several bins of dusty papers and brittle photographs she found in her bedroom closet. All those poorly preserved pictures haphazardly scattered around the home in different places and different boxes—didn't she value them? These were irreplaceable reminders of Louise and Mary. They were all we had left.

From across the kitchen table, I intermittently glanced up at Mom, studying her expressions, trying to discern the unspoken feelings that hung thick in the air between us.

"I remember the wake," Mom began. "I remember the white casket. I couldn't look at her body after seeing Louise in the morgue. That was enough."

I felt her pain but didn't want to appear sympathetic or make her feel weak. I chose my words carefully. "Ugh. That must have been hell."

She nodded slowly, staring straight ahead, her mind in that place where only she and ghosts were allowed to roam.

"She was buried a few days or weeks after the service. I'm not sure exactly when."

My suspicion was fading.

Still, we found no death certificate. I would need to request one from the town hall.

* * *

That night I got little rest. My mind raced with thoughts of Mary's death, her burial, the contract, and how exhausting and overwhelming it was to dig into such a tragic past.

Perhaps that's how Mom felt. The pictures reminded us of precious times with Mary and Louise, but also that they were gone. Maybe she couldn't bear to look at all the memories, or all the loss, at one time, in one place. To look at the whole memory would risk being consumed by the past; relentlessly dissolving you from the edges inward, until you lose all sense of person or place. I knew.

I was sinking into that world, and it was terrifying.

A world where thread-by-thread the family unraveled and scattered; into different caskets, buried in different places.

Chapter 10:

Proof of Death

August, 2015

The Putnam Town Hall is an ornate brownstone building perched on a hill overlooking the French River as it parallels the main street of the quaint downtown. That particular day, I was not interested in marveling at its architecture or admiring its beautiful setting.

I was there to see about death.

The clerk behind the counter was a woman I recognized from high school. It took me by surprise and I instantly felt my cheeks warm. "Hi, Darlene."

As she looked up from the computer screen, she grinned and slapped her palms on the counter. "Julie! How have you been?!"

"Good, thanks." Despite her interest in hearing about my travels, we each managed to share an efficient, 60-second synopsis of the past 30 years. Then I edged closer to the counter and brought up the reason I was there. "I need to get a copy of a death certificate, but I'm not sure how to go about this."

"Is it for a relative? …I need to copy your ID …I never knew you had a sister who died …Just one copy of the certificate? …Do you need any others?"

It was a strange juxtaposition of time periods and people. I felt uneasy. I liked Darlene well enough, but less than a handful of my friends knew about Mary. Was she wondering why I needed the death certificate? Was she judging me? Was it hot in there? This seemed like it was taking a long time.

"Sign here please." She smiled, placed a pen on top of a release form, and slid them toward me.

I scrawled my name at the bottom, and she handed me a white legal envelope. "Okay. Here you go."

I snatched it off the counter. "Thank you. It was nice to see you," I said, waving and turning away from her as I walked out. When I reached my car, I opened the door and sat down. The envelope felt thick and heavy. I opened the flap, took a deep breath, and unfolded the paper.

The autopsy box was checked, confirming an autopsy had been done. I skipped to the bottom where I read a combination of words that I hadn't seen before—*whole-body burial*. Mary was not cremated, not donated. I paused and allowed a feeling of deep relief to sink into my bones.

Below that information was the location of burial, St. Anthony's Cemetery in Webster. Just as Mom had said.

I sat up a little straighter. The search area had gotten infinitesimally smaller.

I drove to Mom and Dad's with the death certificate.

"Did they do an autopsy?" Mom asked.

"Yes."

"What did they list as the cause of death?"

"Mucus in the airways."

Stoic, she nodded. "Right. Okay."

She seemed relieved to some extent. Perhaps validating her recollection was some small comfort to her.

* * *

I left The Compound and drove to St. Anthony's Parish in Dudley.

Valerie read the death certificate carefully and shook her head in disbelief. She made a copy for the parish records. "The next time Paul is at the cemetery I'll have him probe the other graves."

* * *

Life continued in the world above ground. A couple of weeks later, I was attending a faculty outing with Eric and some of my colleagues from the Earth Science Department. We had spent a few days at a remote cabin in the Maine wilderness on the east shore of Sebec Lake. Eric and I had left the camp in Dover-Foxcroft and were heading to Acadia National Park to do some hiking.

My cell phone chimed to alert me of a new voicemail. My heartbeat quickened when I realized it was from Valerie.

I called her back immediately.

"We found your sister Mary. Sorry to take so long to get back to you, but I had to wait until the part-time caretaker, Paul, was working. He probed and found another vault near your grandpa. Mary is buried there."

A deep sigh. Finally, confirmation. *But What did she mean--a vault?* I pressed a hand to my heart. "How do you know for *sure* she's buried there?"

"You can have the grave opened, but it's rather expensive. I would certainly help you arrange it, but there would not be a vault there unless there had been a burial."

I had to remind myself that not everyone is trying to hide things. "Okay. That makes sense."

"Paul cleaned off the markers so you can see them better. Your grandpa is buried in grave number one of plot 18-B. Paul probed the remainder of the plot and found a vault in grave number three. If you have any trouble finding it, please let me know. Paul's not there often, but if we make arrangements ahead, I'm sure he could meet you."

Her thoughtful explanation and soft voice reassured me that we had found Mary. I didn't want to disturb her grave. "Thank you for your help."

"No trouble at all. That's what I'm here for."

Indeed. The network of support stretched far and wide.

* * *

It seemed appropriate that Eric and I ended our vacation in Acadia National Park, for me a place deeply symbolic of life cycles and infused with wilderness. A place where I first observed the ancient intricacies of family dynamics up close, by documenting the lives of breeding loons—a 100-million-year-old species whose pleasures and struggles I saw mirrored within my own life.

Paddling on Long Pond, I dissolved into my surroundings. The surface of the water softly bent into folds of satin, studded with the leathery, saucer-sized leaves and lotus-like blooms of white and pink water lilies. The sky was a cornflower blue and troweled with a few scattered clouds. A pair of loons dressed in their black-tie breeding plumage floated about 50 feet from my kayak and called out softly, *hoo-hoo,* the intimate family call.

* * *

After returning from Maine, I stopped by The Compound to tell Mom and Dad about Valerie's call. They were relieved. I had planned to drive two hours south, to The Ocean House, after the visit, but I took a quick detour to St. Anthony's Cemetery in Webster first. Toward the St. Peter's section. Toward Mary.

I pulled into the cemetery and noticed an open grave, a dump truck filled with soil, and a flatbed truck that had just lowered a vault into the grave. One man operated the chain and webbed harness that lowered the vault. Three other men, one in his mid-late 40s and two in their 60s, stood in front of the dump truck slowly untangling the knot of chains and webbing.

I parked the car, walked toward the grave, and stopped about ten feet from the men. "Hello. Are any of you named Paul, by chance?"

The middle-aged one replied, "Yes. That's me."

Paul had a beard and black hair peppered with wiry strands of grey. His complexion was ashy, and there were dark circles beneath his eyes. "Hi, I'm Julie. I spoke with Valerie about finding my sister Mary's grave."

He nodded. "I can show you where she's buried," he said, anticipating my next question.

I accompanied Paul who was slightly hunched and walked with a limp, toward the St. Peter's section. "You're lucky to catch me here. I'm only part-time, and I've been out sick."

I'm not a big believer in luck. I think Mary brought me there in her own way, perhaps as she had sent a flower garden of encouragement with the driveway petunias.

"Well, this is the plot." He pointed to the markers, and then at the grassy space between them. "There are four graves. Grave one is here. And I found the other vault in grave three, over here."

"Thank you." There was an awkward pause. "I'm just going to stay with her for a few minutes."

"Alright. I've got to help them close that grave." He made his way back to the other men.

I stared at the ground, imagining the concrete vault, the white casket, the satin lining, and Mary. We were only six feet apart. I bowed my head and spoke quietly, but directly to her—an apology four decades in the making. "I'm sorry that we left you alone. I'm ashamed that the person who has spent the most time with you, the caretaker Paul, didn't even know you were here. I used to wonder, *Where are you?* Many times

I've shouted at the clouds and stars in frustration and anger—*Why did you leave me?*

"I don't blame you anymore. I'm sorry you had to leave so soon. I could have been a much better big sister with you in my life. I still miss you. We all miss you. Life has been really difficult without you. There's so much to say. I'm sorry that no one was here for your burial. I'm so sorry."

I was grateful to have a place to visit, to mourn, to feel connected, and to heal. As I stood there, I was struck by a stark reality. This wasn't just the first time I had visited her grave. It was the first time *anyone* in the family had visited her grave.

I was relieved to have found her, but I was also mourning the last bit of magical thinking left over from childhood—that this was all just a long game of hide-and-seek. That she was perhaps under the bed, in the closet, or hiding just around the corner in the lilac bush. That she hadn't really died. But she did, and this was the end of the game. Now I felt the entire weight of 40 years of silence and denial and false hope.

Before I left, I approached Paul once again. "Thanks for finding my sister." I smiled and started to walk away.

"You're welcome," he said, leaning on his rake. "All these years—I didn't even know she was here."

Those words took my breath away. Mary deserved a memorial.

* * *

The first time Dad went to Mary's grave was on August 14th, 2015, a year and two months since we discussed her at the coffee shop.

I picked him up at The Compound, and we bought some red and yellow roses from the floral department inside a nearby grocery store. During the drive to the cemetery, he started complaining about Mom. "I don't know why she won't go. I asked her, and she said she had things to do in the garden today. She can work in the garden anytime."

"Maybe she's just not ready yet. Everyone deals with things in their own way. I'm sure she has her reasons." I knew better than to push the subject with Mom. She's always hated change. She needed time to adjust to things. Breaking the contract of silence was something that would no doubt take a while for her to adjust to.

Once we arrived, it was a short walk over the grass and past the Celko family grave before Dad and I reached the freshly cleared marker that delineated plot 18-B. The three of us had not been in the same place since the evening of March 8, 1976, the evening of Mary's last asthma attack.

Dad and I were both beyond tears, momentarily frozen by the emptiness of *gone*. As if we were waiting for her to climb up out of the ground so we could take her home.

I pointed out the grave that Paul had probed to find the vault.

"Which way is she facing?" Dad asked.

"I don't know." I put my hands in my pockets and looked away. It was a typical Dad question. He had a knack for finding that one flaw—that one spot of dropped paint, that one picture not quite level. And still—I was disappointed that I didn't have an answer for him. We stood there silent for a minute. "I'd like to order a memorial stone for her and Dziadzia if that's okay with you and Mom."

"Yes. I think she should have one. And I'd like to pay for it."

I suggested we split the cost. "I'll let you know before I order it. We should talk about what will be on it."

He looked down at the grass as he reflected, "I treated her just like she was one of my own. No different. She was the sweetest little kid that ever lived." We both had one arm around each other. I leaned my head on his shoulder. "You will never know how much this means to me," he said quietly.

I felt a profound sense of gratitude. The rusty gears in that 40-year-old childhood promise had finally begun to move. We reminisced a bit more and then headed to the car. I drove out very slowly, glancing in the rearview mirror, hating to leave her behind.

On the way home, Dad and I talked about ordering the headstone. The car was quiet for a moment when he turned toward me and said, "We visited an angel today."

I nodded and smiled. "Yes we did, Dad." We were both so grateful to have found her, yet I felt ashamed that I had not searched for her sooner. I wondered if he felt that way too.

Dad and I bonded souls that day. I have always felt close to him, but ever since Mary died, he has been my terra firma, a keystone in the matrix.

* * *

Throughout that summer I had kept in touch with Joanne, a woman I'd met at a yoga workshop. We got together a few times at local cafes around New Haven for lunch and to discuss our writing projects. I was learning how to connect and expand the matrix. So when she invited me to join her at an upcoming book signing in Branford for a local author, I didn't hesitate.

We met in the reading room of the Branford Library, where about 20 middle-aged women stood in intimate clusters and chatted. Joanne and I waited in line near tables set with silver platters of hors d'oeuvres, wine, cheese, and desserts, to have our books signed.

The author, Laura, had kind eyes and a warm smile that invited conversation. I mentioned that Joanne and I were interested in joining a writing group. Laura was enthused. "Oh great! You have to meet Pat." She pointed across the room and waved. "Pat is trying to get a group together. Let her know you're interested in joining us."

* * *

The email arrived on Monday morning. The New Haven Intrepid Women Writers scheduled a standing meeting on the first Tuesday evening of the month at the New Haven Free library. The more we met and shared our writing, the more we learned about ourselves and about each other. Everyone in the group had suffered a significant loss and used writing as a healthy way to process and express deep feelings. I was the youngest and thought of the other women as older sisters. I formed a close bond with my fellow women writers and began to trust them with my vulnerability and with my family story.

I was reaching out, and actions do not exist in a vacuum. They create ripples of energy that move away in all directions until they land on something solid. So many ripples that we cannot know or trace all their paths.

Ironically, Joanne never attended a single meeting of the writing group, yet I never questioned the importance of meeting her. She was the wave that originally brought me to them—an important part of the matrix.

* * *

The petunias in my driveway garden of encouragement continued to bloom at The Ocean House. Meanwhile, a similar mystery had sprouted at The Compound.

Mom told me about it over the phone. "Julie, there are three light pink petunias in bloom near the top of the driveway," she said in a hushed tone. "They came up by themselves."

Instantly—goosebumps. I knew she was connecting it to my extempore driveway garden at The Ocean House. But there was more.

She continued. "The day of little Mary's funeral, I had bought three light pink carnations from the florist on Grove Street and tied them with a blue ribbon. During the service, I walked up and placed them on the casket with a handwritten note that read: "God loaned us an angel."

At that moment, any residual doubt in my evidence-based mind vanished. I believed it was Mary speaking to us. So did Dad. And so did Mom.

The blush pink petunias came up in the exact spot where Mary and I used to lie on our bellies and admire the perfect white bells of the lily of the valley. And the spot where the holy statue of the Mother Mary lands her gaze. Were these two Marys working in unison to build my faith? Up through the soil, without any help from us, the miniature antique gramophones sent a message only audible to those who believe.

We dubbed the flower "the angel plant." Mom mulched it and weeded it. Dad watered it and protected it with an overturned bucket when he mowed the grass. I marveled at their tenderness.

Chapter 11:

Empire of the Barre Granite

September, 2015

I pulled up to the address Valerie had given me on busy Belmont Street in the city of Worcester, Massachusetts, a 30-minute drive from the lake. The Empire Monument Company was located inside a two-story house, hemmed in by buildings on each side, with a lawn that sloped down to the street in front.

As soon as I opened the office door, the pungent smell of mothballs and wintergreen surrounded me. I looked around at the 1960's dark walnut paneling, and the faded, still-life prints of flowers and fruit bowls in frames that matched the walls. I thought about how this place had probably not changed at all since it opened. Appropriate. The office itself was an art exhibit portraying the suspension of time, and the persistence of grief.

I took a seat in the reception area, waiting for Nick.

After a few minutes, he emerged from a doorway across the room, dressed in a well-fitting charcoal blazer and matching shirt and slacks. Nick was six feet tall, thin, and in his early sixties, with wavy, jet-black hair. I stood to greet him. "Hi. Valerie from St. Anthony's in Webster referred me to you. I need a gravestone for my sister." He reached out for my hand and gave it a limp shake.

I followed him into a smaller office where he motioned for me to sit.

Nick slid a pen and a legal pad across the desk. "Please write down your name and contact information. What style monument are you interested in?"

I hesitated. I didn't know the answer to that. "Um. A headstone."

He glanced up momentarily and then took the legal pad from me. "Above ground? A ledger stone? A monolith? A wedge stone?"

I shrugged. I didn't really know what any of those terms meant. I wondered how people even made such an unwelcomed choice.

Nick suggested we begin by looking at the sample monuments they had on site. I was glad to get out of that office. We walked around to the back of the house over a small lawn. It was a rootless garden planted with rows of gravestones. The slabs varied in color, texture, shape, and design. Black, grey, pink, white, rough, polished, tall, wide, heart-shaped, etched, carved, scrolled, and some even had holograms.

A two-bay garage on site was packed with additional monuments. I was overwhelmed by the selection, but one stone on the lawn stood out over all the rest. It was a good size, not too big or small, a classic rectangular shape, composed of large euhedral crystals, and a pretty shade of light grey granite. When Nick mentioned that the source of the stone was an historic quarry in Barre, Vermont, I knew.

That was the one.

I had visited the quarry on a field excursion during graduate school in 2006. The trip was not about gravestones of course, but rather the geologic history of Vermont.

To reach the quarry, you travel Interstate 89 as it meanders diagonally across the rocky, folded spine of central Vermont. Over river valleys and through gorges, with wonderful views of fresh road cuts, their bands of minerals glittering in the sun. Past erector set bridges and weathered homesteads with their corrugated sheet metal roofs waiting patiently for snow. Exit 6 takes you into the town of Barre, famous for an enormous hole that quarrymen dug to reach into the crust with mechanical steel hands to access a beautiful pluton of light grey granite.

The earth's past is recorded in layers of rock like pages of a history book. The deeper you dig, the further back you go. The quarry represented a place to go back in time, to dig up blocks of the past and understand the conditions that formed and shaped them.

The Barre Granite is revered by geologists, builders, and quarrymen for its uniformity, strength, and beauty. It was born 345 million years ago from magma that cooled slowly, deep within the earth, growing large, well-defined, interlocking crystals. Peaceful, protected, honored—it was ideal for Mary's monument.

Nick scratched down some numbers from the side of the monolith, and I followed him back into the land of the lost. With all my geologic distraction removed, I was left with the dented metal office desk, clamshell molding, roll-up shades, and Nick.

He peeled open a dusty peppermint candy from the dish on his desk. I watched as the candy stuck to the wrapper. "Do you want anything else on the front of the stone other than the family name? Anything else on the back besides biographical information?"

The clicking of the candy against his teeth. More decisions. I hadn't considered the front-back notion. "I'd like an angel carved into the stone, and the phrase: *God loaned us an angel*. My mom wrote that on a sheet of stationery and left it on my sister's casket." He didn't look up from the legal pad. He was just scribbling down information like I was buying a used car. That had been the last correspondence my mom had with Mary; that was Mom speaking to Mary and to God, but the importance seemed to be lost on Nick. No doubt he had seen a lot of death--a lot of good people suffering. Maybe he was cynical about God too.

He handed me a three-ring binder of black and white sketches. I slowly leafed through the pages as Nick pointed out images of daffodils and crosses. I rubbed my forehead and shifted in my chair. "I'd really like an angel on the stone."

He glanced toward the clock and flipped to a section in the binder with literally hundreds of different angels—ghostly, pious, cherub, cartoon, large, small, leaning, floating, flying, reclining, pondering.

I flagged several possibilities. My favorite at that point was a dreamy looking cherub that was glancing up and to the right. It reminded me of something I had picked up from Eric about interview and interrogation; up and to the right is the recall glance. Remembering the past. Nick drummed his fingers lightly and rearranged the pens on his desk. It occurred to me that this whole experience felt a bit like interview and interrogation. After a minute or so, Nick pointed to one of the images in the line-up of angels. "How about this one?"

I felt my eyes narrow as I glanced up at him. Was he serious? A laser-cut, hologram angel? Mary wasn't a rap singer. Of course, he didn't know my sister, and was probably just trying to be helpful. Yet I'd waited 40 years; I certainly wasn't going to be rushed into a quick decision. "Would it be possible for you to copy a few of these so I can show them to my parents?"

He nodded. "You'll need to put down a deposit once you're ready to order the stone and pay the balance when it's set in the cemetery. I'll call Valerie and tell her you stopped by."

On my way out, I walked past an older couple waiting to see Nick. They leaned against each other. They seemed fragile, as if their grief was fresh. I knew how they felt—waiting to choose a stone to let everyone know that their loved one had once been part of our world and wishing that were still the case. And they would be charged for it. It wasn't Nick's fault. That was the business.

I lowered my gaze and moved past them to rejoin the bustling crowds on Belmont Street. People too busy to think about gravestones, symbols of life—in all its hurried pace—being brought to a shuddering and irreversible halt.

I was glad to be there on my own. I could not imagine Mom or Dad having to go through that, yet I realized that someone must have done this for Louise.

* * *

Prior to visiting Nick at Empire Monument, the only association I had between stones and Mary was her pet rock. It was smooth, graphite gray, with delicate, white quartz veins, and fit perfectly in my palm. It had a green square of felt attached to the bottom, googly eyes glued to the top, and a simple curved painted smile that made me smile when I held it.

Today, I have an extensive rock collection from around the world. Some of the specimens are rounded river stones, like Mary's pet rock, without the accoutrements. As a geologist, I appreciate the hardships that smooth rocks have endured. It took a long, rough transport, tumbling, abrading, and scouring of their surface for them to get that way.

I wondered about the hardships and sacrifices born by my ancestors. I was enthralled with the family history and became deeply curious about my parents.

For a month straight, one or two mornings per week, I drove to the West Haven Library on Benham Hill and logged on to the patron version of Ancestry.com. I spent hours typing, searching, taking notes, and learning about the path of those before me. Searching immigrant records, births, deaths, and census info.

I had asked Mom questions about her side of the family. She seemed enthused; it was much easier to talk about than her children's deaths. She recounted endless vignettes of life on the farm, foods they cooked, games they played, the way they lived. But I knew much less about Dad's childhood.

"Do you think we could take a road trip to Winchendon sometime?" I asked.

We made the two-hour trip the following Saturday.

* * *

Dad took me on a grand tour of his hometown of Winchendon Massachusetts. It was a now defunct mill town that was once famous for manufacturing wooden toys. Although ironically, most of the residents were too poor to afford them.

We drove through the Main Street and Dad pointed out the sidewalk he used to sweep in front of the drugstore in exchange for being allowed to read the new comics each week. We crossed the train tracks where Dad would wait for the conductor to toss him a brown bag with leftovers from lunch and a few coins. We drove through a grid of streets that hugged the banks of the river where Dad used to fish, and past the *Swamp House* where his family of two parents and nine children lived in five rooms, until Dad's father passed away when he was barely 10-years-old.

Dad leaned forward and directed me when to turn. "Left here. Now right. See that yellow one? We lived there on the first floor." As we wound through the grid of streets, he tapped my shoulder and pointed out the numerous apartments his family had lived in: Pond Street, Algier Street, Poplar Street, and three on Elm Street. With each home, there were stories of the difficulties of poverty and the enduring strength of sibling and family bonds.

We also went to two different cemeteries in town. In the New Boston Cemetery, Dad led me to the gravestones of his birth father, maternal grandfather, maternal grandmother (and two of her three husbands), Uncle Rodney, cousin Patty's husband Kenneth, and their son Richard, who died at 28, two days before his wedding.

At the Cavalry Cemetery, we visited my half-brother Bobby's grave. "If we had time, I'd show you where my brother Ralph's buried. But he's about a half hour away in Winchester, New Hampshire."

"Where's your sister Ruth buried?" I asked. Dad's older sister had died from cancer when she was 28. He still tears up when he talks about her.

"Grammie and Ruth are in Thompson. The cemetery near the four corners. Your Uncle Smokey, Aunt Rita, and Aunt Rachel are there too."

I learned more about Dad in that one day than I had in my whole life to date. I was impressed. He knew where every single one of his relatives was buried. He recalled stories in vivid detail, ripe with humor and heartbreak; and still shed tears over the loss of his big sister Ruth.

* * *

I wanted to get the layout for the memorial stone just right, the font size, style, not too cluttered. The dates—spelled out or abbreviated? Middle names or initials? For Dziadzia--Louis or Ludwig? I needed to ask Mom's preference. I knew in my bones it was important for her to feel that she had control of this. In the events surrounding my sisters' deaths there was a terrifying lack of control. Any little Mom could muster, she held close, trying to keep things stable, familiar, predictable.

Yet this opposes nature itself. I thought about the myriad forces both visible and invisible, at work in our lives. At its very basis, nature is constantly adjusting. Subjected to unfathomable pressures deep within the earth, atomic bonds within minerals break and re-form, creating polymorphs—minerals with the same composition but a different crystal geometry. Taking on a new shape that can accommodate conditions so harsh it's hard for us at the surface to even imagine them. But we see their manifestation—both in *minerals*, and *people* who are so strong, as if forged in the heat of middle earth.

One of those people was Mom.

Another was my sister Tammy.

PART THREE

Fractals

"Learn how to see. Realize that everything connects to everything else."

– Leonardo da Vinci

Chapter 12:

The Weight of Understanding

Mid-September, 2015

Tammy had driven down from Vermont for our younger sister Robyn's wedding, and slept at The Lake House afterward. While I waited for her to wake up the next morning, I thumbed through the living room bookshelf and found "The Artist's Way Creativity Kit". I had bought it almost 20 years ago and carried it with me through several moves. Among other things, the kit contained a package of incense. I removed one stick, stood it in a small burning base, and lit the end. I curled up on my side in the large, overstuffed, round chair, and stared at the smoke as it rose, curled, and tumbled over itself in a graceful dance. The scent of sandalwood quickly filled the room. I closed my eyes, took a deep breath, and Time seemed to crack open.

I recalled being 3, maybe 4-years-old, running barefoot from The Compound along the narrow, wooded path to the clubhouse. I could practically feel the rich, dark soil, between my toes, and the chill of the grey stepping stone at the doorway of the clubhouse. Dad built the one-room cabin for Tammy and Louise, but it had become a magnet for their entire group of friends, and my curiosity.

The exterior had been unremarkable, covered in left-over shingles from one of Dad's construction jobs, but everyone had appreciated the *groovy* interior. Large multi-colored swirls in blue and purple adorned the walls, making you feel dizzy even without the help of any foreign substance. Candles and beaded curtains adorned the windows and the smell of incense hung permanently in the air. Either Mom and Dad had both been clueless, or they had ignored what went on in that clubhouse.

I heard footsteps on the basement stairs. Tammy was awake.

"That room's like a cave. I could've slept all day." As if on cue, her voice naturally blended into my reverie about the clubhouse. "Is that incense?"

I made her a cup of coffee, and we chatted about the wedding and Robyn's new husband. Afterward, the two of us walked to the end of the dirt road to explore the Old Quaddick Cemetery.

Just a few weeks ago, volunteers from the Thompson Historical Society had secured a grant to clear the brush, remove downed branches, and repair some of the broken gravestones. Before their effort, the early 1800's cemetery had been largely ignored and forgotten. Many of its subterranean occupants were victims of smallpox, cholera, or typhus.

Tammy wanted to search for distant relatives on the Tefft side that Mom said might be buried there. I suggested we do gravestone rubbings. Tammy agreed, so we brought pencils and several sheets of white office paper with us. She had always embraced new or different ideas, had always been encouraging. I remembered that. I missed that.

The scent of pine and dry oak leaves traveled with the breeze as we climbed over the dilapidated stone wall and into the cemetery. With each step, twigs snapped and our feet sunk into a plush blanket of moss. Chipmunks darted about and disappeared into gaps in the wall. We meandered among the small, lichen-covered marble and slate headstones, dark with biology, splotches of life in this place that honors death. Tammy and I had not spent much time together as adults, so I was careful to take in as much as I could. I noticed her focus, enthusiasm, curiosity and the way she lingered on the epitaphs. How satisfying it was to spend time with her.

How nice it was to be a little sister again.

With smooth white paper pressed against cold, rough marble, and pencil points turned on their sides, we scratched graphite back and forth until the slow buildup of carbon atoms revealed words worn by centuries of acid rain.

"You are most near and dear to me. I have you in my heart: How can I journey anywhere, if you I cannot see?" – in memory of Jesse Wood, son of Mr. Jesse Wood, and given child to Mrs. Ruth Tourtellot, died 1830.

"Stop reader here and contemplate, how short this life, how sure the slate. In time be wise; seek God most just, ere you are mingled with the dust." – from the stone of Lydia Green, died in 1813, Age 14 years & 9 mo.

"Affliction sure long I bore, Physicians skill was vain. Till God was pleas'd to give me ease and free me from my pain." – in memory of Freelove Green, died 1850, age 60 years; and John Luther, died 1805, age 23 years

The burial dates ranged from the late 1700s to 1800s, and some of the graves honored veterans of The Revolutionary War. Tammy and I pointed out interesting names and epitaphs to each other and talked about loss: the loss of our intact family, the loss of our childhood naivety, and the loss of our sisters.

We returned to the house, poured two glasses of lemonade, and sat outside on the double glider overlooking the lake. We flipped through the pages of gravestone rubbings and compared the sayings and the quality of our work. I paused when looking at the one from little Lydia Green, just 14-years-old.

"Do you still miss Mary?" I asked.

"Poor little kid. She was so sick. The swollen knuckles. The dark circles. At least she wasn't suffering anymore." Tammy sipped her lemonade.

I felt my face get hot. It sounded like something I heard Mom say a very long time ago. I set the papers down on the table and rubbed my forehead. I didn't believe Mary was better off dead. I thought about her being buried without any family there. Tears began to fall, but I wiped them away and sat up straight.

"All of you Tefft bitches deserted me," I snapped.

I didn't even know where that anger came from. I wanted to take it back or make Tammy think I was joking. I cried and laughed at the same time. I didn't want her to think I was angry with her. I didn't want her to think I was feeling sorry for myself. I stared at the spaces between the deck boards.

I could feel Tammy's eyes on me, but she was speechless. Something I had never seen. I hugged my knees in toward my chest and continued.

"You *all* left me. Home, alone. With Kevin—*Mr. No Thanks.*" I stared at the lake surface, mind wandering to the cold depths, devoid of sunlight. "Mom was unreachable. I worried about Dad. Always tried to make him laugh. Shane and Kevin followed Mom's cues and shut down. The new family grew, and I disappeared. I wanted my big sisters back. After Mary died, I had lost all of you. Everything just went to shit." Yes. I was feeling sorry for myself. And it felt good to let it out. To talk through the tears.

That was the first time I ever remember sharing any vulnerability with Tammy; the first time I allowed myself to feel angry in front of her; the first time I allowed myself to cry in front of her.

Tammy slowly pushed the glider back and let it rock gently. "Wow."
She paused, letting the mud settle. "I never knew you and Mary were that
close. I mean, I never really thought about it."

I laughed nervously. "Well, I survived. I'm here." I mopped my
face with my sleeve. "But that *really* sucked."

"I know." Her voice was soft and serious. The voice of true and deep
empathy. She had been there. "I think getting the gravestone will be very
healing for you. I used to go and visit Louise after she died. Sometimes
I'd bring a beer and share it with her. I'd take a drink and then pour some
on the grass. It's important to have a place to go."

The motion of the glider was soothing. I cleared my throat, wiped
my eyes again and turned to face Tammy. "Tell me about Louise. Tell
me a funny story or a good memory."

"Okay." She picked up my stack of gravestone rubbings, gathered
them together with hers, and then set them down in one neat pile. "One
time I remember we were driving around in the Rambler with a few
six-packs of beer and got stopped by the cops. Louise told me to shove
all the beers under the seat. I stuffed as many as I could but there was one
six pack that wouldn't fit." We laughed and Tammy continued. "I tried to
hide them with my feet, but the cop saw the beer of course. Louise told
him it was Bob's, your dad's. She said he liked to drink beer while he
was working on the car. The cop didn't buy it. He wrote her a summons,
brought the beer to the house and gave it to Bob."

"Where did you guys get the beer?" I asked.

"From a Russian kid we were friends with in Putnam. He got fake
IDs for us too."

Tammy continued with other stories that painted a side of Louise
I had not known. About stealing pills from Uncle Jose, doing speed and
smoking pot, and filling an olive jar with assorted alcohol from their
friend's parents' liquor cabinet. They urged Shane, who was only 11
at the time, to drink it. He passed out from alcohol poisoning and was
rushed to the hospital to get his stomach pumped. He could have died.

Tammy chuckled as she recalled many other tales of parties and pills, drugs and drinking. We didn't talk about Louise's death, only her life. But the stories I heard left me conflicted. Louise seemed purposefully reckless; indifferent not only about her own safety and well-being, but that of others.

I tried to remind myself that it was a different time; a time when it didn't occur to us to worry about death; a time before *things like that* happened to *our* family.

The day after Tammy went back to Vermont, I sequestered myself at The Ocean House to process what had come up during our visit. I sat on the balcony and gazed at the vast steel blue ocean of Long Island Sound, extending beyond the horizon and hundreds of feet beneath the waves. So much was hidden below the surface. Eighteen trillion gallons of water, most of it out of our sight, 8.6 pounds to each gallon of truth. I felt the compounding weight of both the known and the yet to be known.

A train's whistle called from behind the house, over the hill, where the beautiful new station is. You can board the train, leave the platform, and be whisked away to a completely new setting. Little cars of escape, transporting you like a dream. Just sit back, close your eyes, and when you open them, your sensory world has changed. Your perspective has changed.

It's easy to remember the good about people who have passed. To polish their memories until they gleam like 24-karat gold. Flawless. My conversation with Tammy forced me to look at Louise from a different perspective. Forty years removed from her murder, I was reacquainting myself with my oldest sister, and not all of it was flattering.

It was 1973. She was only 16.

Chapter 14:

Into the Woods

October, 2015

The more I learned about Louise, the more I wanted to discover and understand the circumstances surrounding her death. Elizabeth DeVita-Raeburn talks about this drive to understand in her book on sibling loss, *The Empty Room*. The author explains that many surviving siblings have felt stifled or stuck when faced with senseless deaths such as an accident or murder, mainly because the lack of information held them in limbo.

DeVita-Raeburn explains that it can be incredibly healing to take time to discover and process the circumstances surrounding the event. Her book includes the following thought from Dr. Pauline Boss, a therapist and researcher who developed the *Theory of Ambiguous Loss*. "Sometimes, the only sense you can make of something is that it *doesn't* make sense. But even that may be enough to help you go on."

* * *

In early October, two weeks after Robyn's wedding, Dad and I were at The Compound moving stones out of the pasture and fiddling around with the backhoe, trying to trace a leak in one of the hydraulic lines.

Satisfied with our work and our analysis, we picked up our jackets from the stone wall and walked down to the house to get a drink of water.

I filled up two glasses, and we sat at the kitchen table. "What'd you think of the wedding?" Dad asked.

"I had a great time. Tammy slept at the lake after. We spent some time together before she went back to Vermont." I went on to tell him about the gravestone rubbings, and our discussion of Louise.

Dad remembered the story about Louise getting the summons and the police officer bringing the beer to him. He shook his head. "She was smart but headstrong like your mother. Hard to get close to." He began to talk about her disappearance and the search that followed.

I waited for him to pause before I asked any questions. "A botanist found her, right? On Wakefield Pond Road?"

"Yes, but at the end, where Wakefield Pond joins the state forest road. I could show you if you want."

I sensed it was important to him. Mom was at work, so I didn't have to worry about upsetting her. "Okay. We can take my car."

From The Compound, we took a left onto Baker Road; past the winding, wooded driveway to my Brother Kevin's house; past the stone wall-lined entrance to Grandma and Dziadzia's farm, where my brother Shane and his wife live; past the gated ghost town of the old abandoned NASCAR racetrack; past an overgrown private road barricaded with three large boulders. Decades ago, that road had led to a few seasonal trailers that have since been torn down. Dad didn't say anything, but I knew he was thinking about it too.

Louise had taken her last breath in one of those trailers.

We crossed over the wood-plank bridge that smells like creosol and spans the main tributary to Quaddick Lake—my lake house sits about two miles away as the crow flies, near the reservoir outlet. We finally reached the end of Baker Road where it intersects Quaddick Town Farm Road. Across the intersection was the gravel access road for the state forest.

It was less than a three-minute drive.

As we inched into the woods, the forest had reclaimed that forgotten stretch of road. It had been a popular route for Louise and her friends going into Rhode Island with their fake IDs to party at one of their favorite bars. There were no road signs or markers of any kind—it was wild and free like the 70s themselves. It had been a beautiful and peaceful place for a wooded ramble. Before Louise had been found there.

Stiff tree branches with dead, brown leaves raked along the sides of my car like nails on a chalkboard. As we continued to creep ahead, the potholes became wider and deeper. The car rocked back and forth like a docked boat on a windy day.

When we had gotten about a half-mile into the woods, the road became impassable.

"It's not much farther. We can walk the rest of the way," Dad suggested.

I nodded. "Okay. You're sure it's not too far? It'll be dark soon." The last thing I wanted was to be out here in the dark. I felt fear brushing against my arms and legs, seeping into my bones. I zipped my sweatshirt and pulled the hood against the back of my neck. I was glad Dad was with me.

He walked along the overgrown gravel path a few paces in front of me, pushing branches aside and holding them so they wouldn't snap back at me. Crows called from somewhere among the grey skeletons of oaks and maples, and the bleach-white bones of the birch. A chilly breeze carried the scent of pine and decomposing earth, damp from groundwater springs.

After a few minutes of trudging further into the woods, Dad slowed his pace and pointed. "She was found over there, on the left." We walked another hundred feet and he stopped. "I drove right past her. Didn't even know she was here." He gestured toward the intersection with Wakefield Pond Road. "I was looking across, trying to decide which way I should go. If I looked to the right, I probably would've seen her."

We stood quietly beside one another. Near the intersection was a dilapidated stone wall, about two-feet high, built a century ago by strong farm hands like Dziadzia's. It was a blessing of a barrier that prevented Dad from noticing her on his search. A day after Dad drove past this spot, a botanist who was out photographing wildflowers found Louise on the other side of the wall.

The side where patches of thick, soft, kelly-green moss coated tree trunks, and miniature, three-inch-high stands of princess pine gave a hint of life to the otherwise greys and browns of the forest floor. Just over the wall on June 20, 1973. Three days after her murder.

Thankfully Dad didn't find her. I'm sure Louise would not have wanted that. It's bad enough he had to identify her at the morgue after Mom left—unable to do the impossible, unable to utter the words—*yes, that's my daughter.* It would have made it real. It would have meant Louise was really gone.

Her murderer served twelve years in prison. Twelve years. The year I turned sweet sixteen, Louise's age when she died, he was released from jail. Free to live his life, as if he had not taken hers. On several occasions, mired in the egocentrics of a teenage mindset, I had imagined what it would be like to find him and kill him. I remember feeling guilty that I hadn't at least faced him, regretting that I hadn't spoken up for Louise, for our family. He is dead now. He died in 1991, nearly six years after he was once again unleashed on society. I am sure he is rotting in hell and will return only to finally answer to Mom, Dad and our family for what he did to all of us.

We stood near the area briefly, both wandering the folds of our own minds. It was getting dark. I imagined Louise lying among the ferns, lady slippers and the jack in the pulpit, left there like trash, alone for three nights. Anger flashed like lightning through my mind.

Although I hadn't known the specifics until my mid-teens, I had always known that something terrible happened. I had been curious about the silence and often hid behind the crack of an open door or around the nearest corner to hear the slightest bit of information. I had heard whispers, things that are not meant for kids' ears. And I knew it was so bad that no one talked about it. I recalled the fierce anger I felt as a teenager, barely 16, the same age that Louise was when she died, knowing that someone had murdered her but never being able to share my feelings about it or discuss it with anyone.

I recalled lines from an article published in a woman's magazine. When Mom had handed it to me, she had simply said, "This is about Louise. You can read it if you want." I stood fixed in place, my eyes scanning every word of the article, a prison interview with my sister's murderer, the 26-year-old Vietnam veteran, titled "Why Men Rape." In the article, he said he panicked. He didn't mean to kill her. Louise told him he was not going to get away with it. She was going to tell the cops. I had wondered if those were her last words.

When I had been in high school, I remember having driven down Wakefield Pond Road on a couple of occasions, alone after a night with friends and beer, looking for traces of her. Not knowing. Not understanding. Only feeling. Anger with no object, driving aimlessly. Carrying a few broken shards of a thousand-piece mosaic, wanting desperately to understand the whole picture. Demanding answers from God—with silence the only reply. Push it down. Hold it there. Years pass. It's buried ever more deeply.

I thought about the DeVita-Raeburn book, and the theory of ambiguous loss as I stared at the stone wall in front of us.

Dad spoke softly. "The detectives came by the house to talk with me and your mother. They said my tire tracks were found near her body—maybe ten yards away. They were suspicious. Asked me why I was there."

I shook my head. I couldn't imagine Dad being questioned. "That's horrible. You must have been so hurt."

He looked at the ground and scraped his shoe back and forth in the dry leaves. "Everyone had to be a suspect until they had more clues, I guess."

I tried to grab hold of my feelings, crushing sadness, for Louise, for Dad, for our family. Sadness doesn't help. Don't feel sorry for yourself. Gone is gone. Such tangled thoughts. There was no organization to them. No order. No logic. Just raw emotions, chaotic and unfiltered in my brain.

The shadows of late afternoon were merging. We walked back to the car and made our way out of the woods. I left with more questions than I had when I arrived. I was beginning to realize the extent of the mosaic, and just how many pieces were missing.

And I left with something else too—rekindled anger. I channeled it into worry about Dad. I wondered how the trip had affected him. He seemed reflective and sad but relieved to have someone to share the experience with. Again, as with Harold and Mary, it seemed as though we were validating each other's grief. Perhaps the drive brought him back to those three days of false hope and desperation.

As we made our way back to The Compound, Dad recalled that several times in the night when the search was ongoing, when he was in between wake and sleep, he would jolt up, thinking he heard the door open, thinking that Louise had come home. But it was just a dream or his imagination playing tricks on him.

For the whole time of the search, she was in the woods with the other wildflowers, behind the lichen-covered, grey metamorphic stone wall, waiting to be found, waiting for justice.

* * *

It was my visit with Tammy, and the visit to Wakefield Pond Road that propelled me deeper into the woods, along the path toward cracking open the 24 karat gold façade, pushing against knotted paradigms that were decades, even *generations* old. Questions drummed in my head— louder and more crowded than ever. Being faced with the cruelty and blatant unfairness of it all made me want to fall into a lake of booze and soak until I was saturated and numb. But I didn't.

I wanted to stop running. I wanted to be fearless. I wanted a reclamation—what exactly I was looking to reclaim was still too large and nebulous to identify.

Chapter 15:

Song of Faith

December, 2015

In an attempt to begin facing some of my deeper, more sinister fears, I attended a weekend writing retreat titled, "Writing from the Heart", at Kripalu in Lennox, Massachusetts. The group consisted of twelve women who met for three sessions per day, each person chained to untold stories.

The schedule provided a balance of support and time for independent reflection. Most meals were held in silence, and cell phone use was restricted to a phone booth near the lobby. A silent lounge on the fourth floor overlooked the pond, hills, and forest in the distance. Aside from the group writing sessions, I strolled in solitude among the evergreens and pines, along a narrow, gravel path arranged for contemplation, with wooden footbridges, altars, and stone statues of avatars and deities. The footpath led to a labyrinth, where each lap around the circular path wound back and forth toward the center of the circle and out again. Like a maze that needed no figuring. The mind could remain focused on a question for the entire journey through the labyrinth. The slow, steady unwinding was critical work.

Kripalu was founded on a holistic approach to mental, physical, and spiritual health. Food was an important part of the matrix of support. It was fresh, sensual, and the selection was entirely novel. The dining hall was a dizzying feast with two, 20–foot-long silver buffets holding a plethora of hot dishes, two salad bars, and separate stations for soup, breads, and desserts. The scones with chunks of spicy, crystallized ginger were my absolute favorite.

Sprinkled in 90-minute sessions between food and contemplation, we sat in a circle on cranberry colored cushions and wrote. We tussled with our inner critics as we transcribed feelings into words, and tried to fashion wings from pen and paper. I felt cathartic and organic to be immersed in the new-age hippie commune, like I was hanging out with Louise and Tammy and their friends.

The most difficult writing assignment was a prompt called "the hardest thing." And for that one, we were encouraged to read aloud. Participants were randomly called on around the circle. My hands trembled. I tucked them under my thighs to warm them up. I hadn't intended to share anything with this group of strangers. It wasn't really any of their business. *Did she just point to me?* I listened as the woman to my left read an emotional piece about her Mom's death from ALS. I closed my eyes and exhaled. And then the workshop leader called on me. The paper shook, and tears trickled down my cheeks through this brief passage:

"The hardest thing...." I stopped and caught my breath. A tear escaped, then another. Breathe. *"The hardest thing is the heart of the story. Finding your way back to your soft insides after life has cast you in bronze."* With one palm pressed against my chest, I took a deep breath. *"After Louise's murder in 1973, we were mannequins buttoned up in corsets of guilt, blame, and despair. Afraid to talk, to love, to leave the house. Mary was the only one who could still see life beyond the immediate tragedy in front of us. Through the alchemy of a pure-hearted 13-year-old, she worked to bring the mannequins back to life. Perhaps she sacrificed too much of her energy for us. 'That's okay Daddy. It will be okay.' And I held him as tight as I could."*

I set down the paper with trembling hands and wiped my cheeks. A contagion of sniffles spread in waves around the circle. Someone handed me a box of tissues.

No one rolled their eyes. No one accused me of looking for attention. Everyone in the group shared deeply personal stories of loss. The burden of grief was a weight that was too heavy for any of us yet seemed manageable within the arms of our collective vulnerability. This was unfamiliar.

That writing prompt brought the unravelling of my family into sharp focus. It was as if I was living through it in the present, able to feel it more viscerally, and see it from a broader perspective.

Dwelling on sadness gives it energy and prolongs it, yet ignoring it does the same. Even as I managed to record that difficult essay, I sat leafing through my notebook, looking for something else to read. Avoidance was a deeply ingrained survival skill.

The weekend events morphed from introspective writing into human bonding over shared loss. At the end of the workshop we sang and danced together with an acoustic-guitar-playing, new-age hippie named Frannie Faith. There was a palpable shift from mourning death to celebrating life. But for me, it was a transition that would need more time and contemplation.

I packed my bag and meandered along the sinuous driveway of Kripalu, past the statues tucked away in the woods, past the dilapidated historic stone gatehouse with the scrolled wrought-iron fence. How do we know when we've properly 'processed' grief? How do we know when we are done grieving? Is it ever done?

***

I found the recipe for the Kripalu ginger scones online and made a batch as soon as I got home from the retreat. Mom found my Kripalu experience ridiculous. She asked me if I was joining a cult. I wasn't surprised. She is a Bardy—new ideas are always the enemy. They involve change and she had had quite enough of that in her life.

She did enjoy the ginger scones though.

Baking, like writing, was acceptable.

I was learning.

* * *

During that visit with the occult accusations and the scones, Mom handed me a photo album. "I found this when I took out the Christmas decorations. Robyn made it a few years ago."

I had seen it before. Robyn assembled it a decade earlier when she had worked as a corrections guard. She printed the murderer's jail record and put it together in a book with several clipped newspaper articles Mom had saved about Louise's murder. At the time, I rebuffed her curiosity. *She wasn't even born when this happened to our family.* Her inquiry was met with the contract of silence. *What kind of a big sister was I?* My stomach instantly knotted.

"Would you mind if I took this home and returned it later?"

"You can keep it at your house, okay? If I want to look at it, I can let you know."

I nodded. "Sure." I leafed through the pages. When I had seen the book years ago I felt detached, distant. But as I read them in that moment, the loss felt sharp, personal, and devastating. Exploring Mary's loss had unexpected consequences. It revealed the depth of my feelings about Louise.

Within the pages of the photo album were articles about Louise going missing, the efforts to find her, the discovery of her body, the search for the murderer, his evasion and capture, and a few sentences describing my sister.

They included short blurbs from teachers, friends, and from Mom about what kind of person Louise was. She hung out with a fringe group.

Liked pretty things. Really smart. A typical 16-year-old. Worked to afford clothes and gas for her car. Within the columns of print, the notion of the mother-daughter-sister bond was clear; but so was the breaking of that bond. This was a record that memorialized a family torn apart. It was the story of a victim.

Louise would have *hated* that characterization. She was *not* a victim.

Was that why Mom gave the book to me? To see how wrong things were so I could set them straight? Was she saying that's not what she wanted to remember anymore? Was she intentionally making room for new memories?

I didn't know. But I felt compelled to create a different sort of record, one celebrating togetherness rather than resonating trauma. Nothing would take away the loss, but perhaps I could shift the focus of the lens—from death to life.

I began scanning, cropping, and reprinting hundreds of family photographs. Grandparents, aunts, uncles, cousins, Mom, Dad, and all of us kids. My goal was to make a true family scrapbook. Where we could all be together in a world I would recreate within the pages.

A world that honored our days at Quonnie Beach.

Chapter 17:

Cup of Fortune

January, 2016

I tucked the envelope from Empire Monument into my coat pocket, brushed the light coating of snow from my windshield and headed to The Compound for breakfast. Max barked enthusiastically at the door as I closed it behind me.

"How was the hill?" Dad asked.

"Fine. Clear. It was just a dusting." I patted Max as he escorted me over to the wood stove. I rubbed my hands together over the heat. "You guys didn't take your tree down yet?"

"This afternoon," Mom said as she pressed the back of the spatula against the bacon in the cast iron pan. It was unusual for her to keep the tree up past the Three Kings Day.

Dad walked into the kitchen and set the table. Mom served the eggs and bacon, and Dad poured coffee.

I took the envelope from my coat pocket. It was a Xeroxed sketch that the headstone salesman, Nick, had mailed to me with a potential layout for Mary and Dziadzia's gravestone. I hung my coat on the back of the chair, sat down, and breached the subject gently.

"I got this in the mail from Empire Monument. From Nick. The guy I told you I met with? We've gone back and forth a few times on the layout. What do you think?" I handed her the sketch and watched as she carefully surveyed both sides of the paper. "If you want anything to be different, I can have him change it; nothing is settled yet."

"No. It looks good as it is. I like the angel."

Her approval reassured me. "You know Mom, if you want to put Grandma's ashes in one of the other graves this might be a good time to do it. No pressure. I just thought I'd mention it. We have some time. They can't do anything 'til the ground thaws."

"They may need to pour a vault for the ashes." Dad knew a lot about cement, and a little about graves. "They could do that the same time as the footing."

That made sense, but I was worried that his comment would upset Mom. I moved my scrambled eggs around the plate with my fork and caught her reaction in my peripheral vision. She was perfectly calm and nodded her head. She seemed to be considering it.

"Hey, did you notice the angel plant?" Dad asked.

Before the first frost, they had dug up the pastel pink petunia that spontaneously sprouted near the statue of Mother Mary and brought it into the house for the winter. I leaned back and glanced at the windowsill in the living room where the plant was flourishing. "Wow! It looks great."

"Your mother's been watering it and pulling the dead blooms off. It's growing up the windowpane."

I smiled. "It certainly seems to like that spot by the Christmas tree."

Mom chimed in, "Well, that tree's been up long enough."

I glanced over at Dad and shook my head. "By the way Mom, how'd your doctor's appointment go last week?"

She had gone for a colonoscopy, which always conjures a bit of nerves for me, and likely her as well, because Dziadzia died of colon cancer. Often, I worry about people close to me dying. Sometimes I worry about my own death.

When Mom met for the pre-op consult, the nurse asked her about her children. She said she had ten, but two died. The nurse asked how.

Mom told her. Softly, she relayed the story to me. Whenever she speaks of those events, it is always with an uncharacteristic softness. As if she is accessing a completely different part of herself. A part that is rarely let out.

"The nurse said she had a daughter who died of a drug overdose at twenty-seven," Mom continued. "She said she knows exactly how I feel."

I nodded slowly. "Empathy is a comfort." I considered her revelation. Mom had only begun to talk about Louise and Mary's deaths with me. To my knowledge, she had never talked about these events with strangers, but that day she did. Was she reaching out for connection? Or, forty years removed, trying to set an example?

* * *

Monday afternoon, I packed my textbooks and laptop and returned to The Ocean House to prepare for the upcoming semester. In the evening, I took a break from work and attended a Mindfulness presentation at the local library.

I walked down a flight of cement stairs to a large meeting room in the library's basement. It was soon filled with a racial and economic kaleidoscope of 35 people, milling about and chatting as they each found a seat within the large arc of folding chairs.

The title of the talk was "The Healing Power of Meditation". The speaker, Dr. Raider, began promptly at 7:00 pm by giving his own bio. "I have practiced and taught geriatric medicine for over thirty years. I have held a faculty position at the University of Connecticut Health Center, authored a chapter in the book entitled, *Meditation as Medication for the Soul*, and lectured widely in the US and Canada about the health benefits of meditation."

He opened the lecture by describing the roots of meditation, how he became intrigued by it in college, and his own mindfulness practice. He presented a wide range of scientific studies that show connections between meditation and emotional, spiritual, and physical health. It was nice to have my personal beliefs confirmed by peer-reviewed research, but the part of his talk that intrigued me was when he candidly revealed how mindfulness deepened his perception and understanding of death.

In his role as a geriatric doctor, naturally he found himself present with many patients at the very moment they died, which he described as the moment that their conscious being left their physical body. One example, however, came from a man who had died but then was resuscitated sometime later.

Dr. Raider visited this man, who was seated upright at the edge of his bed in the hospital room. Looking at the man's chart, the doctor said, "Well, you had a close call in the emergency room." He waited for a response from the patient. A full five seconds went by as the doctor scribbled notes on the chart. The man said nothing.

Dr. Raider looked up to see him staring straight ahead, perfectly still. The doctor waited, curious as to what the man was thinking in a space seemingly so far away. Finally, after about five more seconds of awkward silence, the man spoke—slowly, clearly, and deliberately.

"I remember everything that happened. I remember dying and leaving my body. Looking down on it from the corner of the room. Watching the nurses passing instruments, putting the paddles on my chest. I can tell you what they looked like, I can describe how they moved around the room, and I remember exactly what they were saying."

The doctor stopped writing, and rested the chart on his lap, as the man continued.

"I saw things. Secrets of the universe."

"I'm very interested in hearing about that," the doctor said. "If you're willing to share it with me."

The man was still staring at a point somewhere far beyond the confines of the room. "There is no language for it. There is no way to describe it in the terms that we communicate in. I know we don't just die. There's more."

My eyes began to fill as he told the story. I thought of my sisters, my grandparents, my friends. To think that only their physical bodies died, that they still exist in some form, and that that form can perhaps see the workings on earth astounded me. I had seen both petunias and people appear at just the right moment when I most needed encouragement, but hearing this firsthand account was powerfully affirming.

As Mom had said, people aren't in graves. Only their bodies are there.

I thought about Eric, my sometimes cynical, state-trooper husband, who had lost his brother PJ. I called Eric and repeated the story word-for-word on my way home. He was uncharacteristically silent as I recounted the details Dr. Raider had given. I thought I dropped the call. "Are you there?"

Finally, he spoke. "I have goosebumps right now."

Dr. Raider's talk combined credible scientific research and a few first-hand accounts of the blurry horizon that separates life and death. I know people who either demand evidence or reason by faith. It's unusual to have met someone who could skillfully balance both.

Through his personal story, I recalled my own experience with focused meditation. In 2000, I had gone on a five-day silent retreat at a Sufi community in the Appalachians to ponder a career change. Sitting in stillness helped settle my mind and bring clarity to my decision. I reasoned it might also help deepen my recall of the past. I called the Abode of the Message in New Lebanon, New York, and scheduled a silent retreat for my spring break in March.

One chilly February afternoon, as Eric was making plans for St. Patrick's Day, I poured a glass of wine and opened the word document that contained vignettes of family history. It contained tales that spanned three generations of Mom's ancestors. I spread out some old family pictures on the dining room table and tried to reconcile the written stories with the photos. I wondered what abilities, traits, or tendencies were genetically hardwired, and which were passed down through the emotional cache of family experiences known as 'soft inheritance.'

I recalled the family lore about our fortune-telling abilities. Great Uncle Jim had a career in the circus before he settled down to become a successful entrepreneur in the moonshine business during the prohibition. It's said that his palm-reading skills were passed down from my great-great-great grandmother who used to read tea leaves. Mary Pluta. Another Mary in the family.

This Mary was a fortune teller. She had read the tea and told grandma that she would soon meet a man with blonde hair and blue eyes and would be married. Grandma had met Dziadzia the following week, and they spent the rest of their lives together.

I wanted to learn more about family fortune-telling and moonshine. I wanted to learn more about *that* Mary too. Was I like *her*?

In late February, I happened to spot an advertisement for a tea leaf reading class at a new age shop near The Ocean House. I called to reserve a spot.

When I arrived, there were two square tables perfectly set for a tea party. The store itself was stocked with tarot cards, spiritual books, statues of deities, candles, crystals, and sheer scarves draped tastefully on displays. The strong scent of incense reminded me of Tammy and Louise's bedrooms, except they burned it to hide the skunky stench of marijuana—probably not the case here.

I paid the $20 fee and introduced myself to two other women who were chatting with Ronnie, the owner of the gift shop, and Deborah, the reader. I didn't mention my tea-leaf-reading roots.

As the last of the five attendees arrived and were seated, Deborah began the workshop. She introduced herself, her path to divining tea leaves, and provided some historical context to divination. As she spoke, she continually glanced at her notebook. Dr. Raider didn't need to rely on notes. Maybe she was just a nervous person.

Deborah summarized the steps involved in a reading and passed around some books that depicted hundreds of symbols and defined their meanings. Interesting. She sheepishly admitted to not having the symbols memorized. I squinted, trying hard to keep the skeptic at bay. In any case, when Deborah completed her explanation, it was time to try an actual reading. She preferred Earl Grey. I expected it to be necessary to use some sort of exotic tea or a blend of ancient Chinese tea leaves. But no. Earl Grey would do just fine.

She put roughly ½ teaspoon to ¾ of a teaspoon in each person's tea cup. She explained that the shape of the cup was important. It had to be a similar circumference at the top and bottom. No tapered proper English tea cups here. After the loose-leaf tea went a few tablespoons of water from the Keurig. Hmmm. The spirits didn't need properly boiled water either? There is something to be said for presentation. She was losing credibility.

Deborah instructed us to stir the tea but not drink it. She "didn't want anyone to have an allergic reaction," so she told us to just swirl the tea leaves around the cup and spill the water carefully into the saucer. Deborah came around and assisted us, pointing out how the residual leaves formed shapes, symbols, and patterns.

"The rim is present day. The bottom of the cup represents one year or so into the future." But, as Deborah pointed out, "the universe does not really conform to human time constraints, so it's hard to say."

Convenient. As she instructed us to begin searching for figures and symbols left in the tea, she counseled us to let our imagination and insight come through. I saw an avian circus flying around within the rim of my cup. Songbirds, birds of prey, soaring birds, and a bird that was perched on a branch. I saw a bat that had a scorpion's tail, a Milk bone dog biscuit, and a rose that looked like a Truffula Tree from *The Lorax*.

I didn't think this was what she meant by imagination and insight. I took one of the books and looked up birds, bones, bats, and roses. The symbols apparently indicated: a good journey; taking a chance in life; depression; and success for those who study. Interesting, but vague. I wanted more detail. Okay. Next. Oh. That's it. That's the end of the reading.

Deborah briefly came around to help people see more shapes and symbols; fresh eyes offer additional and sometimes different interpretation, although she seemed to subtly avoid me.

To wrap up the evening, she offered each of us a complimentary crystal reading, another one of her *gifts,* I guess. She shuffled five stones held within a velvet bag.

"Don't look inside," she said as she loosened the drawstring and held the bag in front of me. "Pick one crystal that you are drawn to." I reached in and felt each stone. Four were smooth and one had flat crystal faces in a geometric shape. It reminded me of the smoky quartz crystal I'd found hiking last summer. I chose that one.

"You chose black tourmaline. That's the earth crystal."

I nodded and waited for her to continue.

"You are a grounded person who gets energy from nature, but you are stuck right now. You may need to do some organizing or clearing, or even something as simple as repainting a room."

Ughh. Painting. It takes me an eternity to choose colors. Painting for me is not simple. But stuck, well yes, that's me. Simultaneously trying to recall and understand the old family and how I fit into it, while refusing to face the details of Louise's death? Definitely stuck.

I wasn't convinced that Deborah had a special gift, yet for two hours she entertained me, and introduced me to a form of divination practiced in my own family. Still, I couldn't help but notice her discomfort around me. Did she sense my skepticism? Perhaps she sensed the presence of my great-great-great-grandma Mary looking over her shoulder with a disapproving, furrowed brow, particularly judgmental about the notebook, the Earl Grey tea and the Keurig.

* * *

Still at the beginning of the scrapbook project, I realized how long it would take to complete, and wanted to give Mom something in the interim. I chose about 20 pictures from the stash I got from The Compound and ordered a photo blanket for Mom's birthday, March 10. It was an arrangement of digital photos printed in a quilt-like pattern on a cozy fleece throw. I liked the notion of holding our heartfelt family memories close, wrapping them around us and feeling their warmth and comfort.

I brought it over to The Compound, excited for her to see it.

Mom unfolded the blanket on her lap and looked at each picture. "This is beautiful."

"Let me see it," Dad said. She held it up and turned it toward him. "Where did you find all these?" he asked.

"These are the ones Mom let me borrow. I chose some of the best ones and scanned them."

After a few minutes, Mom folded the blanket and tucked it back in the plastic zippered bag. "I don't want it to get dirty."

After I left, Dad told me she packed it away on the top shelf in their bedroom closet.

* * *

Perhaps before the tea leaf reading but definitely after, I knew Mom was the key to unlocking my stuckness that Deborah pointed out. I also knew there was no rushing the truth without sacrificing its integrity and wholeness. Yet none of us knows in advance exactly how much time we have in this life.

On Saturday March 12, 2016, I cut Mom and Dad's hair prior to Mom's 77th birthday dinner that evening. Even though I got out of the hairdressing business a decade ago, they still enjoy the benefits of having a personal stylist in the family. The following day, I spoke with Dad on the phone. He said Mom was sick. She had been throwing up all morning.

"She was fine yesterday. Did she eat something bad?" I asked.

"No." Dad paused. "But before the birthday dinner, she was helping me with the backhoe."

"Why didn't you ask *me* for help?"

"I only had her putting chains around boulders so I could move them out of the pasture."

The chains were heavy; I had helped him move rocks before. I went over to The Compound with Eric to check on her. She was wincing in pain, but unsure if she wanted to go to the hospital.

Most people have a marked disdain for the hospital. Mom has severe anxiety over it. I don't blame her. It's a trigger for thoughts of many terrifying trips rushing to the ER with little Mary, and one impossible visit to the morgue. In our family, a trip to the hospital meant you probably wouldn't come home.

I stood with my back to the wood stove, deeply concerned, assessing her condition. She was seated at the kitchen table, hunched forward, leaning on her forearm.

"You look scared," she said.

"I've never seen you speechless with pain," I replied. "I think you should go to the hospital."

Normally stoic, pain bad enough to make her flinch would have already driven a normal person to take copious painkillers or pass out. "Okay. I think I'll go." She could barely stand up straight, she was having dry heaves. Ready to go? Nope. Maybe she has to throw up again. Okay. She's ready now.

Mom shuffled outside, and they got into the Prius. Dad started the car and put it in gear. Eric asked if Dad had his cell. He didn't. Dad opened the door and as he stepped out, the car rolled forward. He jumped back in the driver's seat to try to step on the brake and the door hit him in the head. I watched, terrified. It was just too much. His mind seemed unable to focus; perhaps he was reliving little Mary's last trip to the ER. I know it was on *my* mind.

Mom's name is Mary too. I hoped this would not be her last trip.

Chapter 18:

Escape from Day Kimball Hospital

March 13, 2016

After a few hours in the ER, Mom was diagnosed with idiopathic pancreatitis. In other words, her pancreas was inflamed, and they had no idea why. They transferred her to a hospital room to spend the night.

Mom was not pleased. "Do I have to stay? Can't I just come back tomorrow?"

The nurse glanced up from entering data on a tablet. "We need to be able to monitor your condition."

Mom turned toward me. "Well, don't tell everyone I'm here. I don't want all kinds of people parading into my room."

Dad brought her some magazines from the ER, made sure she was comfortable, and we went home for the night. I called my younger sister Angela who is an operating-room nurse in Norwich and told her about Mom. I also sent a text to my other sisters and included Mom's parade comment.

The next day, medical images showed a femoral hernia that needed to be taken care of. I checked in on her around 11:00 am. Robyn had already brought her some back copies of *Mother Earth News* magazine.

The nurse updated me as she changed the IV bag. "We've scheduled Mary for surgery to repair the hernia tomorrow."

Mom was thumbing through one of the magazines and scowled. "I have to stay in here for two more days? I need to take care of my garden."

"Dad can do the watering, and I'll stop over to do some weeding before I head to The Ocean House." I tried to reassure her, but I knew she didn't like anyone else fiddling around in her garden, especially me with my black thumb.

She set the magazine down and looked at me in surprise. "You're going to New Haven?"

Did she feel abandoned? I smoothed the covers on her bed. "I have to teach this afternoon." It didn't really occur to me to cancel class. When it comes to work ethic, I am truly my parent's daughter. I did, however, call the Abode later that day to postpone the start of my silent retreat.

* * *

Mom's surgery was the next day, March 15th. When the anesthesia wore off, she was an emotional wreck and was severely nauseous. She was hallucinating. Hospital staff blamed it on the morphine.

She imagined that clandestine Vietcong were taking over the hospital. She thrashed and flailed, pulled her IV out and became belligerent. Insulting and degrading any hospital personnel who dared to pass into her room and through the curtain. She spewed horribly rank and insolent swears that would make a truck driver blush. The nurses threatened to restrain her and move her to the psych ward. That quieted her down temporarily, but when Dad arrived, she demanded her cell phone and got cranked up again.

She never uses her cell phone—and in fact, has always insisted that she doesn't know *how* to use it—yet she called everyone in her contacts list with minimal assistance from Dad. Aunt Helen, and my sisters old and new--Tammy, Renee, Angela, Robyn, and Nicole--all either heard about the Vietcong conspiracy or received a foul and demanding message from Mom to immediately come and pick her up.

She also called Eric. "Are you on duty? They're trying to keep me here. Come and get me out. Hurry. Bring your badge and your gun." Everyone was upset and worried. Then she told Dad to call me in New Haven.

Before I even said hello, I could hear her swearing at the nurses and doctors, demanding to be able to "leave this prison," convinced that she would be killed in the hostile takeover.

"Is that Julie?" I heard her ask.

"Yes. Talk to her," Dad replied as he passed the phone.

"Julie? Where are you? I need you to come and get me!" Her voice was frantic. It was a mix of anger, paranoia, and deep fear. "They're trying to keep me here."

"Yes, Mom, I can come to the hospital, but it's going to take me a while. I'm just leaving the University." I rubbed my eyes, bloodshot and irritated from lack of sleep.

"Okay. Come get me. Hurry."

"Well, it's going to be a couple of hours. It's rush hour and there's a lot of traffic."

"Okay. Just hurry. Just get here." As she hung up, I heard her say, "She's on her way."

I called Dad on his cell phone. "What the hell is going on with Mom?"

"Hang on a minute." He paused briefly. "Okay. I had to go into the hall. Your mother's been calling everyone, telling them to come pick her up."

"Why? I mean, she's not able to leave, right?"

"No. She's having a reaction to the pain medicine I think, or the anesthesia. Anyway, she was watching a war movie, and now she thinks the Korean doctor is planning to take over the hospital."

"Wow. Alright. I'm on my way. I'll be there as soon as I can."

"Thanks. Eric's on his way too."

Traffic was refrigerated molasses. My fingers drummed on the wheel. I alternated between whichever lane was moving the fastest. It helped keep my mind occupied and made me feel like I had at least some control. About 15 minutes later, my cell phone rang again.

"How soon will you be here?" Mom was desperate.

"I'm going over the Q-bridge now, but it's the rush. It'll take me at least a couple of hours." During the drive, I got a more detailed update on Mom's antics from Eric, who arrived in uniform after work. His presence seemed to help calm both Mom and the hospital staff. But she was still clamoring to get out.

Mom's outburst made me think of my great Uncle, Frank Bardy, and his last trip to the hospital. Uncle Frank served in World War II and earned a Silver Star and Purple Heart in the Battle of the Bulge. A typical Bardy, he was independent and headstrong, living alone with his dog well into his 80s. Until the day he went to the hospital because he was feeling dizzy.

When nurses explained he would have to stay overnight for observation, he panicked and started flailing around and had to be restrained. He ended up having a stroke and died a few weeks later. I feared this happening to Mom. I had already lost her through the tearing and unraveling of our family. But that seemed like it was just starting to change. We had the chance to forge a whole new relationship. If she could make it through this. I drove faster.

By the time I arrived at the hospital, there was a security guard stationed outside her room, and several family members around her bed. Mom was returning to semi-lucidity, although her agitation persisted. She seemed afraid, not the fearless Bardy I had been raised by.

As others filtered out to go home, I spoke quietly to my sister Angela. "What if she has another outburst? I think I should stay overnight."

Angela motioned for me to step outside the door. "That's probably a good idea. I don't know what their staff numbers are, but I'm sure they wouldn't be able to deescalate another hostile takeover." If *Angela* agreed with me, then it was definitely the right thing to do. She rarely agrees with anyone—a true Bardy in that regard.

When the nurse came in to check Mom's IV, I asked, "Would it be okay if I stay here with her tonight?"

The nurse seemed elated. "Sure. No problem. I'll find a bed and bring it in for you."

She was back in a jiffy. She and another nurse moved some of the equipment around to clear a space and wheeled in my bed.

"Wow. That was fast. Thank you." It was the first time I saw her move quickly. It was also the last time I saw her at all, until morning. And it wasn't because I was asleep.

Every 15 minutes or so, I heard Mom get up and stagger toward the bathroom to vomit. "Mom, hold on, you're attached to the IV stand, you'll rip the IV out, you'll trip on the tubes. Wait." The monitor buzzed to alert the nurses, but no one came into the room. I helped get her a pan, made sure her IV didn't get tangled, held my hand on her back as she threw up, helped her brush her teeth, rinse her mouth, and finally helped her back into bed. I tried to get a fast few minutes of rest before she was up again.

It was impossible to keep my eyes from closing. I was exhausted. Yet I sprang up instantly with any hint that she was getting out of bed. My instinct to stay with her was spot on. No one would have been there to help her. She would most definitely have fallen and probably gotten hurt—or worse. Where were the nurses?

Overnight, her condition deteriorated. What if she didn't pull out of this? I needed her to see the memorial stone for Mary. I needed her to know how much I respected and loved her and Dad for showing me the true meaning of not giving up. I needed her to know her daughters would not be forgotten.

"Something is *really* wrong," I told the nurse on her morning check-in. "She's been throwing up dark, foul-smelling fluid every 15 minutes or so, all night long."

The nurse immediately stopped her busy work. "Oh? Let me see it."

I furrowed my brow. Did she really expect me to save it? "Um. It looked swampy and smelled like a sewer. I've been flushing it."

"Okay. I'll let the Doctor know when he arrives for his rounds," she said and walked out.

I sat down in the chair next to Mom's bed. She was nodding off.

The nurse returned just a few minutes later with a coil of clear tubing about the diameter of a drinking straw. "We need to do a nasogastric intubation to suction her stomach."

We? This sounded serious; I stood up near the bedrail. "Okay."

She held up the tubing. "This needs to be inserted down through the nasal pathway, down her throat and into her stomach."

Was she expecting my help? I winced at the thought. Was this the only option?

"Can you help keep her calm?" she asked, as if Mom couldn't hear her.

I raised an eyebrow. Really? Mom had been through a surgery and stayed three days longer than she intended already. Now this? "I'll *try.*"

A second nurse stepped into the room and drew the curtain. "Okay, Mary. This is not going to be comfortable going in, but it *will* stop the vomiting."

I tried to look away as the tube disappeared little by little into her nostril and was pushed toward her stomach. She gagged. I held her hand, empathetically swallowing and cringing for her.

The nurse sounded as if she was lecturing a child. "You *have* to swallow it Mary. If it goes in the wrong way it could damage your lungs."

Mom glared at her with a look I'd seen her give the doctor during the hostile takeover yesterday.

The nurse continued. "Can you take a sip of water? That will help."

Mom acquiesced.

This process looked difficult for both the practitioner and patient. I wondered if that may have been partly why the nightshift seemed to be avoiding the room.

As the nurses taped the tube in place, it immediately began filling with fluid. By gentle suction, the tube siphoned the contents of her stomach directly to a clear plastic cylinder hung on the wall. It was disturbing to see how quickly it filled with the dark, vile substance, 100 mL, 200 mL, and rising.

"It's working, Mary. You should be feeling better very soon." Satisfied with their procedure, the nurses stepped out of the room. One of them returned after a minute or so to retrieve the discarded packaging.

I pointed to the reservoir on the wall. "Do you have another container? This one's almost full."

She glanced over in surprise. "Well, Mary, no wonder you were so sick!"

Yep. No wonder. When the doc on duty arrived, he immediately sent Mom for another scan. The image showed a second hernia that was not previously detected. It may have been missed, it may have been created during her violent outburst, or it may have resulted from the eight hours of vomiting every 15 minutes. In any case, part of her intestine was kinked in the hernia, and it was backing up the contents into her stomach. They scheduled another operation for the next day.

I called Angela to give her an update on Mom's condition. She was on her way to the hospital. I had to lecture in New Haven that afternoon, so after Angela arrived, I bought the biggest cup of coffee possible and drove south.

Later that day, Robyn sent me some selfies of her and Mom from the hospital. Mom was feeling better. Angela assured me that her condition was stable, and she would rest soundly. That night I stayed at The Ocean House to try to catch up on my sleep.

* * *

I had a full day of lectures and labs ahead of me, but as soon as I woke up, I sent the surgeon (one of Eric's friends) a text message. I asked him to call me with a detailed update of Mom's condition.

I kept my cell phone on the podium during Thursday morning's lecture. As I was about to launch into the hazards of pyroclastic flows, the screen lit up. It was the surgeon. I stepped outside the classroom to take his call.

"Hi, Julie. Your mom is stable right now, but as commonly happens she came into the hospital with more than one problem. In addition to the pancreatitis and hernia, she also had an irregular heartbeat. Another operation so soon, although necessary, is very risky, especially considering her age."

He ran down an exhaustive list of potential things that could go wrong. "And then of course there's the fact that she has just undergone surgery. I want you to be prepared for the possibility that she may not make it through this."

I leaned on a table in the hallway and looked out the floor-to-ceiling windows toward the boulders in the courtyard. That was one of the most difficult things I'd ever had to hear. Is this how Mom felt when little Mary's doctor told her there would be a day when she would not make it to the emergency room in time?

"I'm not trying to scare you," he said after a few moments of silence.

"No. I just—have to get back to my lecture. But thank you for being honest." Mom needed the procedure, and I needed her to make it through, but there I stood, on the second floor of the new science building, with much space between my feet and the solid earth. I wiped my eyes, straightened up, took a breath, and returned to the lecture hall. I temporarily disappeared back into the topic of the day—volcanoes and igneous rocks—to get my mind off surgeries, nasogastric intubation, and unfavorable outcomes.

Shifting gears has always come naturally. Perhaps I had to learn to compartmentalize extremely difficult events at a young age. In this case, work was a separate world from family life, and I could easily toggle among the two realities.

I contacted Dad after the volcano lecture, relaying some of the info from the surgeon.

"I'm at the hospital now," he said. "They're taking her into the operating room around eight tonight. Should be done around ten."

I drove north to the hospital after my last class and arrived just a few minutes before Mom came out of surgery. I was the only family member there. Perhaps they were avoiding another hostile takeover? I called Dad to see where everyone was. He said the nurses told him it would be better to visit in the morning. All I could think of was the surgeon's warning. Should I have told Dad about the risks? Would that have changed his decision?

One of the staff helped me navigate the maze of hallways to the recovery room where I spoke with her doctor. He was not encouraging. "She made it through, but her lungs are in very bad shape. She can't go through another procedure."

I was glad I was alone. I would not want Dad to hear that.

"Julie, in my opinion, I think your Mom has the beginnings of dementia, and that's what caused the outburst on Tuesday."

"Dementia? But she's never acted like that before."

The doctor continued. "In my opinion, you are all too close to her condition and probably didn't see it subtly creep in."

I didn't buy it, and when I mentioned it later to my family, neither did they. There was nothing subtle or creeping about this outburst. It was either a bad reaction to too much morphine or something they missed. It wasn't dementia. Mom and I both needed to reconcile the past. We both needed her memory.

The doctor and I spoke for a few minutes, with him continuing to scare the hell out of me. And then I saw the nurses wheeling Mom out, tubes and wires hanging, one end attached to Mom, the other to swinging bags of liquid. Tubes and wires like those hooked up to Dziadzia before he died, like the tangled web I saw when I looked up from my child's vantage point near the cold metal bed rail and reached for his hand one last time.

"She's just starting to wake up," said one of the nurses, shaking her head. "She is *feisty*. Are you her daughter? I think she's been asking for you. What's your name?"

"Julie. My name is Julie," I repeated, happy to think she was asking for me.

"Oh. *You're* Julie. Yes. She was talking about *you*," the nurse said quietly, turned her head, and slunk away.

I felt the heat in my face. I was curious about what Mom revealed under anesthesia.

I had no time to ask. Mom woke up suddenly, swung her hand to the oxygen tube in her nose and yanked it out. The nurses rushed over to her and one tried to hold her arms while the other nurse threw her hands in the air in frustration.

After they got Mom settled again, I asked one of the nurses, "Do you think I should stay the night with her? Will she be okay?"

"She'll rest well. No need to be here. You can see her when she wakes up in the morning."

I went home but got little sleep. *Bad lungs. Asthma. Years of steroids. She's in bad shape. You should be prepared that she may not make it. Beginnings of dementia. She can't go through another procedure.*

Over the next few days, I prayed, but *not* to Jesus—that had proven futile in the past. I prayed to Louise and Mary to do what they could.

During the surgery, Mom had to have a bowel resection, whereby the surgeon removed a dead segment of intestine. Her digestive system needed time to restart. It would take a few days. She was tired of being in the hospital. She had things to do. She was impatient, but at least she wasn't violent.

I brought Mom a magazine ad for a probiotic showing fancy gears and a big, artistic font that read, "Your gut is an engine," and hung it on the wall across from her bed. "It's important to visualize your intestines working."

She narrowed her eyes and gave me the skeptical Bardy glance.

"Okay. Well, I'm leaving the happy Buddha here for you too." I placed the wooden statue on the table near her bed to watch over her. She liked the Buddha. She didn't question why I had chosen that instead of a crucifix. Visualization or not, acceptable deity or not, she was improving and would be released in a few days. A visiting nurse would change her dressings and monitor her recovery.

* * *

With Mom mending and Dad and the new family visiting and keeping tabs on her, I drove to New Lebanon, New York, to spend the rest of my spring break sequestered in an abbreviated, three-day silent retreat at the Abode of the Message.

The farther I got from the hospital, from Mom, the more anxious I became. I wouldn't be able to get any updates—no cell phone, no Internet, no connection to the outside world. I wouldn't be there to filter upsetting news or honest but dark physician commentary. I had to trust that nothing bad would happen. I had to admit that I had no control, and this was something that terrified me.

Chapter 19:

Bridge of Trust

The Abode is a community of practicing Sufi mystics—think Rumi and the whirling dervishes and you're close. Sufism is not a religious construct but a school of experience that seeks a direct connection to the divine by opening the heart through meditation and spiritual inquiry. The Inayati Order at the Abode believe there is one current of truth underlying all people and religions. There was no better place to examine the notion of connection.

Even though it had been 15 years since I'd been on retreat there, I recognized my retreat guide, Don Johnson, right away. Tall, blonde, and fit, he looked like he belonged on a surfboard in San Diego, rather than an abode in New York. His name still made me think of Miami Vice—and of course I still thought better of mentioning it.

I smiled, waved to him, and instantly felt more settled. There was something comforting and familiar about being swaddled among trees, pastures, rocks, and open space; the Abode reminded me of Grandma and Dziadzia's farm.

We hugged and went over truncated Cliffs Notes of our lives for the past decade. He asked about Mom's recovery, and my intentions for the retreat.

"I want to work on a promise I made to help my parents grieve the loss of my sisters and find healing," I began.

Don nodded.

"I'd like to examine anger, resentment, and mistrust. I feel fragmented—cut off from my past. I want to ask God a few things about that."

He raised his eyebrows, smiled, and patted me on the shoulder. "Let's walk. Think for a moment and prioritize your goals for me."

I nodded and took a breath. "Okay. I want to feel less alone. To be able to connect with other people. I want to investigate anger, trust, and the need to control."

"That's better. I think you'll find progress on the goal for your mom and dad by addressing these other things. Sounds like you've thought deeply on this already."

"Yes. But it's become more urgent in recent years. Since the summer of 2014."

"That's good. You'll move further along in this short time."

We walked about a quarter mile down a narrow, meandering footpath edged by mountain laurel, tall grass, small evergreens, and birch trees. The hut was about the size of our tool shed at The Lake House. Don gestured for me to go inside. It was cluttered with a desk, futon, fridge, prayer bench, and zafu (round meditation cushion). The plywood walls were bare except for two framed pictures of Pir Vilayat Inayat Khan, the Sufi leader who founded the Abode in 1975, the year Dziadzia died.

I slung my backpack on the futon and sat down with a thud on the ultra-firm mattress.

Don took a bunch of papers from his leather messenger bag and set them on the desk. "It's early in the season. You're the only seeker here right now." He leafed through the stack and handed me some prayers for the evening. "These are in order. Do you recall the principles of retreat?"

I nodded. "Silence, fasting, isolation, and watchfulness."

"Right. The only communication will be short instructions I give each morning. Tonight, I want you to start with Wazifas. Choose two personal qualities you admire and focus on them while doing purification breaths."

"Okay." I said, quickly scanning the qualities written in Arabic and their translations.

"Follow the evening retreat schedule, including the Kyrie Eleison practice. You can also do any of the other practices that suit you. Sound good?"

I glanced up at him. "I don't remember Kyrie Eleison."

"It's a practice of Mohasaba, asking for divine guidance at the start of retreat. You kneel and bow reciting Kyrie, and then rise on Eleison. The translation is *Lord have mercy*."

I unwittingly gave him The Rumrill Eyebrow. I wasn't quite ready for that one on the first evening of retreat. I don't think Don was privy to my rift with the Lord.

He ignored my sour expression, like a parent ignoring a child who is refusing to do chores. "Okay. Dinner will be dropped off around seven o'clock tonight. I'll see you in the morning."

"Sounds good." Unlike the rest of my family, I was fine with anything that *wasn't* Christianity. That seemed to be a religion where devotion was unrecognized, and where my pleas for help had gone unanswered.

After he left, I poked around the room for a few minutes. I took one of the framed photos of Pir Vilayat off the wall. On the back of the frame I noticed a hand-written line that read "Toward the One." I moved the zafu to the floor in the center of the hut and sat crossed legged with Don's prescription on the floor in front of me. I glanced down the list of Wazifas, and chose *Ya Fattah*, opener of the way, *Ya Hadi*, inner guidance, and *Ya Wali*, mastery.

I began, eyes closed, alternately repeating the phrases in succession. I kept track of the number of repetitions on a string of prayer beads called a Misbaha. It wasn't as fancy as the white rosary beads I had gotten at my first communion. The rosary beads I brought to grandma's for television mass on the Sundays I slept at her house. These wooden beads adorned with their golden tassel felt more organic in my hand—less pretentious to me somehow.

A major tenet of Sufism is the idea of purifying your spirit. To that end, Don left me instructions to do Earth, Water, Fire, and Air breaths. These are done in some combination of breathing in or out the nose or mouth, and are meant to draw energy, expel worry, renew and cleanse the being, and feel connection with the breath of life—breath that God revoked from both Louise and Mary. The next page was Kyrie Eleison. Not ready. I set the pages down and brushed my teeth.

Silence, fasting, isolation, and watchfulness. I journaled and fell asleep on the futon thinking about my relationship with God. I was angry with the divine, and I wasn't sure how that would or could be reconciled in three days.

* * *

On the first full day of the retreat, I awoke to streaky rays of daylight peering in through dusty glass. Outside, a clean sheet of snow had coated the mountainside. The layer of white dissipated in the warmth of the sun, revealing millions of sparkling crystals welded together in rocky outcrops—the truths that lay beneath, emerging as a reminder: sometimes we cannot be seen, but we are always here.

After our silent prayer, Don gave me a goal for the day, to turn inward and explore my connection to others. He suggested I walk up the mountain to explore the community's summer retreat and ritual gathering space.

I roamed past cabins, outhouses, screen houses, and gathering halls. Doors creaked, and slammed against wood shakes, torn plastic sheeting flapped and snapped in the wind. Central to the town that time forgot was a huge stainless-steel fire pit about ten feet across, surrounded by a larger circle of boulders. Don had explained that the Sufi community held a vigil last fall for a member who was seriously ill. They gathered around the contained blaze, chanting and swaying, each person taking turns sitting and praying inside the stone circle.

Mom would certainly have a cult comment to make about that. Yet, joking aside, rituals are important. They help us move forward. They help us grieve and connect with others who are also hurting so we can support one another. I wasn't brought up to cherish traditions or seek connection, but I've felt drawn to those ideas since childhood. Here there was a whole community of support. That notion sounded so comforting.

Walking away from the main summit trail, the land dropped off sharply into a field bordered by woods, hundreds of feet below. An old, dilapidated bridge caught my eye. It was like half a bridge actually; it didn't lead anywhere. It was more like walking "the plank" on a pirate ship. I was curious but twilight was closing in. I returned to the four walls of the hut to sit, chant, and count.

The Abode removed the urgency and turbulence of life, allowing the mud to settle. I realized I had begun to work on my goals, such as connection to self and others, prior to the retreat. That was what I'd been building in my writing groups and other workshops I'd been involved in—community. I had made significant progress connecting in the present, but I still felt the deep past was a formidable barrier.

After dinner, I sat on the zafu and recited *Ya alim*, Arabic for *deep understanding*. I went to sleep on the sandbag, thinking of something Don had said about connection. "Think of yourself as *inheritance*, as the person who carries the *essence* of their parents and grandparents."

* * *

The next morning, after the silent morning prayer, I asked Don about the old bridge.

"Oh, yes. It's exhilarating!"

The Rumrill Eyebrow. "You mean people *walk* on it? Not recently, right?"

"Sure. It's perfectly safe."

I wasn't convinced. My intention for day two was about connecting with the earth, but I did not want that to include plummeting from a dilapidated bridge to nowhere.

Don's instructions for the day included a Buddhist walking meditation and he recommended that I recite it as I walked up the mountain. "Breathe in and take one step, focusing all your attention on the soles of your feet and their solid connection with the ground. If you are not completely in the present moment, don't take another step."

I tried to mask my skeptical expression. I had practiced walking meditation before but across a room or a lawn, not up a mountain. "This sounds like it's going to take a while."

He reassured me of the merits of this tool. "Walking meditation makes you aware of the mind's incessant chatter."

I ambled along the path adjacent to the brook. As I hopped from rock to rock, I recalled Don's instructions. *Be mindful of my steps and feel the contact of my feet with the earth. Breathe. Notice the chaos of the mind.*

Unaware of my pace, it seemed like I reached the ridgeline quickly. I roamed in the opposite direction as the previous day. One of the highlights in that part of the mountain camp was a swing, suspended from a branch at least 30 feet high. It reminded me of the rope swing near Louise and Tammy's clubhouse in the woods at The Compound. I sat down on the smooth, wooden seat, and shimmied back. With one hand on each rope, I pedaled my feet backward and kicked off in flight, swinging forward and back in a long, slow arc like a giant pendulum. Surrender. Trust. Soar. I leapt off the swing in mid-air and continued exploring.

The path brought me in a semi-circle around camp, headed toward the bridge to nowhere. Don had referred to it as the "bridge of trust"; to me it looked like a stunt you might try on *Fear Factor.* It was a precarious half of a drawbridge, made of weathered wood planks and rusty spikes, suspended by twisted steel cables, extended out over the edge of the cliff, hundreds of feet above the valley floor. Thick suspension cables were anchored into several trees and the bridge was marking time with the wind. The knotted branches creaked, and the swaying of the bridge became more pronounced as I inched further away from solid ground, step-by-step, knees soft and heart quivering. Three splintered planks lashed together beneath my feet, with rope loosely draped along the sides for handrails, was all that held my life hovering over the valley below. It was no small feat to trust what Don said, that it was "safe."

Yet once I decided to choose trust over fear, the panoramic view reminded me of the link between risk and reward. I closed my eyes and felt the sun on my face and the wind moving the bridge beneath my feet. Powerful. Free. But the height and the sway weren't conducive to lingering.

* * *

Three nights of sleeping on a sandbag, the mental exhaustion of thinking so deeply, and subconscious worry about Mom were consuming much of my energy. Still, I needed to focus. It was the last full day I would be at the Abode. What was my intention? I stared at the framed picture of Pir Vilayat and recalled the message on the back—toward the One. That day, I chose to work on my disconnection from God.

Even though I was brought up Catholic, I had never made my confirmation. I preferred to skip Catechism and hide in the graveyard, a blatant act of defiance toward God. Even as an adult, I rarely attended church except on occasion to appease Mom.

I thought about how there were strong women on both sides of my family. Grandma and Grammie (Dad's mother). I thought about the incredible difficulties they had suffered, and how they both kept their faith. Even Mom still went to church. Even *she* managed to forgive God. Why couldn't I? That was the question I would spend the day examining.

After silent prayer, Don suggested I walk toward the pond, away from the mountain. Along the way, I stopped to admire the organic garden and noticed the first people I'd seen, other than Don, since I'd arrived. An older man and a younger woman, perhaps father and daughter, were prepping the soil in the garden for planting.

I recalled a picture of Mom and Dziadzia working together in his garden at the farm, a large rectangular, horticultural work of art. He had lovingly tilled, planted, and tended each row and hill. Our connection to the earth, to nature, is at the very core of the Bardy's deep strength. *Wrap the stems of the tomatoes to avoid cutworm. Dust the leaves with wood ashes to deter insects, wait until after Memorial Day to plant.* Despite all the knowledge, skill, and care, sometimes you still get pests, woodchucks, and unexpected frost. Sometimes plants still die.

I continued walking down Chair Factory Road, past the dead-end sign, and found a sunny spot where I sat on a downed tree trunk. A small cemetery across the road held one single grave stone, a tall, obelisk-shaped monument. It brought all the stifled worry about Mom's health under high amplification. I couldn't check in on Mom, and I hated it. But I had resigned to explore the discomfort, working mentally on the idea of connectedness and God's role within the matrix.

If, as the Sufis believe, we are all one with the divine, in an uncompromised state we should feel directly connected to other people and to God—a state of being that Sufis refer to as the One. I was skeptical of course. I had felt shunned by God for quite some time.

But I was open to the possibility of an amended perspective. The gravestone represented more than one human, more than one community, more than even one earth; it represented a belief in some form of life after death.

On the third evening, I knelt on the prayer bench and recited the Kyrie Eleison, asking for divine guidance as I ended the retreat and continued my journey. *Lord have mercy.*

I went to sleep turning over rocks, thinking about God. Christ? Buddha? Allah? Jehovah? I had spent much energy resenting Christianity. Yet I woke in the wee hours with a message ringing loud, smooth, and clear. God is love. Pure love. So simple. *But could I come to understand and trust this?*

* * *

The 8 am bell rang. What is my intention? Along the banks of the swirling brook, bubbles of white foam gathered at eddies. I knelt and with cupped hands splashed the clean, clear, icy water on my cheeks and forehead.

I packed my bag and left the Abode, driving down the mountain toward the Mass Pike. Toward Mom. I called The Compound. It was March 23rd and Mom had just gotten home from the hospital the day before.

Chapter 20:

Providence Earned

Late March, 2016

Eric and I had Easter dinner with his family in Brookfield, Massachusetts. We had asked Mom and Dad to join us, but Mom was still on a restricted, low-fiber diet and didn't feel like socializing or eating a big meal. After dinner I headed right to The Ocean House, and Eric promised to check in on Mom at The Compound.

He called me during my drive south. "She looks fine. Tired, but resting on the couch watching TV."

I was concerned. She was on the couch when we had seen her that morning. "Did she go out in her garden today?"

"No. But she was joking with me as usual. It's all good."

Although Eric seemed convinced, my sharp intuition, honed during the silent retreat, nagged at me. Watchfulness. She hadn't been in her garden. She had undergone two operations. Was it the old wives' tale—things happen in threes?

Within a few hours, Mom was shivering and sweating. Dad covered her up with a blanket and sat in his recliner worrying. Then he went into the back hallway, out of Mom's range, to call Angela.

"Your mother is complaining of pain and she's shivering. I have a fire in the wood stove. It's eighty degrees in here."

Angela was all business. "Take her temperature."

"It's 103.8."

"Take it again." Angela waited.

"It's 104."

"I'll be right over."

Angela lives just across town. When she arrived at The Compound minutes later, Dad was dressed in his street clothes ready to go.

She took Mom's temperature one more time. Without comment on the reading, she turned to Mom. "Let's go. I'm taking you to the hospital. Dad, follow us in your car."

Mom got up slowly, with barely a trace of life. She was a shadow of herself—an exhausted, shivering, tiny woman, in a great deal of physical pain.

Angela pulled out of the drive and headed to the hospital with Mom. Dad followed.

"Angela." Mom's voice was profoundly soft, scared and serious. "I feel so awful. Am I going to die?"

Angela, an OR nurse at a level-four trauma center, knew the gravity of the situation. "We're going to the hospital. I think there's an infection. They'll get you started on antibiotics."

A few hours later, Angela called me to say that Mom was at the ER. She was running a fever of 104 and rising.

I waited in New Haven for news. I couldn't sleep. I couldn't focus. I thought we had rounded this corner. After the silent retreat, I thought God and I had at least reached neutral ground. My family already had a backlog of grief to deal with.

Angela called again from the hospital once Mom was stable. The diagnosis came in at 3:24 am. Sepsis. Infection throughout the body, in her bloodstream. Hospital techs used computerized axial tomography (CAT) to get a three-dimensional image of the affected area. I was familiar with this type of imaging. It's used in geology to map temperature variation in the earth's crust and identify volcanic hazards. For Mom, the CAT scan showed an abscess in her lower abdomen around the incision site of the surgeries.

Her surgeon deduced that the mesh used to repair the hernia had caused the infection. She would spend the next few days in intensive care under close watch, and when stable, would undergo another surgery to remove the mesh. I had a bad feeling.

I trusted the surgeon because Eric said he was one of the best. Angela also knew him and had worked in his office at the beginning of her nursing career. Surely she would have put forth any reservations. Yet doubt crept in. I stepped off the bridge of trust back onto solid land. I called Aunt Helen and Uncle Jose.

Uncle Jose was a retired surgeon, and Auntie was a retired nurse. I had been in contact with them since the hostile takeover. Auntie was the recipient of one of Mom's vulgar get-me-the-hell-out-of-here messages. She had never heard her older sister use that type of language. She had called me back as soon as the shock wore off.

I relayed the new concerns. "Auntie, I need your advice. They want my mom to have another surgery. There's an infection."

"Oh, I don't like that idea. Let me put Uncle Jose on the phone. Hold on." I could hear her explaining the situation to him as I waited.

"Hello, Julie?" Uncle Jose began. "Tell me what is happening with Mary."

I explained what I knew with as much detail as possible. He asked a bunch of medical questions I couldn't answer and used a bunch of medical terms I wasn't familiar with. Google wasn't cutting it. I suggested he speak to Angela. I also put him in contact with the surgeon. It turned out Uncle Jose remembered the surgeon from decades ago when he had helped to train him at Yale New Haven Hospital. I was relieved that they knew and respected each other.

Auntie and Uncle Jose came up from Orange, Connecticut, to review the care plan and check on Mom's condition. They met with the doctors and surgeon and discussed the possible need for a risky surgery to remove the mesh. But on closer review of the CAT scan, Uncle Jose pointed out that the infection appeared to be in a different tissue plane, so another procedure was unnecessary.

With other medical experts to back her up, Angela took charge. She criticized the hospital for using archaic methods. "No one uses bleach irrigation to clean wounds anymore. Why aren't you using a wound vac?" She was referring to a self-contained, portable pump with an attached reservoir that drains the wound as it heals.

They ordered a wound vac and Angela offered to show them how to set it up.

* * *

Mom was finally discharged around 4:00 the next afternoon. She had planned to do rehab, but when she found out that she would have to travel from the hospital to the rehab clinic in a town ambulance, she immediately changed her mind. "I'm not going to have those nose-bags telling the whole town about my business."

I tried to explain that that probably wasn't the best thing to base her decision on, but I knew better than to try to persuade her.

Dad and I took Mom home with her wound vac slung over her shoulder like a purse. She was so weak she could barely walk, but she got into the car and left the hospital for the third time in a month. The old wives' tale of threes was complete.

It seemed that God was on our side for a change, but I still felt a sense of urgency. I knew things could have gone much differently. It made me realize that if I was writing the family history in part to help Mom heal, then I'd better hurry up about it. I had viewed her as fearless and invincible. The hospital debacle made me realize she was far more fragile than I thought.

In the memoir, *Blue Nights*, Joan Didion writes about recognizing her own mother's sense of frailty after surviving a serious illness at 75.

"She was never again exactly as she had been. Things went wrong. She lost confidence. She became apprehensive in crowds."

For Mom, the experience sounded chillingly similar. I could only hope that her sense of frailty would lessen as she continued to regain her health. For once I was wishing for *her* to be more like a Bardy.

Chapter 21:

Set in Stone

On April 8, 2016, Mary would have turned 54-years-old. It was the first year since 1976 that I knew where she was. It was the first time in four decades I thought about celebrating her birthday.

I drove up I-395 from The Ocean House. Before reaching the cemetery, I made a quick turn into the parking lot of the grocery store.

I traced and retraced my path through the floral section three times before I decided on a bouquet of mums. I picked through a selection of small plastic signs and other decorations meant to personalize bouquets for different occasions. So many choices. Nervous indecision. I chose a yellow butterfly made of glittery fabric and a small plastic sign that read 'Happy Birthday.'

While the cashier rang them up, I ruminated. Would Mary even know? Was I being ridiculous? I should just bring the flowers to Mom. I ordered a caramel macchiato at the adjacent Starbucks kiosk and, while waiting for my drink, mulled over the decision. Whether I left the flowers or not, I was going to visit the grave and could decide there.

I drove into St. Anthony's Cemetery where Mary's shell was resting in St. Peter's section, still unmarked, as if her life—or her death—was a secret. A single robin chirped loudly and flitted among the gravestones in the adjacent section. I stepped lightly over the grass with my birthday offering, past the Celko, Hughes, and Dragon family plots toward Mary and Dziadzia.

I knelt on their plot and pushed the stem of the happy birthday sign into the soft moss covering the soil. It felt like the deep-green, velvet patches in the woods at The Compound, whose cool sponginess Mary and I could feel on the soles of our bare feet and between our toes. I set the stake for the yellow butterfly into the earth next to the happy birthday sign. Its wings began to flutter and sparkle in the breezy afternoon sun. I walked back to the car to get my Swiss Army knife from the console, clipped one pink button mum with a yellow center from the bunch, and set it down on Mary's grave. Three offerings to my once-older sister who was 13. Again.

Part of me still felt the familiar sadness, but there was also a deep comfort, a peace, to being there with her on that day. It just felt good to be able to sit quietly among the birdsong and gentle breeze and celebrate the seven years we spent together. She was not forgotten.

The morning before I drove up from The Ocean House, I had thought about calling Mom to remind her of Mary's birthday. But I was afraid it would make her sad. After visiting Mary's grave, I knew it was okay to reach out.

I stopped by The Compound before going to the lake. Max mauled me with attention as soon as I walked in the door.

Dad grabbed a magazine, leaned forward in the recliner, and swatted at him. "Get down!"

Mom was lying on the couch, wound vac at her side. She, Dad, and Max had been watching a western on TV. I held the bouquet of button mums behind me. "How are you feeling, Mom?"

"Okay. Tammy's on her way. She should have been here already. Robyn's bringing lunch. Are you going to stay?"

"I have to bring some stuff to the lake, but I'll be back."

Dad got up from the recliner and hugged me. He eyed the flowers. "Who are those for?"

"I bought them for Mary. For her birthday. I left one at her grave and wanted to bring the rest here and put them near her picture."

Mom looked a bit surprised, maybe a tad embarrassed, but then smiled. "Oh, how nice."

"They reminded me of the flowered wallpaper that was in her bedroom."

Dad smiled softly. "That's right. How do you remember these things?"

I patted his forearm, looked into his eyes, and smiled. "Do you have a vase?"

* * *

The letter arrived two weeks later.

It was buried in a pile of mail that Eric finally brought in from the cache in his pickup truck. I sat at the table with a cup of tea and opened it. The return address read *Empire Monument Company*.

I hoped it was a Xerox that showed the changes to the stone I had requested in our last correspondence. When he had received the changes to the layout, Nick called me and said he needed an additional deposit before he could order the stone. I refused. I had paid the initial deposit—and would pay the rest when the gravestone was in place. That was the deal we made at the office on Belmont Street this past summer. Had I offended him? Was he sending me a note to say *Thanks, but no thanks, I'd rather not do business with you?* The envelope was small, not like the previous business-sized ones.

I took a breath, and slowly unfolded the contents.

It was a triplicate copy of an itemized bill for $1,916.56, stamped with the company's name. The last line read, "Your monument has been set in the cemetery."

I folded the bill and placed it back into the envelope. I paused and thought about the last line—could that be true? Was it really in place?

Was that what the line said? No. They would have told me. The stone had been set? When? I knew nothing about it. Did I officially approve the final layout? How long had it been there? A week? Two weeks?

I sat there, frozen. Unable to attach meaning and let it sink in. *Your monument has been set.* But he was *supposed* to let me know. I tapped the edge of the envelope firmly on the table. I felt angry and left out. Things just happened, and I was excluded. Like Mary's burial—no one was there to see the stone set in place.

I opened the envelope again and read the last line just to be sure. I placed the bill on the table. The sun was setting. I grabbed my car keys and turned to Eric who was in his recliner watching TV. "I'm taking a run to Webster."

"What's going on?"

"According to this bill, Mary's stone was set in the cemetery. I need to see if it's really there."

"Can I come with you?"

I turned back, already headed out the door. "Okay, but let's go." We got into the car. What was I feeling? Anxious. Confused. I was trying to imagine how I *should* feel. Should I be sad? Should I be crying? What if the letter had been sent by mistake?

The car was silent. No radio. No conversation. Internally, my mind blared with noise. Eric asked several questions in quick succession, but then gave up when I mostly just asked him to repeat them. I kept trying to anticipate how I would feel. Was she really going to have a monument after all this time?

I turned the car into St. Anthony's Cemetery. The blinker seemed really loud. I noticed the sign for St. Peter's section on my right, drove toward the end, and scanned across Mary's row. Celko, Hughes, Dragon, and yes, a fourth stone. A speckled grey, glittering slab of Barre, Vermont, granite that hadn't been there before. We got out of the car and walked toward it. I proofread the front, Dziadzia's family name, Rzeszutko, with a dreamy angel leaning on folded forearms and looking up to the right, recalling good times. On the back, Dziadzia, Grandma, and Mary's names and dates, and Mom's sentiment—*God loaned us an angel.* It was exactly right.

Eric put his arm around me. "What do you think?"

I kissed him on the cheek, leaned toward the stone, and rested my palm on the cool granite. The feel of the stone reminded me of the many walls Mary and I climbed over at The Compound, and at Dziadzia's farm, picking sweet, ripe blueberries in the summer sun. I thought of my visit to the quarry in Barre, Vermont. The enduring nature of quartz. My past was slowly crystalizing in the present. A huge piece of the family mosaic had just been set down.

Finally, she was recognized. If a heart could possibly smile, mine was grinning widely at that moment. Tammy had said this would be very healing for me. I had been skeptical at the time, but there was no confusion that evening. As the sun set behind the clouds, distant rays of sisterhood splayed wide across the sky like arms from heaven. As if to say, *We can still reach you.*

The Barre granite, composed of a matrix of interlocking quartz, would endure for billions of years. Everyone who came to the cemetery would know that Mary had lived, she would always be loved, and she would never be forgotten.

* * *

I called Mom the next morning. "So, I got a letter in the mail yesterday."

"Yes?"

"And it said that the monument was in place."

"Really."

"I went to see it last night and it's beautiful." I couldn't veil my enthusiasm. "It's light grey Vermont granite, has an angel on the front, with Grandma, Dziadzia, and Mary's names and your quote on the back."

"Oh." She paused. "Will they want Gramma's ashes to be emptied to bury them? I don't want to open the container. I don't want to *look* at the ashes."

My heart felt her angst. It was not the Bardy fearlessness. It was a struggle with vulnerability. "Whatever you're comfortable with, Mom. I'm sure we can bury her ashes in an urn." I tried to imagine what was going through her mind.

I wasn't sure if I should ask her if she wanted to go see the stone. I wanted to tell Dad about it, but he was up at the barn, feeding the pony. I was hoping she would have shared some of my happiness, but I guess there wasn't much to be happy about. It was a gravestone. She seemed preoccupied with the dread of another burial, one that had been delayed since 1996. I decided against asking her.

"Can you let Dad know that if he wants to debug his computer, we can take it to Worcester later this morning?"

"Okay."

I knew she probably wouldn't tell him. Sometimes she gets anxious about being alone for long stretches of time, and he already had plans with a friend to practice guitar later that day. He would be away long enough.

Perhaps she also knew I would tell him about the gravestone. He would want to go see it. And he would want her to go. She would need time to consider visiting the grave.

* * *

A week later, I was on I-95 when Mom called, her voice bubbling with energy.

"Guess where Dad and I went?"

"Were you guys picking through the swap shack at the dump again?"

"No. We went to the cemetery in Webster."

Did I hear that right? "What?"

"We saw the stone for Mary and Dziadzia. It's beautiful!" She sounded genuinely excited. Proud of herself even. She mentioned planting some petunias there over the summer. I fought tears of relief, joy, sadness, and triumph—a whole slew of emotions. Goosebumps raced up my arms and I felt queasy. I wasn't sure I could utter a coherent sentence.

This was the first time she had ever been to Little Mary's grave. This was the first time she had ever been to her father's grave. This is the first time she had been in a cemetery since Louise was buried in 1973. And she and Dad were there together.

Big, wet tears fell from my face onto my shirt and into my lap. My nose ran. I was stunned. She sounded elated, happy, relieved.

"Julie? Are you there?"

"Yes," I replied between sniffles. Overwhelmed with gratefulness. I wasn't sure if she would ever go. But she went. *They* went. Rusted gears breaking free after decades of stillness. Did it help ease their pain? I hoped so. It was all I'd wanted.

"Julie? Hello?"

"Yes. Yes. I'm glad—so glad you liked it." I wiped my eyes.

After Grandma had died in 1996, Mom told me that she and Auntie decided they didn't need to have a service or bury Grandma right away. They had the plot and didn't need to run out and spend money on a gravestone.

I got the reasoning, but as Tammy had pointed out, monuments are also for the living. For those who want to go and have a quiet place to sit and reflect and appreciate those who have passed on. Monuments help people grieve.

Yet more meaningful than the monument itself, was the fact that Mom *went* to the cemetery. She visited her father and her little angel—the girl who bears her own name and the name of her great-great grandmother, the tea leaf reader.

The origin of the name Mary has been debated. Some say it is an Anglicized form of Maria, derived from the Hebrew Miriam. Although it seems that *sea of bitterness or sorrow* is the most probable meaning, some sources define it as *wished-for child*, and *mistress or lady of the sea*. In any case, Mary remains one of the most popular names in the Christian world. Like the smoky quartz crystal I found on the Franconia Ridge trail. Enduring.

It was clear in her voice that Mom and I felt a similar joy in seeing the stone in place. It was freeing, liberating. Perhaps she built it up in her mind that it might bring about feelings of shame for not visiting or might be sad or frightening to go there. Perhaps I felt that way. Regardless of any trepidation, the unbreakable mother-daughter-sister bond that had seemed dormant was reawakening.

I hope she realized that this little angel of hers will always be remembered. Somewhere amidst the swirling emotions of that day, I felt a sense of mending, but I also felt a quiet sense of foreboding. For as the frayed edges of our family tapestry were smoothed and stitched, I could no longer ignore the full extent of the damage. Family tapestries are a complex and pure art form. As with much art, they are best understood from a distance, where the viewer can reflect upon the significance of the feelings and emotions evoked by the piece.

My clearest vantage point turned out to be half-way around the world.

Chapter 22:

Temple of the Heart

July, 2016

Following the workshop at Kripalu, the silent retreat, and Mom's health debacle, I had been practicing yoga at least twice a week at the studio in New Haven. One evening before class, as I milled about in the hallway, a fan of colorful postcards on the bulletin board grabbed my attention. They showed a lone yogi facing a rugged spine of mountains, hands to the heart in prayer, the delicate fabric of her Hindu sari flowing in the wind. The cards advertised an upcoming yoga and service retreat at a mindfulness-based environmental school in the Indian Himalayas. Highlights included: volunteering at the rural K-8 school, trekking in the tallest mountains on earth, temple visits, a remote location, and yoga twice a day. It sounded like a great balance of giving and receiving, teaching and learning, but what stood out most of all was the idea of *service to others*. It was the theme of Mary's entire life. A theme that was left incomplete. I tucked the card in my bag and filled out the online registration that night.

* * *

Weeks passed. I lounged in bed after slapping at the snooze alarm for the third time. The sci-fi ringtone of The Compound pulled me from dreamland. I pressed the phone to my ear and rolled over. "Hello?"

Mom's voice. "Julie, why are you going to India? It's not safe there."

I growled. "What time is it?" She loved to brag to Aunt Helen about my trips once I returned, but the time leading up to my departure riddled her with worry.

I peeled away the covers and sat up. "Who told you about India? Robyn?" The quickest way to get any news around the family was to tell Robyn. Because she would tell Mom, and Mom would tell everyone else.

There was a pause. A chair scraped against the floor in the background and Dad asked about breakfast. "Don't you think it's a little too dangerous?" she continued.

"I won't be in the city. I'll be at an ashram in the mountains." The faucet was running. She was probably filling the kettle for coffee.

"I thought you were doing yoga in New Haven. Why do you have to go to *India*?"

That was a good question. And I knew just where her angst was rooted. Sadly, rape was a frequent crime in India, and the news had publicized a particularly brutal incident less than a year ago. Mom was probably thinking about Louise. And she was right; I certainly didn't *have* to go. But I didn't feel like sharing the deeper reasons for the trip, how I wanted to do more for Mary's memory than just the memorial stone. "It's more than just yoga. I'm also volunteering at a school."

She rattled through some pans in the cabinet. "Alright. Well, I have to make breakfast for your father." With that, the conversation was over, but I knew her worry was not.

* * *

Eric and I celebrated the Fourth of July with a cookout and fireworks cruise at the lake. I received my Indian visa by email a few days later, and on July 10th I boarded a plane in Boston, bound for New Delhi.

At the Indira Gandhi airport, the line for customs was an immiscible mass of people inching forward, crowding and nudging. Baggage claim was a repeat of the same. At the exit, I slogged through the rough sea of congestion—humans, traffic, air, people waving, hawking, pushing, following on my heels—as I attempted to find the *one* driver who held a sign with my name. The clamor of people and vehicles, shouting and honking, was dizzying. Finally, dragging my suitcase behind me, I made my way over to a blocky middle-aged man who held a white paper sign with my name scrawled in black marker.

"Okay. Julie?" he asked.

"Whew. Yes." I smiled, nodded, and we shook hands.

"Yes. We wait."

Wait? I had been on a plane for the past 16 hours. Was he just running the idea past me?

"I must pick up one more person for transport in just more than one hour."

I hoisted my backpack over my right shoulder. "Nahn. I'm tired from the flight. I need to go to my hotel."

"Okay. We will go." And just like that, he grabbed the handle of my suitcase. The "one more person" was suddenly not important.

As chaotic as the airport seemed, the taxi ride into the city of Delhi was worse. The air conditioner wasn't working, and the car smelled like sweat and Dad's old aftershave. Dharam, the driver, blared Bhaṅgrā Indian pop music on the radio. The roads were flooded with traffic moving as turbulent rapids and eddies, past obstacles any and every which way. People never stopped honking and drove the wrong way, like a continuous game of chicken, approaching head-on and swerving at the last second.

I arrived in the capital city of New Delhi, senses overwhelmed.

"Amax Hotel? You are positive?" the driver asked.

"Yes." I handed him the paper with the address on it.

He read it aloud. "Eight-one-four-five-dash-six Arakashan Road, Multani Dhanda, Paharganj, New Delhi, Delhi." He shook his head and passed the paper back to me. "Oh. That area is not good."

Great. I was alone in a city of around 20 million people, in a bad area; I didn't speak the language or have any Rupees. "Um. Okay." It's not like I had any options. "I'll be careful."

Dharam glanced in the rearview mirror. "Are you traveling alone?"

"No. I'm meeting a group at the hotel tonight. We're going to Uttarakhand."

He seemed relieved. "The country is beautiful. You must go to the Ganges River and bathe. It removes all stress."

All stress? Impressive. "Thanks. I'll try it."

The rest of the way into Delhi, Dharam helped me practice a few Hindi phrases and used his horn *way* more than anyone in New Haven—an impressive and unlikely feat.

The taxi weaved through a tight maze of streets clogged with people, vehicles, and motorbikes. It was a disorienting combination of few signs and many turns. Dharam pulled over at the side of one of the streets, got out, hoisted my bag from the trunk, and pointed down a crowded, crooked alley. "Amax. It is there."

I took the handle of my suitcase. "Thank you." I wandered toward the narrow passage and glanced back at Dharam, my only landmark in the clamor of sensation, but he was already gone, the void fast flooded with the chaos of life in Delhi. I inched through the congestion, glancing up at store fronts and street signs written in Hindi. Pedestrians, trucks, and rickshaws navigated as one mass, past heaps of cement bags and other building materials, and feral dogs stretched out on their sides in the roadway. Rays of sun filtered through a dense fog of pollution, and condensation from air conditioners dripped from overhead as I dragged my suitcase through rank puddles strewn with trash, past several other small hotels.

Floor-to-ceiling windows served as the front wall to the lobby of the Amax Hotel. It *looked* like a nice place. I wondered why the taxi driver referred to this area as "not good."

Considering airport transfers, I had been traveling almost 24 hours without much sleep. I was looking forward to a cool shower and a bed. As soon as I checked in, the computer screen flickered, and the lobby went dark. Power outage. I leaned on the reception desk in disbelief. Air temps felt like triple digits with 100% humidity, and the elevator wasn't an option. Welcome to India.

I slung my backpack over one shoulder and dragged my hulking suitcase, *step-clunk, step-clunk,* up the narrow, winding stairs, toward the third floor. My shirt clung to my back, and I raised my arm to wipe my forehead just as one of the waif-like boys from the reception lifted my bag over his head as if it was empty, whisked past me taking two steps at a time, and placed it outside my room.

I unlocked the door, dragged my bag inside, flopped down on the bed, closed my eyes, and fell asleep. I woke to the lights on and the ceiling fan teetering unevenly. *Clank, clink chink. Clank, clink, chink.* It occurred to me that I had no idea when the others in the group were arriving. I felt caged in by self-doubt, like a prisoner of my own fear and perhaps Mom's as well. To overcome the emotion, I needed to face it. I splashed water on my cheeks, covered up with some India-appropriate clothing, wolfed down a granola bar, and walked down three flights—over the white marble floors, past the brass-trimmed reception desk, through the glass doors, and into the city.

Jet-lagged and dehydrated, I slogged through streets that looked like slot canyons carved through outcrops of buildings by the flow of motorbikes, rickshaws, tuk-tuks, and people—very few of them women. Wet garbage and mud, warmed by the heat of the day and slick under my feet, oozed into my sandals and between my toes.

Stall owners strung-up red chickens dusted with chili powder, turmeric, or paprika. Errand boys carried five-gallon tins retrofitted for water, and chai boys navigated skillfully as they carried stainless steel trays with steaming cups of tea. Diesel exhaust, fumes from burning trash, and the scent of food cooking over barrels of smoldering charcoal, combined to produce a smell that seemed uniquely India.

I brushed away the beads of oily sweat that collected on my forehead and cheeks. I continued to walk, not too fast, not too slow, not making eye contact. *Why am I not safe here?* Was it real danger, or was I in fear of a thinly veiled stereotype? Amidst the continuous honking and endless clamor, sacred cows with bells swinging slowly, *clunk-clank, clunk-clank,* hip and shoulder bones protruding through tissue-paper skin, lumbered unconcerned down the center of the street.

An Indian friend had enlightened me on some of the dichotomies that existed in her country. From extreme wealth juxtaposed with abject poverty, to ruthless violence against women contemporaneous with the cultural worship of female deities, to the lighthearted notion of *sacred cows*—"tourists believe that sacred cows roam free because they are precious and honored," my friend began, matter of factly. "But that's just a sham so owners don't have to feed their pet cow."

Back at the Amax Hotel later that evening, I got an email from Mohan and Khushi, the retreat organizers. I was to meet up with them and the other six retreat participants, who just happened to be women, Amanda, Anne, Christine, Deb, Jamie, and Mary, in the lobby of the Amax. Instantly, I felt anxious. I became aware of the familiar wall I habitually placed between myself and others.

After brief introductions, I learned that Mohan and Khushi had known each other for years, Amanda and Anne were mother and daughter, Christine and Deb were both public health professors, and Jamie and Mary had just completed their K-8 teaching certification. It seemed like everyone was paired up. Except for me. We gathered into several rickshaws and dissolved into the lemon, cobalt, ruby, and electric violet saris and fabrics flowing from the kiosks and store fronts along the streets. Steeped in the vibrant pulse of energy humming through the capitol city, we reunited at an open-air restaurant to experience our first meal of true Northern Indian cuisine.

Nine of us sat at a table for eight, and shared several tasty hot dishes like samosas, vegetable biryani, palak paneer (spinach and cheese curry), naan bread, and roti (a fried bread). I mostly listened, nervously waiting for opportunities to contribute to the conversation. Khushi insisted we try the lemon soda and she bought a round for the entire group. Soda in India is not your average Pepsi. She sang the praises of this drink as a health tonic for upset stomach or a digestive aid after a large meal. "It's made with fresh lemon, spices like turmeric and ginger, and black salt with sulfur. Oh! And they sprinkle silver flecks on top." She sold all of us on the drink. Until it arrived at our table.

The strong rotten egg stench of sulfur bubbled over the rims and to our noses like frothing volcanic fumaroles in front of us. We glanced at each other; no one wanted to take the first sip. Khushi lifted her cup. "Cheers! Welcome to India. You guys will love it."

"What are the metal flecks made of?" I asked.

Khushi shrugged. "I don't know. Silver?"

That's toxic, I thought. I watched the others sip the fizzy cup of rotten eggs with lemon. And then I lifted my cup, swept the metal flakes to the side with my finger, squinted, and took a sip.

"Wow. You can really taste the sulfur," Amanda said, eyes wide, setting down her cup.

"It's really *earthy,*" I added and chased the sip with a healthy swallow of bottled water.

"This doesn't taste right." Khushi winced and called over the waiter. She chatted with him quietly in Hindi and then turned to us and said, "Let's get some water and go shopping for saris."

Ah, the impermanence of India.

* * *

Early the next morning, we packed people and bags into a caravan of tuk-tuks and headed to the station to catch the train to Haridwar. All roads seemed to lead to the station, and they were all jammed with traffic. We muddled through checkpoints, with no time to run our bags through the x-ray. No problem. The coolies cruised right past security guards, hefting one bag on each shoulder—a few extra rupees greasing the gate.

The platform was congested with travelers and hawkers. Street vendors sold bananas, rice, and chicken from pushcarts. Suppliers ferried linens, fruit, and other wares between vendors in huge baskets or rectangular containers balanced on their heads. Men in western shirts and shorts, and women in sapphire and saffron saris and hijabs bought food and waited in clusters for the next train. The smell of charcoal chicken, roti, and curry hung in the air. There was shouting and selling and endless honking.

We nudged and squeezed our way through a dense blockade of wheeled bags and people and boarded the first-class train for the five-and-a-half-hour ride to Haridwar. Our group was clustered together, and Amanda sat in the seat next to me. At first, I was intimidated by her, as I was with the entire group of intelligent, confident, creative women. I wrestled with the discomfort and tried to rationalize it. I'm not an elementary teacher. I don't wear my vulnerability openly. I'm not like them.

Being outside of the circle was a familiar feeling of disconnection. A feeling that I had become acutely aware of during the 4th grade science fair in 1979. To participate in the fair, each student was tasked with crafting a presentation. Mine had included a life-size, paper-mâché model of the human body, highlighting the circulatory system—specifically, the heart.

I had molded the base out of scraps of chicken-wire and covered it with strips of old newspaper soaked in a flour and water paste. After it was dry, I painted blue veins, red arteries and a fist-sized heart.

Mom and Dad had raised a beef cow and had it slaughtered at the same time I was working on the project for school. Mom suggested I include the cow heart in my presentation. What a great idea. After all, it would allow people to get a close-up look at reality. We found a clear plastic cylinder with a lid, placed the heart inside, and transported it to school in Dad's lunch cooler. It smelled like a bloody steak.

I proudly placed the heart right next to my paper-mâché model at the science fair. The reactions were varied. The boys picked up the container and stared at it, the girls squealed and turned away, and the adults were oddly quiet.

After a while, the teacher suggested we store the heart in the cooler. It hadn't occurred to me or Mom that some folks may have been shocked or repulsed by the reality of slaughtering a cow. There was a good reason for *that* death, it was food. I didn't think it was scary. The cow's death was not an accident or a tragedy. This was normal—in my family. But it wasn't normal to everyone else.

The science fair didn't *cause* the disconnection, but it brought my feeling of being an outsider into sharp focus. As with the 4th grade science fair, meeting the group in the hotel lobby, and the previous night at dinner, again I felt like I was a poor fit, an oddball, lacking skills that came so naturally to others. Right there on the train to Haridwar was the first time I consciously recognized this gut reaction and paused. I was envious of the emotional freedom and organic sense of belonging that others enjoyed.

I glanced out the window of the train, the landscape of Uttarakhand flickering and passing by like the filmstrip of an old movie. I felt a growing distance from the confinements of the past, even if it was only temporary. I clipped my pen to a page in my journal and tucked it in my bag. I wrapped my arms around my shins, pulled my feet up onto the seat, and turned toward Amanda who sat to my right. "Where do you live?" I began.

She set down her book without hesitation. "I live in Guatemala."

We chatted like sisters who had not seen each other in years, sharing details and stories about our homes, our aspirations, and our travels. The city faded away into a series of endless fields of Amaranth and Millet and two-story cylindrical chimneys connected to crumbling brick kilns whose usefulness had passed.

At Haridwar station, the skies unleashed a drenching downpour. The last leg of the trip would be by vehicle. Coolies strapped our bags to the roofs of two four-wheel-drive jeeps and attempted to cover the bags with tarps. It was monsoon season—the season of swollen rivers, deluges, and landslides.

Our path into the mountains at times paralleled the river valley of the mighty Ganges. I thought of what Dharam, the taxi driver had said, and smiled at the thought of bathing to remove all stress. Swiftly moving water is considered sacred and purifying in Hindu culture. It is thought to both absorb impurities and take them away, starting a new. As Rumi has said, "…back to the root of the root of yourself…"

Twilight had ended and the downpour had diminished to a light rain when we finally reached the butter-yellow, two-story, cement-block building of the Ashram Paryavaran Vidyalaya (APV) in Tehri-Garhwal, Uttarakhand. Cooks prepared hot chai and a dinner of chapatti, lentils, green beans, potatoes, and sweet rice. After dinner, we checked into our sparse yet quaint rooms on the second floor. Each room had two beds, a night-table with a lamp, and a bathroom. The rooms each had a door that swung out to one common balcony running the length of the building.

I opened the windows to hear the many layers of sound drifting up to APV; dogs barked, monkeys howled, crickets sang, and I heard the distant sound of drumming, like a heartbeat beneath it all. I lay in bed and fell asleep to the twinkling lights of the villages in the valley below that sparkled like jewels set into the hillside.

The first morning at 5:30 am, the chai man arrived with a gentle knock and delivered a tin cup of hot tea to my door. The structure of our days on retreat was similar. Chai was followed by morning yoga, breakfast with the retreat group, and then off to climb the ten flights of stone steps up the nearly vertical hillside to the school building. The first few days, everything was exotic and wonderful. The power outages and lack of Wi-Fi gave me a chance to read. The water dripping from the ceiling onto the bed was no big deal; I had another bed I could sleep on. The chai delivery was a dreamy way to start each morning, and the hike to the school was great exercise.

By the fifth day, my rose-colored view of APV was more grounded. The smoke from daily trash burning drifted into my room through the balcony door, left open to air out the mold from the leaky roof, which now dripped on both beds. Not a morning person by any stretch, I came to dread the 5:30 am knock from the chai man, and the chai itself. The thick buffalo milk, overabundance of sugar, and scalding hot temperature of the tea—served in a lip-searing metal cup.

"No, thank you," I said, pillow over my head, curled up in the blankets on the dry part of the bed away from the leaky roof. But the offer was non-negotiable. He just responded, "Chai." *Knock-knock-knock.* "Chai." *Knock-knock-knock.* Until I opened the door.

The ten flights of stone stairs would have been a great workout, if I wasn't struggling to breathe at nearly 6,000 feet elevation, and I wasn't suffering from a lung infection, and if it wasn't monsoon season and I didn't get soaked to the bone most mornings on the way to the school.

Once at the school however, the difficulties and annoyances were easily forgotten. I followed the children's lead and remembered what was important. It's not about mold, or bronchitis, or burned, peeling lips. It's about recognizing the impermanence of both pleasant and unpleasant experiences, learning from each other, and enjoying connection.

Everyone left their shoes outside the door, filed into the assembly room, and sat around the perimeter, cross-legged, on wool blankets that covered the floor. The guru, Anand, lead the children through meditation, and then it was time for assembly. A few students passed out drums while one of the teachers placed the harmonium in front of Anand. One student chose the song, Anand began on the harmonium, and the rest of the students started playing the drums, swaying back and forth, and singing.

That day, the musical selection was one that had been written at APV. The combination of the words, the message in the song, the way they belted out the tune, eyes shut tight, chin up, chest out, sitting around the room so that their voices mingled somewhere in the center, just made me cry. They sang so passionately about an ocean they had never been to, connecting to the ocean of salt water that bathes all our cells, grounding our happiness firmly in the earth. The words to the song are:

> *"Somewhere, deep inside, an ocean is singing by....*
> *There are a trillion shining suns; all you need is to look*
> *in the sky*
> *When you are on a lonely desert*
> *When the river of life runs dry*
> *Look deep deep inside*
> *An ocean is singing by...*
> *There are a trillion shining suns; all you need is to look*
> *in the sky*
> *When in darkness the path is lost*
> *And you have no friends, nor a guide*
> *Remember you have a trillion suns*
> *All you need is to look in the sky*
> *Somewhere, deep inside, an ocean is singing by....*

After assembly, the students split up by grade and went to the various classrooms. I spent the first day observing, but each subsequent day I taught these children, who live among the tallest mountains on earth, about geology.

By the end of the week I had given a two-hour lesson on the rock cycle. The students collected samples of each type, drew a poster-sized diagram, and prepared a short skit. I was an expert on separation, classification, and discerning differences. They were experts at connection and wholeness. We had plenty to teach each other.

The children referred to the teachers as Ma'am. At the beginning of each school day, they would enthusiastically crowd around me, sometimes holding pebbles in their outstretched hands. "Ma'am, this is igneous?"

Since igneous rocks seemed to capture their imagination, I also taught a lesson on volcanoes, where the students learned about the formation of volcanic chains such as the Andes of South America. We sat on the classroom floor together, and I used my 4th grade paper-mâché expertise to help the students build models of explosive stratovolcanoes. I had gathered the necessary supplies the previous day by finding useless garbage and turning it into a science lesson. One-foot squares of old cardboard boxes served as the base, plastic bottles became the volcanic reservoir and pipe for lava. The children tore two-inch strips of newspaper, soaked them in paste made of flour and water, and layered them from the top of the bottles to the cardboard base. After they built the volcano models, the glue needed to dry. We planned an eruption for Friday, the last day of class.

Each day after that, as I visited the school and worked with different grades, students ran up to me, tugged at my shirt or grabbed my hand in excitement. "Ma'am! Ma'am! We *blahst* the volcano today?" Or, "Ma'am! You come to my home? Please! You must come to my home! Please!"

It was such a lesson to experience their innocence and openness. Because of the language barrier, we relied more on expressions and other more intuitive cues. The children helped me recall what it was like to be, for a brief time, completely free and vulnerable, before the family contract was written.

* * *

Each day after our work at the school, the retreat group took different cultural excursions or treks, followed by the evening yoga session, and a late dinner. Finally it was time for rest, which was never long enough and always interrupted by early morning chai, which seemed earlier, sweeter, hotter, and buffalo-milkier every day. About mid-way through the retreat, between the mold from the leaky roof and the trash burning outside my window, I developed bronchitis. Climbing the ten flights of stairs to go to the school each day, I wasn't sure I had the breath in my lungs to see this through.

I wanted to call home. I was sick and wanted to hear the familiar voices of my family and husband. But Verizon had no cell service at APV, and between power outages and spotty Wi-Fi, I couldn't even send regular emails.

For the next couple of days, I slept in, skipped yoga and the coughing school kids, and took some antibiotics wrapped in a paper napkin that Mohan had delivered to my room. I regained some energy and felt good enough to join the drive and a trek to the Chandrabadni temple in Jhanau.

In Hinduism, temples are believed to be the seat of a deity, where people can leave offerings and be with the gods. It is a special place in which our inner and outer worlds commune. Akin to the notion that if we want to examine the workings of a cell, we go to a lab and use a microscope; to examine the human relationship with God, we go to a temple. That site was one of the designated places to honor Shakti, the inherently female universal energy of creation—the energy at the root of the mother-daughter-sister bond.

Traveling along switchbacks, higher and higher, we surveyed the terraced, emerald green landscape in all its fertile, monsoon glory. A few of us rode on the roof of the jeep, clinging to the luggage rails. Up, up along the winding mountain pass, the sun warmed our cheeks and wind whipped through our hair.

At the end of the road we parked the jeep and walked further up a winding gravel and cement path with several flights of stone steps to the temple entrance. We took off our shoes, rang a brass bell overhead, walked through a grand archway, and climbed up another tremendous flight of red sandstone stairs where there was another brass bell over the entrance to the heart of the temple. The inner sanctum was the realm of a Hindu pujari (priest). He sat in a dim alcove, surrounded by statues with offerings of flowers left at their feet. Strings of gently swaying brass bells chimed from above and the scent of burning incense filled the air. We knelt in front of the pujari who blessed each one of us in turn by tying a red string around our left wrist. As he tied the string he chanted in Hindi and smudged saffron powder on our foreheads. Khushi said the blessing was good for one year. Over time, temple ceremonies are believed to change the patterns of karma dating back many past lives, removing seeds that weigh heavy on the soul.

It may have been something burning along with the incense, but I did feel lighter after the blessing. A 360-degree view edged by strings of oscillating bells and flags flapping in the breeze. From the breathtaking perch we surveyed rugged, Himalayan peaks topped with pristine white glaciers to the north and the deep gash of a river valley with its broad floodplain splayed in sage, olive, and deep avocado-green across the landscape to the south. Several Hindu men sat on crates and palmed drums as our group explored and photographed and celebrated the female energy of Shakti as it resonated through a vibrant, fresh-peeled citrus sunset.

The trek scraped away the film that had obscured the bold colors of life. I was in the tallest mountains on earth, within the cradle of spirituality, closer to God than I've ever been in any church, with truth unfolding all around me. The concepts of Life, Earth, and spirituality appeared boundless, and inseparable.

From that perspective, I found it difficult to imagine a higher power was anything but love. Yet there was no denying what my family had been put through. Like the mighty Himalayas themselves, my mistrust in God seemed insurmountable, with deep roots and a convoluted history.

* * *

The final day of school was the last day the students ran up to me, tugging and hopping, "Ma'am! Ma'am! Volcano blaahst?" The last day of assembly, each class took turns showing the rest what they learned. The Indian teachers sang Garhwali songs to us, passed down by family members, celebrating their rich traditions.

It brought forth a tender time, frozen in place where many of my family traditions stopped. Baking Christmas cookies, making pine-cone wreaths, teaching someone to field grounders at short-stop, and reading *The Shy Little Kitten*. But did they really *end*? I *had* tried to continue some of these things, passed them down to the new family or my nieces and nephews, but something was missing. The shadow of loss diluted all traditions by unfairly comparing them to what was or what might have been. Perhaps they could be revived. Maybe I could begin by expanding my narrow definition of family.

When it was the fourth grade's turn, we knelt in a semi-circle in front of our audience, filled the "volcanic pipes" with baking soda and dish soap, and then all together added the vinegar and *whoosh*! The models erupted in streams of frothy lava. The students turned to each other, hopping, squealing and giggling with delight. This was a tradition that I wanted to continue. Using skills I learned from Mary to take discarded materials and give them new life, eliciting connection and happiness out of thin air.

*** * ***

For our final yoga practice, Khushi led us through a sequence which focused on opening the heart through the back of the body. The hall was dark and damp, the smell of mold and white sage hung heavy in the air. Strings of smoke from the incense rose slowly and bent into deformed spirals as they expanded to fill the empty spaces within the room. Hindu chants from distant loudspeakers rose in a ghostly echo from the valley below.

Khushi spoke softly. "Sit with your shins crossed in front of you, breathe in, reach the hands overhead, and lengthen the spine. On the exhale, fold forward, reaching the arms long on the mat in front of you. Open the back body, to soften and shine the heart."

She moved around the room, only a cool breeze and the swish of her sari announced her presence. She paused by my side, leaned over, and gently placed her palm on my back. I felt the warmth of connection.

"Breathe into the places you have closed off. Let the light in."

At that moment, Khushi's soft voice and gentle touch seemed to draw truth to the surface. Tears appeared without warning, made paths down my cheekbones, and fell onto my yoga mat. I was confused. I thought I knew the contents of my heart—yet here was this pocket of strong emotion. A last holdout tucked away within a shell of old Bardy stoicism, the "stuckness" that Deborah referred to in the tea leaf reading. It was like the right key had just turned an ancient lock and an enormous heavy door cracked open. At that place in my heart was the trauma of Louise's death.

I tried to organize my thoughts. Louise had a headstone, a burial, and I had visited her grave many times. Yet the stream of tears told me it was more complicated than that. After all my digging, I had finally reached the *foundation* of the contract.

Feeling like a rag doll gripped and shaken hard by the jaws of truth, my arms and legs trembled. An old pathway had been cleared. One that had been blocked even before Mary's death. Khushi had reintroduced me to a forgotten part of my 4-year-old self. How could she reach in and pull it to the surface when I had not been willing to acknowledge it? Perhaps she had some help from the pujari at the temple.

Some events in life resonate so strongly it's as if they have seeped into the marrow of your bones or have woven their way into the thick fibers of your heart muscle. They may forge connections so powerful that even when you have been apart for decades, the scent of lemongrass, the song of a mourning dove, or perhaps the gentle warmth of a friend's palm resting between your shoulder blades can engulf your mind in a torrent of jumbled emotions and sharp splinters of truth.

Learning and knowledge are powerful agents that operate within the matrix I had built, able to dissolve our fears and float them downstream on the Ganges, to join the ocean that sings by in celebration of our unfolding. But first, those fears had to be broken free and cast into the river to tumble and smooth their sharp edges.

* * *

Our scheduled departure the next morning was delayed by a teeming rain that pounded against the stone stairs and walkways. We all milled about in the dining area after breakfast. We chatted and waited through several more delays. We prepared lunch. We ate. Silent with worry about the solid mountain breaking apart and burying us. When we could wait no longer, we hurried through the wind and deluge, splattered with mud as we loaded the land cruisers with bags and people. Big steel drops of rain hammered the roof as we clutched the seats, the dashboard, leaned away from the doors, and crept our way down the hairpin switchbacks of the mountain road.

Banks of dense fog rolled in and shrouded the peaks behind us. Knife edges of rock disappeared and reemerged, ominous and heavy over our heads. Mohan and Khushi sat in the front, leaned toward the driver, and whispered to each other in Hindi. Windshield wipers pulsed at full speed in vain, hearts raced, eyes scoured the hill slopes for danger—for things that were moving but shouldn't be. Hypervigilant.

Twice we had rounded corners to find the road ahead was gone. It had slid down the mountain. Emergency crews with backhoes and bulldozers shaped the void back into a road. *But how stable was it? How many people had been swept away?*

The third slide we approached had happened just moments before—a thick, muddy stew of boulders and whole trees were still tumbling down the slopes below. It would be a while before crews could reach us. We sat on that narrow mountain pass, with the road just a huge raw gash in front of us. Tenuous, the group got out and stood near the vehicle. I walked to where the road fell away and stood there, humbled by the power of nature to be so unpredictable and cruel. If we had arrived moments earlier, we would have been thrown thousands of feet downslope by the force of the debris and buried. Mohan called to me. "Julie, we should stay in the car. To be safe."

We were the lucky ones. The following day, the front page of the paper was covered with news of the cloudburst, stories of villages buried by tens of feet of mud and giant rock slabs, and cars shoved off the side of the mountain by the force of debris flows. Friends, daughters, sisters—gone in an instant.

Why were we traveling down a mountain during monsoon? Why didn't I think more carefully about the timing, the conditions? Senseless risks. A lifetime of burden for the survivors. You go to sleep with a big sister and wake up alone.

Why did Louise put herself in danger? How careless. Why didn't her friends try to stop her? Why would the APV choose this time and potentially put us all in harm's way? Why would anyone hurt my family? Why would someone take Louise from us?

A pressure-cooker of emotions boiled and frothed and obscured my previous sense of clarity. In a complex heap of emotions at odds with each other, at odds with my own peace. A tangled, dark, seething, hateful, beat-you-into-the-ground-if-I-had-the-chance anger that Khushi's practice had wrenched from its hiding place in the back of my heart.

I had given myself to India, and perhaps that's what India had to teach me in return. That this journey wasn't over yet. The raw nature of the bandaged place had just been exposed.

PART FOUR

Charybdis

"He who fights with monsters might take care lest he thereby become a monster. And if you gaze for long into an abyss, the abyss gazes also into you."

—Friedrich Nietzsche.

Chapter 23:

August, 2016

Tucked in bed with a blanket of textbooks and sticky notes, I was engrossed in the science of tsunami. The cell phone rang and startled me. It was only 10pm, but Robyn *never* called that late, and her tone was never serious. My mind raced through the death gamut.

"Hey--did you hear about Greg?"

"No. Why? What's up?"

"He's in UMASS on life support. Gunshot to the head." Robyn has Dad's lack of subtlety.

I shifted and sat up straighter as—*thump, plunk*—a textbook hit the floor. "Greg Renshaw? You sure? Who told you?"

"WINY radio announced it."

I skipped right over the grave implications of the term *life support*. "Is he going to be okay? What happened?"

"Not sure. Doesn't sound good. He was found at the Fall's Mill—the one he's converting to condos? They were talking possible suicide attempt."

"Who's *they*?"

"I don't know. The police? People on the radio?"

"Suicide? No way. That's bullshit." I first met Greg two decades ago at a costume party. He was dressed as George Washington, complete with the powdered wig, velvet knickers, and nylon stockings. He had spent the entire night gyrating his hips, biting his bottom lip, making eyes at and purposely bumping into every woman on the dance floor. His ego and reputation arrived at the party with him, neither of them favorable. Despite the awful first impression, we quickly became good friends when he briefly dated Robyn a few years later.

Before Greg was married, his love life was a continuous session of speed dating. In a similar fashion, he dealt in European antiques and bought and sold real estate like most people buy shoes. Greg invited Eric and me over to his storage warehouse one evening for a drink. We walked in to find he had cleared out half of the first-floor and set up a sprawling antique mahogany bar from Ireland smack in the center of the room. After an evening of cocktails and colorful conversation, we dressed in suits of armor, piled into a panel van, and had one of his workers drive us to Dunkin' Donuts at 1am.

His undiluted penchant for the outrageous continued, but his love-life settled down. He married, had three beautiful boys, and adored his wife Leanne. I knew Greg. He took incredible risks with money. But not with his life. It could not be suicide.

I called Eric after I hung up with Robyn. He was at the Cape on business but had already heard about Greg.

"I want to go visit him. Make him laugh," I said, filled with the ignorant hope that humor would be a cure all.

"Julie, it's not like that." Silence while I waited for him to continue. "He's on life support. He was shot in the head." Eric didn't intend to be blunt, but he had spoken with the local police. He knew Greg was never going to laugh again.

After a week in the hospital, Greg's organs were donated, and his life was unplugged.

* * *

One of the cruelest parts of life I've had to endure is that it doesn't slow down for death. Two days after Greg was shot, while my emotions were in a tailspin, my youngest sister Nicole had her fourth child, Ava. The family buzzed with excitement.

During Ava's fifth day on earth, Greg took his last breath on the ventilator. Life and death side by side, impossible for me to reconcile. Nicole called to ask when I was coming to see Ava. She sounded so happy. I smiled as I listened to the message. And then my mind flipped back to Greg. Anger and guilt crept in. What right did I have to be happy at a time like this? I sunk into the past, looking back, trying to make sense of his death, mind stuck trying to bend, to yield, to peer around one of the most incomprehensible ways to die—murder.

I railed at the senselessness and the injustice. I knew it wasn't suicide, and Eric confirmed that. The main suspect was the last person to see Greg alive, the one who called 911, the sole witness, the likely perpetrator. Yet Greg's murderer would likely never be held accountable for his actions.

There was no case against that man. When they had arrived, EMTs and paramedics unwittingly trampled on the crime scene trying to save Greg. Local police officers were confused by the initial call of suicide and failed to collect and preserve key evidence. And, even if they had made a case, justice is rarely served.

I thought about Louise, how her murderer took a plea bargain and served less than twelve years in jail. Then he moved to Florida to sell drugs and guns. That was the justice my family got.

Greg's business tactics and childhood trauma seemed magnets that drew him toward difficulty and, eventually, his death. But Louise was only 16, a teenager, a child. What could have possibly drawn her to her killer? A 26-year-old Vietnam vet, who was hanging around with high school kids.

A vulnerability that had been brought to light in India was now fully exposed and sore to the touch. I wanted to crawl inside the deepest hole I could manage to dig and hibernate. I couldn't convince myself to go to the hospital to see Ava. It wasn't a time to be happy. Happiness makes people angry. Be quiet. Behave.

I needed to craft syllabi, organize my office, and prepare for my classes that were starting at the beginning of the next week. But then again, maybe I just needed to be pissed off about Greg's death. I wanted to show Nicole that I was happy for her, but I couldn't figure out how to do both. I was breaking to pieces inside. Rubble weakly cemented by single-pointed distraction. I had work to do.

The semester began in its usual frenzied manner, with anxious students, long office hours, endless emails, and constant interruptions. The distraction and distance were soothing, but Greg's services were the following weekend, so I had to go to the lake. The weather was as perfect as late summer gets, and Eric invited Mom and Dad over for a boat cruise.

As I untied the dock lines, Mom asked if I'd gone to see Ava yet.

I coiled the slack rope and flung it near the silver metal cleat. "No. I haven't had time," I said as I stepped onto the boat, pushing us away from shore. "School started this week. Fall is really busy." All of that was true, but I left out the snarled mess of feelings surrounding Greg's death that I'd been struggling with. It was no one else's business. I sat back in my seat and searched the shoreline. "Do you guys see the resident heron anywhere?"

Eric motored slowly around the lake. "It's a pterodactyl," he stated, searching for a ball game on the radio. Mom and Dad chuckled. I raised an eyebrow at the intentional way he butchered proper terminology.

We cruised along past the Old Quaddick Cemetery and came to the spot where the towers used to be. Mom pointed and turned to me. "Louise and Tammy and their friends used to swim there. They took you along too."

"I remember the towers. But there was only one building. Why was it called the towers?"

"That's just what they called it," Mom said.

"Were there *ever* two buildings?"

"I don't know. I don't think so."

I shrugged and peered at the line of shrubs and the vacant space behind them on the shore where the grey, concrete, one-story building shaped like a saltine box used to sit. I remember what the trip had been like to get there.

At 4-years-old, I would stand up on the front seat of Louise's Nash Rambler as it kicked up dust, bumping down the narrow gravel access road. The real purpose of the 'towers' had been to house the gears and pumps for the dam that controlled the water level in the lake. For *our* purpose, it had been an Olympic diving platform. A ladder made of rebar allowed access to the top for jumpers. The audience, including me, sat on the gravel near the water's edge or floated in the deeper water with Louise or Tammy or one of their friends. After the competition, they spread out towels on the small patch of tall grass and we basked in the sun like seals.

"I used to love watching them jump and splash into the water," I said.

Mom's voice was low and serious. "Arthur Taylor went swimming with you too."

The name sucked all the heat from the warm summer breeze. I felt the cold breath of evil with the mention of his name. I never used it. To me, he wasn't a person. He was a manifestation of stinking, rotting evil. *I swam with the filth who murdered my sister? Did his hands ever touch mine? I shuddered at the thought. How could no one see what a monster he was? How could Louise have trusted him?*

Mom's voice broke the incessant mental barrage. "You know, there was a reel to reel recording with Louise's voice on it."

The thought of being able to hear Louise's actual voice brightened my mood. I leaned in, waiting for Mom to continue.

"But it wore out."

Hope extinguished. Did she or Tammy play it over and over? Trying to pull Louise close? Trying to cuddle up next to a time that made more sense, was less frightening? Did Mom throw it away in a fit of anger? When she heard it, was it a reminder of what was no longer here? Of the cruelty and injustice?

Eric's question pulled me from the quicksand. "Jules, did you remember to take the hamburger out of the freezer?"

Dad instantly chimed in with a snicker. "Yeah, I sure could go for a nice burger."

* * *

At Greg's wake, people gathered in small groups within sheltered alcoves of the funeral home and spoke quietly to one another. A large room with Victorian wallpaper and wood paneled wainscoting housed Greg's casket. The sheen of the satin lining caught my eye. I slowed my pace. Open casket? Head wound from a gunshot. Putty. Makeup. I forced air into my lungs. Bracing myself for the visual reality of *gone*, I adjusted the sweater draped over my arm. One hand gripped the strap of my purse, the other fidgeted with my scarf. My breath became shallow and fast. I worked to slow it down.

I passed a group of people as I drew closer to the casket. From a distance, it didn't look like him. He looked much older than the last time I had seen him, carefree and bouncing his new son on his knee, sipping iced tea on my porch. As I got closer, I thought for a moment, maybe there was some mistake. I had never seen Greg without a smile. Ever.

I knelt by the casket. I felt socially obligated to pray, but my mind was blank, numb. I paused and thought. His children. Of course. Pray for Greg to watch over his children. Under my breath, I asked him what happened, why he left so soon, and told him that I would always remember the good times, the laughs, his outrageous sense of humor.

I grasped the carved shellacked mahogany railing with both hands, stood up, and turned toward the receiving line. There were five people in it: Greg's wife, Leanne; his mother-in-law; and his three sons, between the ages of 5 and 10. The sight of those children, wide-eyed, scared, confused, trying to stand with their emotions buttoned-up and lint-brushed, in their navy-blue, three-piece suits, like little soldiers against loss—it was too much. I felt my heart break open. I hugged Leanne and knelt near each of the children. I thought about what to say besides how sorry I was, but what thrashed around loudest inside my head was how their lives would never be what their mom wanted, what Greg wanted, what they wanted. How they would have to try to be so tough, so strong. How they would desperately try to control the sadness around them. How they would try to fill the silence, the empty space. How they would try to be good, be quiet, behave. How they had already started constructing the saddest wall that can be built; the wall to protect them from feeling this type of hurt again.

A dam broke in my mind. Memories flooded in and I imagined what it was like to be a child near the casket of someone who meant the world to you, your protector, your teacher, your best hugger. A person you could always snuggle up with after a bad dream—dead, cold, waxy—lying about ten feet from you. And what you want to do more than anything is take them out of this place. Take them home and tuck them into a warm bed and cuddle up next to them and feel their back expand with breath and feel their arms around you and know this was just a horrible dream. But here you are, and there's the casket. And they are gone.

I tried my best to compartmentalize the emotion but it was too strong. My mind toggled unpredictably between past and present. Greg was gone. Gone like Louise, in an instant. Her absence left us with an empty seat at the table, a gaping, bottomless sinkhole in our routines, and an unshakeable fear that no one was safe. Routines provide a frame. Like Greg's routine of pre-warming his mug with hot water when he stopped by for coffee. It reminded me of the routine Mom and I had where we scrubbed and pre-warmed Dad's lunch thermos. The tall one that held coffee with evaporated milk and sugar, and the short one that held Beefaroni or Ravioli or homemade American Chop Suey—one of his favorites. We packed a couple of sandwiches and an apple or other fruit so he could slice it with his paring knife he held in a leathery palm, calloused by honest, hard work. Construction hands that could build the steel frame of a skyscraper, or take apart the tiny gears in the motor of Drowsy's voice box. Dad could fix anything. Well, nearly anything.

Dad only missed three days of work. That was when he was out looking for Louise.

The injustice of another person being ripped from the arms of their family made me anxious for Greg's killer to be caught—to pay. It blew the cover off the teeth-gnashing, wall-punching rage over Louise's murder. The blame just wouldn't land. Blaming evil was easy, but what was God's role in this? Wasn't he supposed to deliver us from evil? Bullshit. There was no scapegoat mountain top vista here. My mind was a stinging swarm of questions about the circumstances and culpability surrounding murder. Greg's murder. Louise's murder. I lived in a state of angry distraction, lost in resentment.

* * *

A week later, as I made our morning coffee, Eric mentioned an event in town.

"I went to Fort Hill Farm last week. The owner, I forget her name, the blonde lady…"

I rummaged in the fridge for the creamer. "Kristin?"

"Yeah. She said to tell you about The Day of Peace. And that you should go."

"Oh, yeah. I saw a sign on the common. It's today." I paused, hoping he would offer to join me, but his attention was fixed on his laptop. I asked anyway. "Wanna go?"

"I have a presentation to work on. But you should take a ride over."

Fort Hill is less than two miles from the lake, but I had yet to visit. It's owned by a friend of Tammy and Louise and frequented by Eric, who will never forget the taste of their homemade blueberry ice cream but apparently could not remember Kristin's name.

When I arrived at the farm, I drove through the gate and parked with about 30 other cars in one of the pastures. As I walked along a gravel path to the ice cream shack, people milled about and the scent of fresh cut hay and the sound of folk music filled the air. I heard someone call out to me.

"Julie?! I'm so glad you finally made it!" Kristin jogged over, arms outstretched, and wrapped me in a big, tight, lingering hug. A familiar, genuine free-love hug, straight from an era that belonged to Louise and Tammy. After a minute of rocking back and forth and laughing with joy, she leaned back, holding on to my shoulders. "I see Eric all the time. He loves the blueberry ice cream. He told me you went to India! I want to hear *all* about it. I'm so glad you're here!" She led me by the arm. "Come on, I'll give you a tour of the farm and we can talk."

She asked a million questions about India, especially my excursion to the Chandrabadni Temple to honor Shakti, the energy at the root of the mother-daughter-sister bond. I asked her about the farming business and her family. We walked around the grounds, to the ice cream and gift shop, and talked about her lavender fields. "I sell my lavender to France! It's *that* good. The labyrinth has these amazing rocks I found in the cornfield. And the tower on the hill, do you know what that's used for?"

I didn't.

"It's a radar beacon for aircraft. Cool, huh?"

I nodded. "Absolutely."

She vibrated with boundless energy. And then that energy opened an interesting door.

"Hey." She patted my back. "How's your sister Tammy? I've wondered how she's doing. Do you see her very often?"

"She's great. Still in Vermont. Has some beautiful land."

Kristin nodded, listening intently.

"You went to school with her and Louise, right?" I asked.

Kristin slouched a bit and gave me a sympathetic look. "Yes. My sister Cathy and I were friendly with them. It's a small town, you know. They were close in age like me and Cathy. So close."

I smiled and nodded. She knew who I'd lost. She knew Louise and Tammy.

Kristin continued. "Where ever you saw Louise, you saw Tammy. Not one without the other." She lowered her voice. "Well, until Louise died. That was so sad. Then Tammy was different. Quiet." She leaned in close as if to tell me a secret. "It was like she dissolved."

Tammy never talked much about Louise's death, and I didn't want to push her. She and Louise were only one year apart. Their relationship had to have been like Mary and me—even more so. Missing a huge part of her matrix, she dissolved. It made sense. Her fearless Bardy nature, her birth right, was compromised.

I wanted to find the truth, to be able to put both my sisters in a permanent, confident space in my memory. That was the window and I took it. "Did you know Taylor?" The sound of his name made my stomach turn. "I mean, why did they hang around with him? Trust him?" Every molecule of my being was still, anticipating her response.

"Cathy and I went to Marianapolis Prep. We didn't hang around with the same group of people." Kristin looked down for the first time in the conversation. My defensive brain instantly interpreted the meaning as: *'I'm embarrassed and trying to hide the fact that I'm judging your family right now.'*

I was hoping to get some insight on the piece of garbage. Something that would make sense. But nothing about Louise's death made sense to me. And it was about to get worse.

"It was Wendall who found her. On Taylor Road." She shook her head. "He was getting stones for the wall."

What? That wasn't right. It was Wakefield Pond, not Taylor Road. I knew that. Dad took me there. So was it really Wendall? Her brother? That didn't make sense. What else did I not know? The way she mentioned Louise's body being found struck a deep chord with me. She seemed to be talking about it like I didn't live through it. Like I was too young to remember any of it. Too young to grieve the loss of my sister, the loss of my family as I knew it.

Perhaps she sensed my mood. Her bubbly enthusiastic tone returned in a jolt. "Does Tammy come to visit Connecticut? Please tell her she has to stop in. I would love to see her!"

"I'm sure she'd like that. I'll tell her." I hadn't seen much of The Day of Peace, spare some drumming in the background, but it seemed like a good time to leave before I got more confused. "And thanks for the tour. I'll be back for ice cream sometime."

"Oh! Take some home!" She clapped her hands together. "Yes! Come with me. You have to try the new *Haymaker Hash*!"

* * *

The conversation with Kristin prompted me to take stock of what I knew and what I didn't know. It made me think more deeply about the subjective nature of truth—how it changes with independent recollection, filters, and re-telling. I needed a guilt-free, credible, firsthand source of information.

It was late afternoon when I returned to the lake and joined Eric out on the deck.

"How was The Day of Peace? Did you see Kristin?" His back was to me as he scrubbed the grate on the gas grill.

"Yeah. It was good." I pulled two chairs out at the table, sat in one and put my feet up on the other. "Has there been any progress on Greg's case?"

"Well, I know they're working on it."

"Yep. How hard?"

He stopped scrubbing and faced me. "As hard as they can." He turned back to the grill. "There's not a lot of evidence. They have to document everything. Build a case. It takes time. Do you want chicken or steak?"

I folded my arms. "I'm not hungry." I stared down at a small clump of feathers near the stone wall on the lawn. "The hawk killed another songbird. I feed them and just set them up to be prey."

Eric glanced at the feeder. "That's nature."

"I don't understand why it's moving so slow. Articles in the news every day say the same thing. Why do they keep printing the same shit? Just like when Louise died. Making the family read it again and again."

"Cops don't control the news." He lit the grill and closed the cover. "They only get one chance. If they don't make the case, the charges get dismissed."

I pulled my feet up onto the chair, knees against my chest. "How can I get a copy of the police report for Louise? I asked you a while ago."

"I had Mike check. It's not at headquarters." His answer trailed off as he walked inside to the kitchen. "It's probably in storage somewhere. I'll try to find out."

* * *

214

Moving into October, the days continued to shorten, life events weighed heavy and I sunk deeper into a shadow space. I read several grief books with first-hand accounts from mothers, fathers, and siblings of all age ranges. I recognized behaviors in my parents, my sibs and myself. The knowledge was affirming but heartbreaking.

A visit with my nieces Lauren and Sophia could always lighten my mood with their high-octane silliness. I loved them as if they were my own children, but I hadn't seen them in months, and it felt like a cruel punishment. My sister Nicole had not responded to any of my messages since August—probably mad that I didn't go visit her in the hospital for the birth of my youngest niece Ava. It seemed as though she just wrote me off. It felt the familiar heartbreak of people I loved being taken away.

I reached for my phone and called Eric. Lately he had been away more than home, giving leadership presentations for law enforcement agencies around the country. His simple presence was a comfort I had taken for granted. The phone went straight to voicemail. He was at a workshop in Indiana but called me back after he finished lunch. "You seemed upset earlier in your message. I'm getting a vibe."

"Yeah, well, it's not you. I've been doing a lot of introspective stuff. Reading some heavy books, meditating, mindfulness, and starting yoga tonight—"

"Oh, okay. I feel better. It has nothing to do with me."

Hmm. I ignored the dismissive tone. "I'm almost finished with the book on sibling loss and—"

"Hey, can I call you later? I'm going through evaluations. I just want to get them done."

"Sure. Okay."

From the second-floor perch of my writing desk at The Ocean House, I looked down Fairview Avenue toward the waves crashing on West Haven Beach. At times I felt the doom of complete detachment. I knew much of that was my own doing. The titanium shell that holds the pain in, also keeps others out.

Chapter 24:

Sisters of Wisdom

That same October, I had begun yoga teacher training at the studio in New Haven and the demanding schedule was a welcomed distraction. The class met as a group two weekends a month, but we also had to attend at least three yoga sessions a week, keep up with a heavy reading load, maintain a journal, schedule and attend study sessions, and meet with mentors. It helped to lift my spirits, giving me a whole new group of connections.

The New Haven writing group had also been meeting regularly, either at the Wilson Library or at the Lawn Club in New Haven. We planned a social gathering, dubbed a 'Kibbutz,' where we could talk about our lives beyond our writing projects. Manju volunteered to hostess and everyone brought a dish to share. We had Indian samosas, garden salad, potato salad, ginger scones, apple pie, and vanilla ice cream. I still felt the burden of social anxiety, but it quickly lightened in the company of strong, successful, supportive, and compassionate women. They were like the older sisters I didn't have.

As we sipped wine and milled about, talking about travel, work, goals, and family, one of our members, Debbie, placed a stack of brochures on the coffee table. "These list upcoming programs at the Wisdom House," she said.

"Oh, I've gone there." Diane grabbed a flyer and started browsing. "It's really great. Haven't been in a while though."

Two of my writing sisters had now endorsed it. I tucked a brochure into my purse and continued a conversation with Manju about the India retreat.

Later, at The Ocean House, I sunk into the loveseat with a cup of tea and read through the Wisdom House offerings. An inset box announcing a full-day program on grief grabbed my attention. The title was "Healing the Heart after Loss," and it would be led by a woman with a private practice in Litchfield specializing in bereavement and loss. I was deeply curious to learn how other people dealt with grief. Did it unravel their families and make them feel like outsiders also? I reached for my laptop, navigated to the Wisdom House website, and before I could change my mind, registered for the program.

* * *

It was a raw, drizzly fall morning as I drove north and west, across a 450 million-year-old, geologic collision zone called *Cameron's Line,* and into the marble belt of Connecticut. The fault marked an ancient coastline that once supported extensive coral reefs. But the pressure and heat of plate convergence transformed the coral into marble, crumpling it, burying it, and leaving it far from the comfort and conditions it enjoyed during its early existence.

The road kept company with dense forest on both sides, aflame with leaves of gold, rust, and tangerine, whose colors became more intense with increasing elevation. Deep into the Litchfield woods along Clark Road, I reached the Wisdom House, an interfaith retreat center sponsored by the Daughters of Wisdom, a community of Catholic sisters. It is a place of contemplation and self-exploration. With some trepidation, I planned to do both.

I arrived at 8:45 am and pulled into a parking space in a large gravel lot. Several buildings, including a two-story red barn, a colonial-era farmhouse, and a three-story retreat building, sat around the periphery of the parking area. As if a million pipes had burst at once, the sky unleashed buckets of rain. I sat in the driver's seat, engine still running, gripping the steering wheel, second-guessing my decision, and waiting for the rain to slow. I rummaged through my bag to make sure I had tissues and checked my cell phone. I scanned my email, answered a few, and scrolled through Facebook.

Two more cars arrived: two women in one, and a man and woman in the other. I wondered if they were attending the grief program. Would I be the only one arriving alone? I considered the possibility of sneaking out at the lunch break. After organizing the console and glove compartment, I grabbed my umbrella and purse, hurried across the puddled gravel, and stepped inside through the basement-level entrance.

A small, unmanned desk stood like a guardian, half blocking a hallway that stretched the length of the building, with several doors on each side. A 50-something woman with brassy, cropped hair and an inch of exposed grey roots paced nearby. She had a wet jacket partially stuffed under her left arm and clutched an unsteady armful of phone, keys, notebook, several pens, a purse, and a travel mug.

She dropped several things onto the desk and swept a damp shock of hair from her eyes. "I haven't seen anyone to check in with." She waved a hand through the air. "Pffft."

Just then a pleasantly round woman emerged from a doorway near the other end of the hall and shuffled toward us, her wet shoes squeaking across the slick tile floor. "Are you here for a program?" She smiled warmly and her eyes took the shape of little crescents.

The disheveled woman sheepishly avoided eye contact.

I hesitated. I couldn't remember the title. "Um. Yes. The grief program?"

"Oh, yes. What is your name, dear?"

She crossed my name off her list and handed me a marker. "Please make yourself a name tag." The disheveled woman was signing in for the same program; her name was Mary. She looked to be between five and ten years older than me, but it was hard to tell. Loss can age you, but some people, like my family, seem to wear it more on the inside.

It was early, so I went up to the second floor and browsed around the Marie Louise Trichet Gallery. The current exhibit was a collection by artist Elisabeth Moss, titled, "Inviting the Great Dance: Paintings on the Path to Letting Go." A video kiosk looped an interview with the artist recorded at the exhibit opening. To create each piece, she used old journal pages, magazines, fabric, decorative papers, and acrylic paint. Moss explained that she did not approach her art with a plan; it emerged and changed as she progressed. As she created, she let go of expectations and allowed energy to channel through her and manifest its message onto the canvas. Moss's approach to art was skillfully applied mindfulness. The opposite of stuckness.

As 9:30 neared, I wandered back toward the program room. It was bustling with people. A tall, thin woman with shoulder-length, tousled blonde waves and a warm smile stood in the doorway. "Welcome. I'm Eileen."

I shook her hand. "Hi. I'm Julie. Nice to meet you."

"Sit anywhere you like. We'll get started in a few minutes."

The chairs were set up in a wide circle. I surveyed the room and chose a seat across from the door. There were about 20 others in attendance, mostly women, most of them at least ten years older than me—only a couple were younger, and only by a few years. How might their struggles shed light on mine?

Sister Joanna, short, thick, and grey, shuffled in. She spoke about the history and mission of Wisdom House, introduced Eileen, handed each person a donation envelope, and then slipped out. Eileen gave us a brief overview of the program as she passed around pens and paper. "Write down your name, the name of your deceased loved one, when they died, and what you hope to get from the program." She paused. "I would also like you to write down one word that you would use to describe yourself today that you would not have used before the loss of your loved one."

We were each expected to read it aloud to the class. Aloud? Which loss did she want me to write down? I glanced around at others, scratched behind my ear, and pulled at the collar of my sweater.

As participants shared names and dates, a list of words emerged that revealed some of the commonality of grief—words such as empty, sad, vulnerable, scattered, uncertain, and terrified. Although their loss varied—parents, friends, children, or siblings—their experiences sounded eerily familiar.

I bit my nails and studied my sheet as my turn approached. I could barely concentrate on what the person next to me said. My heart was slamming against the inside of my chest so forcefully I was sure others could see it. I glanced around the circle of faces; pairs of sad, glossy eyes fixed on me like spotlights. The paper shook. I smoothed it down onto my lap. This was *not* a betrayal.

"I'm Julie. I lost my two older sisters, Louise and Mary." I started crying, but I fought the tears and kept reading. "They died in 1973 and 1976. I hope to feel more comfortable talking about them." I cried harder. Someone placed a box of tissues on the floor next to me. "One word I would use to describe myself today that I would not have used before loss is *incomplete*." I sniffled and laughed nervously. "I'm sorry." I wiped my eyes. "I'm really *not* a basket case."

Eileen shook her head. "Oh, no. I will have none of that. No one here is a basket case. We are grieving. Tears are a normal and healthy part of grief." She looked around the circle. "We are *expected* to cry in here."

Normal? Hmmm. Not in my family. I needed to ponder that a bit. But her assurance did make me feel better.

A middle-aged woman named Beth, who had lost her son in a car accident, spoke softly. "Julie, how did your sisters die?"

It took me a moment to realize what she had asked. That she was talking to me. I swallowed hard. I hated this question almost as much as the *how-many-brothers-and-sisters-do-you-have* question. "Mary had an asthma attack, and Louise was murdered." I could hear the subtle collective holy-shit gasp. The worst of the worst. The one time you don't want to win a superlative. And then she followed it up with an all-too-familiar reply.

"Your poor parents."

Yes. I looked at the floor and nodded. It was a typical concern. I was a child at the time, so it was often assumed that I didn't know what was going on. But as DeVita-Raeburn points out in the book *The Empty Room*, children cannot process the event in real-time. They store it until they are older, typically around midlife. In the meantime, as children they must live surrounded by the confusion and suffering of others and later, as adults, come to terms with their own.

After the heart-wrenching introductions were complete, I already needed a nap. Eileen handed out a single page with three questions on it. She asked us to think about the first time we experienced a loss in our life, how we grieved, and what messages we heard in our family about grief.

"I was only four-years-old when Louise was murdered," I began as tears instantly pooled, and the pitch in my voice wavered. "I didn't grieve. I tried to be good, be quiet, and stay out of the way."

Eileen commented. "It's been more than forty years, and your pain is sharp."

I nodded.

"What can you share with people in the room about the grieving process?"

I stared toward the blank space in the middle of the room and skillfully allowed mindfulness to gather and free the truest thoughts from decades of solitary confinement. "Don't keep it a secret. Cry, bang your fists, throw things, yell—do anything except hold it in and pretend you are fine. Because the longer you pretend it's not bothering you, the deeper it is buried, and it will contaminate everything that happens after. Every relationship. Every experience."

When I finished that grief rant, I took a deep breath and wondered where the hell that all came from. I glanced up at Eileen. She gave me an affirming nod.

Jane, another participant, spoke. "I agree with Julie. After my brother Ben died, no one wanted to bring it up. It just seemed easier to hold it inside. Like if you let it out, you might fall apart or lose control. We wouldn't have put it out in the open if the counselor hadn't told us how important that was."

Even though I had read about the pervasiveness of silence after loss, it was truly helpful to hear it firsthand from real people suffering with grief. My family did not *invent* the contract of silence. It was a natural human reaction to loss. And it made so much sense now.

Many of us were living with a pervasive disconnection from others and the fear of death. Betrayed by our own imaginations run amok—accidents, illness, violence. A fear of the dreaded phone call. When will it happen again? Will I be next? We *all* felt this way. Just realizing I wasn't alone was a comfort.

Eileen encouraged us to write down these fears and how they had affected our lives. I glanced up and watched people feverishly scratching down sentences, paragraphs. I didn't think they were selfish to acknowledge pain and I didn't view them as attention mongers. I empathized with them. Could I afford myself that same compassion?

A third box of tissues went around the circle as Eileen explained the "grief loop" and how it is unpredictable and changing. She passed around a graphic developed by Jeanne M. Harper that depicts the ebb and flow of grief as a tapered corkscrew. According to Harper, entering a *loop* represents feelings such as despair, withdrawal, anger and depression, and can include experiences like disrupted sleep, disorganized thinking, and restlessness.

Breaks in the grieving process are depicted as segments of the coil between loops, when the intensity of grief lessens or subsides. In these times, the bereft may experience some level of relief, adjustment, or may strike out to try to form new relationships.

Eileen explained that many triggers can pull us into another grief loop, such as coming across a loved one's belongings, holidays, birthdays, anniversaries, special songs, scents, or places. Over time however, the grief we experience when entering successive loops becomes less intense than the initial feelings.

When grief is pushed aside however, as when in denial, the intensity of feelings remains elevated. You are literally stuck in the tentacles of grief. Welcome to the last four decades of my life.

Eileen also introduced the concept of *anticipatory grief.* When a loved one is gravely ill and they are not going to get better, grieving begins when doctors reveal, or the prognosis becomes obvious, that death is imminent. Perhaps Mom and Dad were grieving long before Mary's last trip to the ER.

The program continued after lunch break with more discussion, sharing, short video clips about loss, tears, patience, active listening, and lots of empathy and compassion. Eileen read from a poem called "We remember them" from the Gates of Prayer, a Jewish Prayer book.

> *In the rising of the sun and in its going down,*
> *We remember them.*
> *In the blowing of the wind and in the chill of winter,*
> *In the opening of buds and in the warmth of summer,*
> *In the rustling of leaves and the beauty of autumn,*
> *In the beginning of the year and when it ends,*
> *When we are weary and in need of strength,*
> *When we are lost and sick at heart,*
> *When we have joys we yearn to share,*

When we have decisions that are difficult to make,
When we have achievements that are based on theirs,
As long as we live, they too shall live,
for they are a part of us,
as We remember them.

As another box of tissues was sent around the circle, like a wave of relief propagating around the room; a tide of hope and renewed energy. Then Eileen posed the question to Staci, "If your tears could talk what would they say?" Staci was so choked-up over the loss of her husband that she couldn't even speak. She blew her nose and tried to catch her breath.

I leaned forward, forearms resting on my thighs, looking down. I felt like I was invading her privacy.

"Julie," Eileen said.

I straightened, and looked up, wide-eyed. *Did I miss something?* "Yes?"

"What advice would you give her right now?"

Without hesitation, I glanced over at Staci. "Talk through the tears," I offered softly. My own tears had all questions and no answers, however. Why did they go so far away from me? Why do I feel so disconnected? Why did Louise take such risks? How could she trust him? How could he destroy my family? How could God let all this happen?

A woman named Evelyn spoke next. "My tears would talk about guilt. I had two people close to me die, one right after another. I couldn't deal with the second funeral. I walked out. I just couldn't be there."

That was probably how Mom felt. No burials after Louise's. That was more than enough.

Eileen read a poem called "Allow," by Danna Faulds.

There is no controlling life.
Try corralling a lightning bolt, containing a tornado.

Dam a stream and it will create a new channel.
Resist, and the tide will sweep you off your feet.
Allow, and grace will carry you to higher ground.
The only safety lies in letting it all in—the wild and the
weak—fear, fantasies, failures, and success.
When loss rips off the doors of the heart or sadness veils
your vision with despair,
Practice becomes simply bearing the truth.
In the choice to let go of your known way of being,
The whole world is revealed to your new eyes.

To me, this was about surrendering to grief. Allowing myself to feel the emptiness, rather than run, deny, or replace it with guilt or shame. It was about holding grief in my open palm, and lifting it up to the light, examining it, learning how to carry it.

The first line of Fauld's poem put forth the idea that "…there is no controlling life." *No* control. By man or God. I began to deconstruct my unfair judgement of the church. Through this workshop promoted by the Sisters of Wisdom, it became clear that God's power is not in causing or preventing the storm, but in the recovery. Serving as a hub of community and support. A critical substance of the matrix.

Then Eileen asked us to write the next part of our lives.

I wrote about incorporating rituals into my life. Rather than focus on the time of year or date of my sisters' deaths, I wanted to celebrate their life somehow. Perhaps a small service on their birthdays. Letting the space that they occupy in our hearts be a place marker for love rather than pain. I wanted to honor them by finishing the family book I had started to write.

Everyone took turns speaking about their own next steps. Jane wanted to visit Ben's grave. Staci wanted to start a scholarship in her husband's name. Yes. We need to honor their legacy. They should not be forgotten.

Eileen asked us about a concept she believed was often overlooked in grief. "How will you take care of yourselves? Because those who are working through grief need extreme self-care."

Some folks responded by saying they would seek counseling. Some said they would spend more time with friends. I wasn't sure. Plans sometimes proved futile in my life, like there was some other driving force that was always steering it. Nevertheless, I was committed to writing, and that, for me, seemed to be the best therapy of all. She asked us to list five restorative places we could go to recharge—that was easy. But the next request was tough. She wanted us to list five supportive people we could reach out to. I tapped my pen against the notebook. It was difficult to name five people I was willing to open up to--that itself was telling.

As people thanked Eileen and filtered out, I watched how she interacted with them. How she was so considerate of their feelings. How she reminded me of Mary. I browsed the pamphlets on grief that were spread on the table near her. I took several, some geared toward children. I thought it would be valuable knowledge that I was never exposed to. I also took her business card.

Today was the first day I spoke openly with strangers who had also suffered a traumatic loss. I felt the strength and support of that connection but feared it would be relegated to this unique world—this room of people living in purgatory, just like me. People who, reeling from loss, weren't sure where they fit.

Once there was space, I approached Eileen. "Thanks so much. This is important work you do."

She smiled and put a hand on my shoulder. "You've clearly been working hard. You're a very open person," she said. "Thanks for sharing today."

Open? That surprised me. "I always think I'm closed off and shut people out."

"That might be how *you* see yourself, but believe me, others see something much different. Can I hug you?"

I smiled and reached out. "Of course." I was happy to hug her. It was yet another small token of reassurance that I was on the right path. Eileen reminded me of how I would want a big sister to be: caring, smart, successful, compassionate, and kind. I wondered how my younger sisters saw me. I cringed. I've been a seeker most of my life, bumping off the edges of philosophies and ideas, without really internalizing them. Wanting so badly to build bridges to and from my heart, but unsure how to even sketch the blueprints. The openness that Eileen saw was a recent development within the past two years. That kind of vulnerability would have gotten you ripped to shreds in my family, and potentially still could.

I walked to my car. The clouds remained, but the rain had stopped. The leaves were flaunting their fiery beauty against a steel-grey canvas. I drove away, the angular gravel of the drive and the weathered split-rail fence in the rearview giving way to smooth pavement and sturdy guard-rails. Huge extended families of oaks, maples, and ash lined both sides of the road, celebrating another season, honoring the old while embracing the promise of fresh new leaves in the spring.

Chapter 25:

Crash

Late November, 2016

The gusty winds of late fall howled up from the shore, and the thick branches of the ash tree in the backyard swayed and pointed angry stick fingers at my house. I made some tea and headed into the living room to work on chapter six of the family history. I hadn't written anything since Wisdom House. It was as if I'd gone dormant like the trees.

As I rearranged the cushions, I balanced my laptop precariously on the arm of the couch. I knew it was a bad idea. As if in slow motion, I watched it crash to the floor, mangling and jamming the flash drive containing my writing files into the USB port. After weeks of avoidance, I had finally decided to write, and in an instant that decision was taken from me. I stood there staring in disbelief before I picked up the laptop and plucked out the remains of the tiny, defunct, electronic file cabinet. Just to be sure, I plugged it back in. The computer couldn't read it.

Memories spanning more than four decades of my life, and two generations before me, were coded in computer language, imprinted on that tiny little circuit board—and now it was lying in pieces. Instantly inaccessible. No. I didn't back it up to the cloud. I had a more open mind than most members of the Bardy clan, but anyone with any shred of Bardy DNA would never trust some invisible voodoo like *that*.

I sat on the edge of the couch, hunched over, forearms on thighs, and stared at the remains of the flash-drive. Gone were transcribed interviews, tearful personal recollections, and two years' worth of family research that made up the rough draft of my family history. Gone were my detailed journal entries documenting the entire experience.

It might have been possible to piece together the fragments, but I didn't have the energy. If I decided to start over, it would have to be with a brand-new foundation. Usually, renovations aren't worth it. Dealing with walls that aren't square, mouse skeletons, and sink traps filled with the decomposed sludge of food waste? No. I'll not start with that.

The files were gone. What did I have to say when the words were broken? I sat there on the couch, with nothing to show for the last two years, utterly baffled that I wasn't crying. I wasn't emotional. I was still. Exhausted. Was it stoicism inherited from Mom? Or perhaps something simpler. If I didn't cry, I could deny the tragedy a little longer. Push it down. Hold it there.

If I didn't cry, perhaps my sisters hadn't died.

A bass drum resonated within my skull. It had been pounding intermittently all day. I *knew* the laptop was going to fall—a premonition I ignored. Maybe that's why I wasn't crying. Buried within that knowing were confusing, guilt-ridden flashes of relief. The burden of all that heart-wringing work lifted.

Was that why Mom didn't cry? Anticipatory grief? Perhaps she imagined it several times over. And when the dreaded day finally arrived, she was still. Exhausted.

There's no comparing the loss of a book and the loss of a child—I knew that—although I couldn't help but ponder some sort of parallel. I coiled up and burrowed into the cushions of the overstuffed sofa, teasing apart my feelings over the loss of the work I had done to find my sisters. In a cruel blow of irony, they'd been lost again.

Grief has a lot to teach us about the balance between giving and getting, gaining and losing. About remembering not just what we've lost, but more importantly, cherishing what we have. And there was no more painful example at the present than the deterioration of my relationship with the new family.

* * *

As often happened, when there was strife in my waking hours, there was little peace at night. In a particularly vivid dream, I watched the sun rise through cathedral windows overlooking the lake. All was silent until the arrival of a glossy black raven with a cobalt blue feather on one wing. Plunk-plunk-plunk. The raven hammered on the glass and hovered, its beady eyes fixed on mine.

To the native northwest coast people, the raven is a symbol of transformation. It was often called upon by tribal elders for insight into problems or conflicts for its ability to reveal underlying truths. They also believe the raven is a long-distance healer who helps expose secrets that could potentially harm the keepers.

* * *

I don't have much knowledge of spirit animals, but the raven dream was a harbinger indeed.

It was early December and I had not spoken to my youngest sister Nicole since her daughter Ava was born in August. I had since called and left a few voicemails and sent several text messages, but they went unanswered. I had assumed she knew I was keeping up with her through discussions with others and posts on Facebook. I was wrong. She had become deeply resentful, but like Mom, kept a lid on it, until the pressure was too great.

The day after the raven dream, I got a phone call from Nicole and felt the full force of her indignation. "I want to know why you didn't come see me and Ava? I know you were mad about something."

"I wasn't mad. I was busy."

"How could you be too busy to visit me in the hospital? Or when I got home?" Her voice boomed with frustration. "I asked you to come and visit three times!"

"I had to go to my office, to get ready for classes starting. You had lots of other people there. Renee went. Angela...." I tried to explain, but there was no space in her anger.

"I *know* you were in Thompson. You could have stopped by," she lectured.

I tried to remain calm, but the judgement overwhelmed my patience. I raised my voice. And she raised hers. Months of pent-up frustration were hurled my way at the speed of sound.

"I have two other children but you only spend time with Lauren and Sophia. I know you're angry about something and lying to me!" Caught off-guard, I felt she should have brought all this up sooner. Maybe she tried, and I just didn't hear her.

She had no way of knowing all that I was carrying around and trying to work through. I hadn't shared my struggles with anyone, except maybe Eric. I felt like no one would understand, and I didn't want to be a burden. It was *my* problem.

When she finished testing the strength of my eardrums by shouting out exactly how neglectful and hurtful I was, she hung up. I felt like I had been pummeled and thrown into solitary confinement. I knew visiting with my nieces was out of the question until this could be resolved. Yet it seemed more hopeless than ever.

The more I thought about the raven dream and Nicole, the worse I felt. In truth, she was celebrating one of the most amazing life events, yet I was too busy digging up the past to notice that I was covering my present with a big pile of dirt.

Apparently, it was time to challenge some of the assumptions I had made and look more objectively at my relationships with my younger sisters and the role I play in their lives. More than ever, it felt like I was desperately chasing what I had lost, rather than focusing on what remained.

* * *

There was some encouraging news about the flash-drive though. It turned out that one of my fellow students in the yoga teacher training course was an IT manager. He offered to take the memory stick to work to see if someone could repair it. Not to be outdone by another man, Eric ended up bringing it to a computer shop near the police barracks, and they were able to retrieve 90% of the original files. The strength and variety of my support network continued to surprise me, even if it was occasionally fueled by male ego.

Despite the resurrection of the files, I scattered my energy among classes at the university, weekend jaunts with Eric, bonfires, theater, and my responsibilities as a budding yogi, such that I had no time left to write. Was it intentional? Maybe I just needed a break.

Mired in guilt, I felt that *not* writing meant moving further from Louise and Mary. On the other hand, continuing to write seemed to isolate me from the new family.

I argued with my stuckness. Why was I even writing a family history in the first place?

I was writing for Louise, for Mary, for Mom, Dad, the old family, the new family, and for me. Because no one else will. And, for many reasons, perhaps no one else *can*. I needed to continually remind myself of this.

Chapter 26:

Pieces of Us

Late December, 2016

"**A**re you ready to go?" Eric asked from his recliner. I exhaled, reached for a glass on the table beside him, and brought it to the sink. "I think so."

Eric slipped on a fleece jacket while I grabbed my long wool coat from the closet. He held it up so I could find the other sleeve. "It's not that cold out. Are you sure you need this one?"

I pulled the collar up against my neck. "It'll get cold later."

The annual family Christmas Eve party was at Nicole's house that year. It was always a lively celebration with Mom and Dad and the new family. But since Tammy always celebrates in Vermont, it was also an annual reminder of who's missing--my older sisters.

The rift between Nicole and me added a new depth to my typical holiday anxiety. We hadn't spoken since she hung up on me four weeks prior. Discord within the new family was never a secret. I spent the entire twenty-minute drive to her house picking at my cuticles and rifling through old emails on my phone.

When we arrived, Nicole opened the door and greeted Eric and I with a fleeting, one-armed hug and a smile so forced it looked almost painful.

"Merry Christmas!" Eric offered with naïve enthusiasm.

"You too," she managed, fixing her glance on the shrimp cocktail I brought. "I'll put this in the fridge." She snatched the container and disappeared into the kitchen.

"The roads are icy. Are Mom and Dad going to make it?" I called out.

No response.

Others arrived and within about 15 minutes, the living room was filled with the chaotic energy of a typical family party. I said hello to Renee and Angela and their significant others, but they were immersed in their own conversation, so I made the rounds. I spoke with everyone except Nicole, although I tried. When I walked into the room she was in, she would walk out. If I sat next to her, she got up and moved. I enjoyed seeing everyone, but I couldn't deny that her rejection crushed my spirit. This used to be my favorite time of year.

As kids, excitement had started to build right after Thanksgiving. Mary and I couldn't convince *Mom* to begin celebrating that early, so we started by decorating Grandma's house. Up into the snowy woods we trudged, with a small handsaw to find the perfect white pine. With teaspoons and tiny, sap-covered fingers, we dug into the frozen gravel of the driveway. We dropped a few cold, grey rocks— *plunk, plunk*—into an empty three-pound can from Eight O'Clock Coffee.

We brought the tree and our makeshift stand into "Siberia," the term Grandma used for the lonesome living room that stayed shut after Dziadzia died. When we stayed over, Siberia teemed with life. We crumpled sheets of newspaper into balls and placed them on the grate in the fireplace. A layer of kindling over the paper, and a few sticks of wood on top. Mary struck the match and lit several edges of the paper. In no time, the fire was crackling and chasing away the chill of that lonely room. We wedged the trunk of the white pine into the coffee can and stood it up among the rocks, straight and proud. It was ready for decorations.

With dull scissors and nimble fingers, we sat at the round oak dining room table and cut red and green construction paper into inch-wide strips.

Mary stirred flour and water in a glass bowl to make a thick paste. We bent the paper into loops and linked them together with our homemade glue to form a chain. Meanwhile, the sound of kernels pinging against a metal lid, and the smell of popcorn let us know that Grandma was doing her part. She shook the cast-iron pot over the top of the woodstove until the lid started to rise, then filled a mixing bowl with hot popcorn. One by one, I handed the fluffy white kernels to Mary. With patience and precision, she pierced each one with a tiny silver sewing needle and threaded them onto a length of Christmas-red string.

The last decoration was my favorite. Mary sketched and cut out a star shape from an old saltine box. We peeled just the right size piece of reclaimed tinfoil from the conglomerate silver ball that smelled of lard. I wrapped the edges of the foil around the star shape and Mary secured it to the top of the tree with a bread tie. The light from the fireplace glinted off the wrinkled foil and made our star look as if it was studded with twinkling rhinestones. Perfect.

When my younger sisters were old enough to traipse into the woods with me, I rekindled the tradition of the white pine. But I could never quite rid *Siberia* of a particular hollow chill, no matter how great a fire I built.

Last year, I shared the tradition of the handmade star with my nieces and basked in my memories of what had once been the happiest time of the year.

But tonight, all I felt was the icy draft of resentment.

After the entire family exchanged gifts, Nicole helped her youngest children, Jackson and little Ava, tear the paper off their presents. She took time to admire and comment on each one. I watched in anticipation as the pile diminished. When she got to the gifts I brought, she pushed them under the chair next to her.

Her oldest daughter Lauren noticed them. "Mommy, you have two more presents."

Nicole didn't even glance up. "We'll open those later."

Crushed. There was so much joy in the room, but I felt as though I was standing outside, hands pressed against the cold glass of the picture window, looking in. It was time to leave.

* * *

The alarm blared at 4:30 am, on that cold January morning, reminding me how much I hate to get up early. I uncoiled myself from the warm covers and got into the shower. I had to leave by 5:15 to meet my friend Julie (whom I bonded with at the Kripalu cult retreat) and her husband Scott at their house in Worcester. Julie had to undergo a wire-guided lumpectomy at Newton-Wellesley Hospital in Boston. I needed to bring all the compassion and vulnerability I could muster. For me, it would be a day spent as the antithesis of a Bardy.

Julie was a self-admitted chicken. She wept openly at the thought of anesthesia and cried hysterically with the mention of the procedure itself. After the nurses checked her in, it took some convincing before she allowed Scott and me to leave her side. She clutched the tail of Scott's un-tucked, button-down shirt. "Don't go," she begged.

I leaned outside the curtain of her room. "Excuse me, nurse? Can you give her something to calm her down?"

"We've tried. She refuses to take any sedatives." The nurse waved her hand through the air and muttered as she hurried away. "Your friend brought a bunch of herbal supplements with her."

Of course she did. That's Julie. My gluten-free, dairy-free, nightshade-free, organic, free-range friend. I turned to Scott. "Maybe they could slip something in her IV?" I suggested.

He laughed. For both Scott and me it was an anxious day of waiting, whispering with nurses, and bargaining with doctors about how to present information so that Julie would not freak out.

It was also a day of my trying to bridge the emotional canyon left when Julie's Mom passed away a few years earlier. They had been best friends, and I knew how much she needed a strong female presence. Julie's only sib was a distant younger brother.

As I sat by her bedside, she squeezed my hand. "Thank you for being here today. Without my mom—" She teared up. "Well, I couldn't have done this without you. You're the big sister I never had."

I thought about what kind of a big sister I had been to Nicole lately. How could I be so right and so wrong at the same time? The new family was tough. Bardy genes for sure; begrudging, judgmental, nary an apology. I had no idea how to reach her.

* * *

The next morning, after Eric left for work, my frustration reached crisis stage. I begged out loud to the person I knew was best at resolving arguments. "Mary, please, I don't know what to do. How do I fix this when she won't even talk to me? If you can hear me, if you can help at all, please." I lay in bed face into the pillow, wallowing in frustration, until I heard a knock at the door. Startled, I raised my head, wiped my face, and sat up. This was The Lake House, on a road with seasonal homes, a treacherous hill, and a wintertime population of three—Eric, me, and one other hardy, year-rounder a few houses down. No one happened down this road in the winter. I peeled back one corner of the blind and saw a strange truck parked out front.

As I made my way down the hall, the second knock brought more concrete thoughts—danger, harm, and home invasion. I glanced at the keys nearby and imagined how they could be used as a defensive weapon.

I opened the door and a short, squat woman with a round face smiled at me. Hardly an attacker; she looked more like the Campbell's soup girl. "Do you want to know about life after death?" she asked.

The Rumrill Eyebrow. I couldn't help it. No introduction or anything, and she comes out with that? Images of Mom spouting off to the Jehovah's flashed through my mind. I had no intention of swearing at this woman, but I wanted her to leave. So I threw out a white lie. "I follow Buddhism—infinite possibilities. Not enough time to talk about all that."

"Well that sounds—"

"Peace to you." I started to close the door.

She leaned to the side and peered in through the remaining space. "Well, it's a lovely day isn't it?"

Return of The Eyebrow. A change in tactics? "If you like mud and dirty snow."

"Don't you get lonely down here, all by yourself?"

Peculiar question. Peculiar little woman. I thought more about her inquiry. What did she mean by *down here*? Initially, she had asked me about life after death. Did she mean *down here* on earth as opposed to heaven?

"Lonely? No. I live with my husband." Bardy paranoia took over and my thoughts changed from Campbell's soup girl to Jehovah's to *she's casing the joint.* "And we have many neighbors. Have a good day." I backed away, closed the door, and went to the window to watch her leave. She got into the passenger seat of a red, late-model, Dodge pickup truck. A man wearing a Daniel Boone hat was driving. I didn't think to get the plate number—I was distracted by the hat. Rookie mistake. Eric wouldn't like that.

I stood at the counter and rehashed the way that stranger's questions eerily mirrored my struggles. My niece Lauren's 14th birthday was only a few days away, and I wanted to see her. I thought about how important birthdays are to kids. I didn't like to miss the celebrations. I *was* lonely down here.

I paced in the kitchen until I finally decided to call Nicole. One ring, two rings, three rings, and then an annoyed, scratchy voice on the other end. "Hello?"

Wow, okay. She answered the phone. I paused, overwhelmed by muddled feelings—shock, gratefulness, relief, and resentment. "Hi, Nicole. It's Julie." I spoke fast, afraid she might hang up again. "I'm not going to be able to make Lauren's party. I had planned to go away this weekend. I wanted to see if I could spend some time with her before I leave town tomorrow."

"I think we need to clear up some things before that happens."

"Okay. Well, I've been trying. But you haven't called me back or returned my text messages."

"I don't have time to get into a conversation right now."

Avoidance again. I was despondent. "Fair enough."

"Fair enough?!" she erupted.

I doubted I could say anything that she would agree with. "Yeah. I mean, I get it. You're too busy."

A long pause. I waited. Nicole explained how abandoned she'd felt when I didn't visit her and Ava in the hospital. "Everyone else came to see us, *except* for you. I *know* you were mad that I asked Renee to stay with Lauren and Sophia when Tim brought me to the hospital."

"No. You *believe* I was mad. But you don't *know* it." I rubbed my forehead. The Bardy shortcut—in the absence of information, you don't need to find the truth, you just need to decide what *you* believe to be true.

After several minutes of angry venting, I realized nothing would change until I opened up. "It's the book I've been working on. Sometimes I feel like I'm drowning in the past. I lose whole days to thinking, recalling, writing. I wish Mary hadn't died. I wish Dad never had to drive her to the hospital. I miss her so much." I grabbed a box of tissues and sat at the kitchen table, head in my hands. "I'm glad Renee could be there with you. I'm glad you weren't alone. Being alone sucks." I blew my nose.

Nicole spoke with a soft, concerned tone. "Why didn't you tell me?"

I cleared my throat. "I'm not trying to get pity. I wasn't ignoring you. I was trying to balance things. I was doing okay. And then Greg. The murder. Brought *everything* back."

"What about Greg? Greg *who*?"

I took time to explain some of how Greg's murder had swamped me with dark memories and emotions.

"Why do you keep everything to yourself?" she lectured. "It's not healthy. You can talk to me anytime."

Hmmm. Anytime? I wasn't about to argue. In any case, I knew I would probably never feel comfortable divulging all the details of my struggle. It seemed to me that relationships in the new family were sometimes like those on the TV show *Survivor*: people suspicious of other's motives, always forming and dissolving secret alliances. I never felt like I knew where I stood with anyone. Or maybe my perspective was skewed by a maze of emotional walls—theirs and mine. In any case, I hated to waste time mired in misunderstanding. I knew how quickly sisters could be taken away.

I made arrangements to visit Nicole and her family, Lauren, Sophia, Jackson, and Ava, the following day. Nicole opened the door and greeted me without words, but with a two-armed, lingering hug. We sat on her living room floor around a blanket where Ava stretched and giggled. Jackson shuffled back and forth from the toy box, bringing an assortment of rattles and soft toys. We talked about dates for a sleepover as Sophia passed around a plate of warm chocolate chip cookies. Lauren eagerly tore open the early birthday gift I brought. I felt bad that I would be out of town for the party, but Nicole seemed to understand. For that afternoon we were all together huddled around Ava, lying on our bellies, eating cookies, making plans, and holding hands.

Quietly to myself, I thanked Mary for sending the encouragement I needed to mend the rift. This journey was teaching me about a powerful kind of truth that lives within intuition and speaks the language of blooms; a truth that science cannot explain.

Apparent roadblocks like the rift with Nicole or the loss of my writing files, were guidance in disguise, that begged for my attention. Suddenly, the purpose of my writing came into focus, sharp and close. I needed to change the storyline of the book from a family history to a memoir of this journey. A journey of mending family connections, both old and new. A journey whose power could only be fully realized when the details were shared.

* * *

Five minutes into my niece Lauren's birthday party, Robyn posted photos on Facebook. A tinge of guilt rippled through my mind. I scrolled through the pictures as I sat alone on the floor by a fireplace at The Apple Tree Inn in Lennox, Massachusetts, on a weekend scrapbooking retreat. I added a few more logs to the crackling fire. It popped and snapped; tiny orange cinders burst forth like miniature fireworks. The flickering shape and radiant glow of the flames made me feel warm, safe, and comforted, not lonely. Much like the fireplace at Grandma's house, beside which stood the little pine tree with its handmade decorations.

The purpose of the retreat was to make progress on a family scrapbook for my parents. Months earlier, I had gathered photos from the various caches at The Compound—closets, attics, old trunks, and drawers—and brought them to the loft at the lake house and sorted them. The pictures had been a convenient excuse to talk with Mom and Dad about dates, places, people, and events I was too young to recall. Like a good scientist, I had taken detailed notes to help recolor a faded family history.

Women filtered into the "round room" at the Inn, lugging crates and totes stuffed with scrapbooking supplies. Windows lined the entire perimeter, like the bridge of the Starship Enterprise, providing a panoramic view of a sprawling evergreen carpet dusted with snow and pierced by the jagged spine of the Berkshire Hills. The curved wall of windows rose about seven feet to a cone-shaped ceiling much like a circus tent, supported by a sturdy post in the center of the room. The big-top was lined with ghostly panels of sheer, cream-colored fabric and strings of miniature white lights. I found my reserved seat, unpacked my crafting tools, and began to arrange the past in front of me on a six-foot table.

I started with pictures of Louise. I placed pieces of her life on the page as she had lived it; from the time she came into the world when Mom was only 17, through her first communion photo, big, bright aquamarine eyes and hands clasped together in prayer, to the end of her junior year in high school when she got her driver's license and the Rambler.

Working on photos of the old family was like being away for over 40 years and then finally returning home. I felt as though I was physically stepping into pages of the past, captured in reverie as I studied each image, dissolving into the smallest detail. The values I had admired and the fashion I had emulated as a child surrounded me once again. Peace signs, tie-dye, bright yellow smiley faces, bell-bottom hip-huggers, and fringy suede vests. Home.

A budding little hippie flower child, I hung around my big sisters and their friends. I had a huge social network for a 4-year old. Always one of a group, whole and complete. A time and place where I belonged and was cared for, when I first learned about caring for others.

When I looked at pictures of Louise, I didn't see the reckless, risky side of her that Tammy had described. There were pictures of Louise with her horse, Gidget, with bunnies, and kittens, and our dog, Dusty. Tending, nurturing, and holding them close as she did with me. A big-hearted, fiercely intelligent, nature-loving tomboy. That was the big sister I remembered.

The big sister who would at dusk trudge along the narrow path into the woods, fighting sticky spider webs and slapping at mosquitoes to help me find the perfect sized branch to toast marshmallows. We would sit around the fire-pit that Dad had made of leftover bricks from one of his job sites.

The stars were pinholes of light in the black velvet sky as we roasted hot dogs and chased after fireflies. Like stars in a bottle, we gingerly caught the little twinklers in between our cupped palms. We transferred them to a canning jar whose metal lid Dad punctured with an 8-penny nail so our new friends could breathe. Grass clippings placed in the bottom allowed some privacy in their temporary home. A magical lantern. A magical life. A life that tragedy had exiled me from.

But *that* weekend—the past was alive under a big-top sky. I arranged, glued, embellished, journaled, and liberated over 20 pages of family history that had been fragmented, pushed down, and locked away. As I began to work on pages that contained photos of my younger sisters, I realized that this was the only scrapbook with pictures of both the old family and the new family. In my mind, assembling the book was like constructing a bridge that joined these two different families, these two separate lives.

For that weekend, I felt unmistakably whole. I was hovering somewhere between heaven and earth. Using permanent, double-sided adhesive, I glued down one happy photo after another—no illness, murders, burials, contracts, or rifts. I didn't want the retreat to end.

Chapter 27:

To Bend Like a Rock

February, 2017

Compared to the Berkshires, the Himalayan Mountains are brutish, towering giants. A crumpled chaos of serrated knife edges capped by a dense pack of ice and snow, they stand stoic and unreachable. It may seem that this is their nature through and through. Yet geologists know that deep within the core of the mountain belt, great rock slabs mull and churn under intense pressure and heat, folding and flowing like soft chocolate. Exposed to the most horrible of conditions, they are able to bend instead of break. People can be like that too.

* * *

It was Super Bowl Sunday and I planned to head down to West Haven to watch the game at a pub with some friends. I decided to call Dad first to ask if he needed a haircut. Although he's mostly bald, he claims that no one else does what he wants.

Dad swept the bits of hair into a meager pile of clippings. "You didn't take off very much."

"Well, you're half bald. If you get rid of the comb-over, there'll be more to sweep up."

247

Mom snickered, but the shrill ring of the phone interrupted her fun. She shuffled into the living room to answer it. I heard her say "Hello." I wound the cord, slowly and silently, around the hair trimmer as I listened for reassurance that it wasn't a death call.

Glancing around the corner, my attention was cued to detect any micro-expressions that might betray Mom's stoic façade. Dad mentioned something about the Super Bowl, but his words trailed off as I walked ahead of him into the living room.

Mom stood with her back to us, one hand on her hip, looking out the window. "Yes. Who is *this*?" She turned toward Dad. "Oh. Hold on. I'll give the phone to Bob." She tossed the handset over the coffee table as if it was red-hot and lowered herself onto the edge of the couch. Max slunk behind the recliner and curled up on his bed, chin resting on his front paws.

I sat in a chair across from her, and we both watched Dad, intent on his words.

"Mmhmm. Oh? When did that happen?" Dad tucked the phone between his ear and shoulder and searched his pocket. I knew what he was looking for—his fingernail clippers.

I whispered to Mom. "Who is it?"

It was my cousin Dianne calling from Florida. Her son Butch had been killed in a car accident. This was exactly why we sometimes feared answering the phone. A death call could arrive anytime. They clamped their jaws around the back of your neck at the precise moment that all seemed peaceful in the world.

Dad made his way slowly toward his recliner. "Mmhmm. Mmhmm." He sat down. "Hold on a minute, Julie's here. I'll put her on the phone."

Seriously? Dad was known to pass the phone when he was in the middle of a TV program and didn't feel like talking—but at a time like *this*?

My gut reaction was to raise a hand and wave it away. For a split second, every neuron in my brain was firing with the same question: *What could I possibly say?*

Messages I had grown up with about grief flashed through my mind. Be strong, be good, and put up walls. Continue as if nothing happened. Act like you're fine when you're really sad, scared, and confused. Push it down. Hold it there. Don't feel sorry for yourself. Same old feelings.

But then I recalled the Wisdom House program and read from a different script. Don't keep repeating the same bad advice.

I reached out and took the phone. Dad sunk back into the recliner. I felt his and Mom's attention land on me like a blinding spotlight. As soon as I heard my cousin's voice—the tenderness, the raw truth in her pain—I knew that *my* words were not what mattered. Dianne needed her grief to be recognized.

She talked through her tears and told me a couple of stories about Butch, his work as a teacher, as a mentor for children, his love of bowling. I had met him maybe twice in my life, when we were kids. Dianne seemed to want affirmation that his life had purpose; he was loved and would not be forgotten.

After a few minutes, she paused to blow her nose. "I'm sorry to be a blubbering fool."

"Don't apologize. Please. You're going through something awful." I thought about Eileen from the grief workshop. "You're expected to cry. What else can you do?"

"Okay. Thank you." I heard Dianne trying to catch her breath.

"Sounds like Butch was an amazing person. He helped a lot of people."

"Yes. He is—was—he did."

"I'm so sorry this happened. I'll send you strength and love."

She thanked me again, and I told her I loved her. I handed the phone back to Dad, my head and heart flooded with emotions. It was my turn to observe.

Dad acknowledged the difficulty Dianne had already faced in her life. Her mother was Dad's older sister Ruth, who died at 28. Dianne was only 13 at the time and essentially grew up on her own. Dad didn't offer any of the ignorant clichés that make me want to punch someone, like *everything happens for a reason*. He offered empathy and compassion from life experience. "It's hard to lose a child. Mary has lost two, I've lost two. We know what that's like."

Dad hadn't gone to Wisdom House. He hadn't been on silent retreat or to a tea leaf reader, or mindfulness classes. He had lost children. He also knew what it was like to lose a sister. Yet he naturally showed tenderness and empathy, a vulnerability that could fold and flow like soft chocolate. He was definitely *not* a Bardy.

Mom was still sitting on the couch, leaning forward with her arms folded, staring off into that place she goes. The place where no one else is allowed.

At the end of the call, Dad asked about the services and, before he hung up, said, "I'm sorry" and "I love you." Sometimes that's what needs to be said most of all.

Dianne's loss was palpable in that living room. It was *our* loss. Acknowledging her pain and trying to help her was like validating our own grief, like giving ourselves permission to hurt. For the first time when faced with the news of death, I felt what it was like to experience it in real time with Mom and Dad. I felt what it was like to show compassion. To be *normal*. To face death together as a family rather than alone.

* * *

On April 8, 2017, Mary would have turned 55. I intended to call Mom and remind her, but she called me first.

We chatted a bit about what was on television the previous night and about the warm weather ahead. "It's Little Mary's birthday today," she said softly. She caught me off guard. She'd never reminded me of Mary's birthday.

"Yes. I'm going to bring her some flowers. Do you want to go?" I winced. The question escaped without reservation or planning.

After what seemed like an unbearable pause, where possibility—of confirmation or rejection—hung in the air like a smell you haven't figured out yet, Mom answered, "Yes."

Yes? Really? I might have let out an audible sigh of relief or surprise.

"I have to take care of the animals and let Miss Lilly out of the barn first."

Of course. Yes. The pony. "No problem. I still have to eat breakfast and get dressed. I'll pick you up in about an hour?"

"Okay," she said with what seemed to be a slight hint of reservation, or maybe I just imagined it. "I'll be here."

I ended the call and leaned against the kitchen counter to let her response sink in. After 41 years, it would be the first time that she and I would be at Mary's grave together. It was also the first time in 41 years we would celebrate Mary's birthday.

I devoured a small bowl of granola, set the dish in the sink, and got dressed. I hoped she wouldn't change her mind. I arrived at The Compound and walked into the kitchen where Max jumped and scratched at me.

"I'm in here," Mom called out. She emerged from the hallway and joined me in the kitchen.

I reached on top the fridge and grabbed a treat for Max.

She eyed my outfit. "Should I wear a sweatshirt too? Will this be enough?" I knew she had just been outside at the barn.

"The wind is fierce; you may want a sweatshirt under your vest." I tossed a dog treat in the air. Max snatched it and trotted over to his bed, tail wagging.

Mom draped the vest on a chair and got a heavier jacket out of the closet. With her layers in place, we embarked on our trip.

On the way to the cemetery, Mom reminisced. She talked about how Grandma refused to call Tammy by her name because it wasn't from the Bible. "She used to call her 'Sissy' until Auntie named her second daughter Janet. I pointed out that Janet wasn't a Bible name either. After that, Grandma never brought it up again."

I wondered what made her think of Grandma today. Was it because Grandma tried to control both Louise and Mary's services? How, in Grandma's opinion, they *should* have been open casket? I wondered about the root of this control. Perhaps Grandma's behavior could be attributed to her own experience of loss.

Several years ago, Tammy had mentioned that Grandma's first baby died. Maybe Grandma regretted not having a formal service for her eldest daughter—Mom's big sister that she never had the chance to meet.

I turned to Mom. "Grandma lost her first baby in childbirth, right?"

Mom fired a suspicious glance my way. "How did you know about that?"

A flash of heat spread from my cheeks to my earlobes. I needed a scapegoat. "I think Tammy told me. Did Grandma name the baby?"

"Yes. She named her Helen."

"Helen?" Strange. That was also Mom's younger sister's name.

She seemed to pick up on my puzzled expression. "Yes. I'm so glad they didn't name the baby *Mary*. I think that would have been awful to have the same name as a dead baby."

I nodded. "You're right."

Mom continued. "Renee was born just six months after Louise died. Grandma insisted that I name her Louise."

Control and regret. How it tangled, cinched, and suffocated relationships.

"Did she and Dziadzia bury the baby?"

"Yes. Grandma mentioned it to me and Auntie once. She said they buried the baby in the big cemetery across the street from St. Anthony's.

I don't think there was a service. She never took us to visit the grave. I don't know where it is or if there is even a marker."

I knew exactly what that was like. Abandonment. Denial. Sealing your heart inside the saddest wall that can ever be built. In this light, Mom's and Grandma's controlling and stoic natures were understandable. Perhaps even an effective survival mechanism, albeit with the unintended consequences of soft inheritance for the succeeding generation.

"I can ask Valerie from the Parish to check the plot plan. I'd like to know where the baby was buried. I can let you know what she says."

Mom nodded "Okay. Yes. Let me know."

We stopped at the grocery store to pick out some flowers to take to Little Mary's stone. I didn't want to pick out the wrong kind. I didn't want to do anything that might make this a bad experience for Mom, so I asked her which ones *she* thought we should get.

She didn't need time to browse. "The pussy willows. I remember you guys liked to bring them home from the swamp."

Pussy willows it was. In the checkout line, we chatted about the weather with an old man wearing a Russian fur hat that reminded me of one Dziadzia used to have. The cashier chimed in, a pleasant woman in her mid-fifties, with straight blonde hair and kind eyes like Mary.

Strange coincidences. Life seemed full of them. Maybe it always was.

On the way to St. Anthony's cemetery, Mom divided the bouquet. She left half of it in the car as we walked side by side to the monument, carrying our birthday offerings. Mom bent over and set the pussy willows on the grass. I took a smooth quartz stone and a small pink seashell from my pocket and set them on the small ledge at the base of the Barre Granite. "Happy Birthday, Mary," I said.

"Yes. Happy Birthday, Little Mary," Mom echoed as she brushed her fingers thoughtfully across Mary's and Dziadzia's names on the monument. She walked slowly around the grave, treading lightly. I wondered what she was thinking, and then she asked, "If Mary lived, what do you think she would have done for work?"

I'd thought about that often and didn't hesitate. "She would have been a teacher. Mary loved teaching. Remember how we always played with the Little People schoolhouse? I learned so much from her."

Mom nodded, uncharacteristically engaged in my response. "And now *you're* a teacher."

"Right." Was she drawing a parallel? I had often wished I could be more like Mary, but it seemed an impossible goal. "What do *you* think Mary would have done for work?"

"I don't know. She loved arts and crafts. Maybe an artist."

"Hmmph." I shrugged and straightened the angel ornament that sat on the edge of her stone. "Maybe." I was hoping Mom would say *teacher*.

She folded her arms. "Jeez, that wind is cold."

"It is. Do you want to head home?"

"Yes. But let's go the long way, through East Thompson."

Having grown up in East Thompson, Mom reveled in stories of her youth: the school bus route, the families who used to live in various houses, and the location of the old Shoddy Mill. And then we passed Wakefield Pond Road.

It was where Louise's body had been found on June 20, 1973, three days after her murder. It was the road Dad and I had driven down last year, while Mom was at work, so he could show me the exact location.

I didn't pretend that Wakefield Pond Road wasn't at the forefront of both our minds. "A botanist found Louise, right?"

"Yes. A botanist from the University of Rhode Island. He was photographing wildflowers."

"Kristen Orr said her brother Wendell found Louise."

"No. Why would Wendell be on that dirt road?"

"She said he was picking up rocks for a wall."

"No. The state police told me it was a botanist."

That's what was written in the newspaper clippings as well, but I was glad I could ask Mom about it. Until recently, I wouldn't have dared to bring it up.

"Do you care if I drive through the state park?" I needed to shift to something positive.

"Okay."

It was the first time we had driven into the park together in over 25 years, yet my heart felt the joy of a 10-year-old. I told Mom how I loved when she took us there as kids. My younger sisters and I ate ice cream sandwiches from the concession stand, splashed in boat wakes, and buried each other up to our necks in the sand. It was the closest we had ever gotten to the carefree days at Quonnie Beach, when our family was still whole.

When Mom and I returned to The Compound, we walked into the house chatting about upcoming errands and appointments. She grabbed a vase from the kitchen cabinet and put the rest of the pussy willows in water. "I think I'll go out and get some greens and some forsythia to put in here too."

I knew it would be a tasteful arrangement, just like in the mid-70s, when Mom, Mary, and I made festive wreaths out of princess pine together. I also knew it was her way of saying she wanted to be alone to process the day.

* * *

Eric and I went back to The Compound later that night after a call from Mom. She asked if Eric would check on a suspicious car that was parked in front of their house. I hoped the visit to the gravesite and our conversation earlier that day hadn't caused her anxiety to flare up. The drive past Wakefield Pond Road. The reminder of everything that murder takes from you. The nagging hyper-vigilance—who'll be next? Will it be me?

The questionable car turned out to be someone with engine trouble, and they were waiting on a tow truck. Eric and I went into The Compound for a quick visit. Mom made coffee for Eric, doting on him as usual. I followed Dad into the living room and sat in the chair next to his.

"I found something today that I think you'll appreciate." He lifted a cardboard box from the floor beside his recliner and handed me a winter collage scene that Mary had made in December of 1973. It depicted a town square with a Christmas tree, a church, and a group of carolers. I ran my hand over the surface, knowing that her nimble, careful little fingers had once held, cut, and pasted every scrap of paper in that scene. Amid a holiday season where the entire family was reeling from the loss of Louise, Mary was a spark of hope in a dark time. My eyes filled with joy. It was a priceless gift to be able to hold something she created, to feel Mary with us in this small, but thoughtful way, on what would have been her 55th year on earth.

* * *

Good Friday marked the third time that year Mom and I went to church together. On each occasion, when I left the yard, I thought about the suffering cat in the ditch and having to turn around so Mom could get her shotgun. Thankfully, none of our subsequent trips involved maimed felines or firearms and I haven't seen her shoot anything since.

After Good Friday mass, as we walked back to the car, I tried to think of a way to tell Mom I wanted to visit Louise with her. We had just gone to visit Mary a little more than a week earlier; this was either the best or the worst timing, and I wasn't sure which. The cemetery was just behind the church, but I still needed a concrete reason or Mom would probably refuse.

In the parking lot I unlocked the doors, started the car, and fiddled with the heat. The window of opportunity had nearly closed when it finally occurred to me. "Hey, Mom, I want to get the manger that I put on Louise's grave for the holidays. Would you mind?" I squinted a little and held my breath—a conditioned response.

"That's fine."

"Thanks. Okay. Great." This was a huge step for us. Mary's death had buttressed the contract of silence, but Louise's death had originally forged it.

I had visited Louise's grave many times as a confused and desperate teenager looking for advice, but I hadn't known of a single time Mom had been there since the burial. We had never gone together. I felt like crying. I felt like hugging her. I felt like asking a thousand questions. But I knew better than to do any of those things.

As we got out of the car, I grabbed my Swiss Army knife from the console. We wandered past two rows of gravestones toward the small wooden manger with moss glued to the roof that stood on Louise's memorial stone. I knelt, picked up the manger, and cut some old grass away from the edges of her footstone. I swept the clippings away from her name. "We miss you Louise, and we love you." I had never spoken to her in front of anyone, especially Mom.

Mom stood quietly beside me. I wondered what she was thinking, but there was no step big enough to liberate *that* question.

She seemed curious or surprised. As if she didn't realize that I had ever brought anything to Louise. "Where did you get that?" she asked.

I tucked the manger into a small cardboard box. "At the Dollar Store in town."

"It looks like the one Shane made that Christmas. In 1973."

I was glad she noticed. "I thought so too. That's why I bought it."

She stood over the grave for a moment and then meandered around the nearby headstones, reading the names. "I think Keith Szpyrka is buried in this cemetery." He was the 11-year-old son of our neighbors next door to The Compound. He died from a heart defect in 1963.

"Do you want to see if we can find his grave?"

"No. That's okay."

I placed the box on the floor behind the driver's seat, and we got into the car. It was a quick visit. I hoped this would help—her, or me, or both of us—but truthfully, it was impossible to see through that stone slab of an exterior. And I was wading in uncharted emotional waters.

On the way home, Mom brought up other folks whose children had died. We went back and forth, naming names. The Picard family lost a son in a motorcycle accident last summer, and the Gagnes' daughter was murdered by a neighbor in 1981. That was the same year a local serial killer began a four-year spree, kidnapping and killing teenage girls. He was caught in 1985. The same year Louise's killer was released from prison. No rest for the hypervigilant.

And what about little Andy Amato, 4-years-old, who wandered off in 1978 and only his little toy *Weeble* was ever found. Neither Mom or I could forget nor let go. It was the one place I felt like I still belonged. Where memories lived on within the emptiness of a blank stare, owning that space where no one else is allowed.

Talking about loss to others just seemed to tear at a wound that refused to heal. Our companions in unresolved grief all lived behind the saddest wall that could ever be built. That was the nature of our tribe—our only connection being one of disconnection.

But maybe that could change. As we drove up the long incline on Route 200, the song by Pink, *Just Give Me a Reason*, came on the radio. Mom stared out the window, and I shook my head in wonderment as I listened to the lyrics. Maybe like the rocks of the Himalayas, we could learn to bend without breaking. Maybe we could learn to love again.

Chapter 28:

A Paper Time Machine

Late April, 2017

The sun loomed near the horizon, casting a narrow arc of blood orange that softened into a pink-grapefruit and lavender sky. That morning I needed to walk. To banish a horrific nightmare where three little blonde-haired, blue-eyed boys were run over by a cargo truck. One was killed, one was severely injured, and I don't know what happened to the other.

I wandered down the hill toward the beach, past the neighbor's perfectly tended beds of butter-yellow daffodils, until pavement gave way to the soft, yielding, forgiving sand. Ocean Ave was deserted. No cars, no sound of engines in the distance. Seagulls squawked and chattered, still arguing over leftovers from low tide several hours earlier. I sat amongst a hash of quartz grains, tangled seaweed, and broken shells at the strand line.

I thought about my friend Greg who had been murdered the previous summer. His children were the boys in my nightmare. That's what death does to those left behind. Some are lost. Some are fractured. Some never recover.

Waves approached, grew taller and collapsed, zippering themselves to the sand. Fingers of foam reached out only to be dragged back and drowned by the next breaker. A departure from their typical gentle, lulling rhythm, the waves that day were unusually large, scouring, and erosive. There was no local wind to explain their tantrum-like nature. Rather, they manifested from a storm far offshore. Confounding indignation provoked and released unexpectedly.

* * *

Thursday evenings at The Compound were fairly predictable, like the subtle background rhythm of small waves strumming the shores of Long Island Sound. Mom and Dad could be found in the living room, binge-watching a drama series on TV called *Blue Bloods*.

The show followed the lives of the Reagans, a family of NYPD officers, and the moral dilemmas they faced at home and work. Mom and Dad's favorite scenes were when the family gathered around the table for Sunday dinner, sharing celebrations, problems, and stories. The episode that week was atypical. It tracked the Reagan's efforts to catch a serial killer who preyed on young women. One particularly violent scene triggered Mom.

She barked at Dad in the middle of the show, seemingly without provocation. "Turn it off, or change the channel."

Dad was confused. "But I'm watching it."

Mom got up, shut the TV off, and stomped out of the room.

Within a few minutes, she called my sister Robyn, crying. "All I could think about was Louise—if she had suffered, if she was calling out to me."

After hanging up with Mom, Robyn immediately called me at the lake. That was one of the few times I was thankful that Robyn never kept things to herself. When she finished spilling all the details, I headed to The Compound.

I could hear the television blaring from the walkway. It sounded like an old Western. Dad was in his chair and didn't even look up from the TV when I walked in. The air was stiff with the discomfort of people at odds with each other.

"Hi. Where's Mom?" I asked.

He waved a hand through the air. "She stormed off into the other room. Pissed about something."

"Julie?" Mom called to me from the bedroom. "I'm in here."

She was sitting on the edge of the bed, hunched forward, holding her elbows.

"I talked to Robyn." I smoothed the blanket next to Mom and sat down.

Her toes rested on the old, oak floorboards with the glossy, oil-based paint I had applied many years ago. Always trying to help them fix things. Paint was easy.

"Why didn't you explain to Dad *why* the show upset you?"

"I *have* told him. He *knows* that stuff bothers me. It makes me think of Louise." She buried her face in her hands and wept. "I wonder if she suffered."

I closed my eyes and nodded, resting my hand on her back. My heart hurt for her, and I wanted to fix things. I didn't want her to blame Dad. It was my fault she was upset. I never should have brought her to Louise's grave. How stupid to think that would be helpful.

"Dad wasn't purposely being insensitive." I paused, waiting to see if she would respond. "Eric is like that sometimes too. He just doesn't pay attention. I'll talk to him."

Max followed me through the kitchen and into the living room. Dad sat upright in his recliner, clutching the remote.

"Do you want some coffee?" I asked.

He shook his head.

I sat on the cushioned arm of his chair. "Mom has things—worries—hidden away. She doesn't share them. But they bother her."

Dad bristled; he and his stubborn nature, staring at the TV. "If you lean back, you're going to break that."

I countered with my own inherited stubbornness. "I won't lean back." An uncomfortable pause. "She doesn't mean to be unreasonable."

He shot me a sideways glance and then back to the TV. "So this is *my* fault?"

"No. Of course not." I patted his shoulder.

He wiped tears from his cheek with the back of his hand—a strong, leathery, construction hand that had poured concrete, strummed chords on the guitar, and wiped plenty of tears from my own cheeks. I rested my head on his shoulder and draped one arm across his chest.

"How am I supposed to know what bothers her if she doesn't tell me?"

Of course he was right. I knew his struggle well. It was mine too. "I'm trying to help her work on that." We sat together for a few minutes and watched the end of the western.

The argument blew over, but in its wake an unanswered question emerged. A question Mom still carried—unimaginably heavy and harrowing—more than four decades after Louise's murder.

Did Louise suffer?

Finding the answer to this question was of paramount importance. If the answer was no, perhaps it could help to defuse one of Mom's major triggers. But I was only 4 at the time and recall scant details of Louise's death. The situation must have been impossible. Needing to know the truth, but not wanting to hear any of it. Trying to continue with life, balancing on the edge of a huge hole in the universe.

If only there was a way to go back and collect the truth for her. Without dragging her back with me, and without her knowing about my effort. I needed a time machine. I knew it was literally impossible, but perhaps there was a virtual proxy. I had asked Eric about the police report a while ago. Mom's palpable anguish compelled me to follow up.

The report was a potential means of organizing and processing fragments of memories and feelings I had stored as a child. A passive way to learn about Louise's death without creating emotional turmoil for others in the present. A proxy for time travel made of paper and ink.

After I told Eric about Mom and Dad's argument, he promised to see about getting a copy of the report.

* * *

A week or so later, as Eric and I watched the birds and finished our morning coffee at the lake, he set his mug on the windowsill. "Oh—I made a few calls about your sister's report." He reached over and thumbed through some papers in his computer bag resting on the floor. "All of the old case files are usually stored out of state, and there's a backlog of requests. It could take up to a year...*if* they can even locate it." He handed me a double-sided sheet of paper as his phone rang. He glanced at the screen. "That's one of my sergeants." He grabbed his bag for work. "I gotta go. Fill out this form and leave it on the counter for me. I'm running late."

I glanced at both sides of the form, got up, and rummaged through the junk drawer for a pen. I leaned against the counter and began filling in the request. Each line pulled me closer to 1973.

Case number. I don't know. She was my sister, a person, not a number. I hated this already. *Date of incident.* Incident? Father's Day, 1973. June 17. The end of her junior year. The end of her life. The end of my mother's firstborn child. *Name of any principal party.* How was his name spelled? E-V-I-L. *How involved.* He murdered my sister. He took away her life, my family, our sense of safety. *Date of birth.* He was 26. I paused and pulled the collar of my sweater snug against the back of my neck. *Provide any additional available information.* I didn't have any. *Approximate time.* What time did my sister die? Gut punch. What was the *plate number* of her car? The car that she loved. The car that her murderer fled in. The car he later abandoned. *Incident type /description.* Homicide. The murder of my 16-year-old sister when I was 4-years old.

What did it mean to be Louise's sister? Did that meaning change after she died?

I pictured my nieces Lauren and Sophia as they rocked together on the hammock at The Ocean House this past summer. They are sisters, two years apart. They share friends, secrets, dreams, quarrels, and nightmares, celebrate accomplishments, giggle about their crushes and their quirks. Lauren and Sophia are individuals for sure. Yet as sisters with their lives so intertwined, they also intrinsically define themselves through their connection to each other.

As my previous conversation with Kristin at Fort Hill Farm revealed, when Louise died a large part of Tammy seemed to dissolve. Tammy couldn't definitively say what parts were still there and which ones were gone. I was too young to even recognize that dissolution in myself, but I certainly felt it now. Through all the empty space that Louise and Mary and the old family used to fill, our connection lives on. It is a phenomenon every bit as powerful and enigmatic as the strong nuclear force that cements all the matter in the universe. The *mother-daughter-sister bond*.

* * *

After nearly six months of cropping, cutting, arranging, gluing, and journaling hundreds of photos in the family scrapbook, it was finally complete. On Mother's Day, I slid the scrapbook into a brown paper shopping bag—it barely fit--and lugged our five-pound, behemoth of a life back to The Compound, where it originated.

Max's frenzied welcome and the warmth of a cheery fire in the woodstove greeted me just inside the door. "Mom, can you tie him up out back? I want to show you something, and I'm afraid he might ruin it."

"Okay. Come on Max." She grabbed his collar and led him outside.

I set the bag on the coffee table with a thud and carefully slid out the scrapbook. "This is the family album I've been working on."

"Oh, whoa. Let me get my glasses." Mom returned from the kitchen, sat on the sofa, and hunched over the album savoring it—page by page, picture by picture.

Dad came in from feeding the chickens. "We got six eggs today." He set them on the counter and joined our reverie. "Is that the scrapbook you were working on in January?"

I gave an emphatic nod. "Yep. It's finally finished."

Mom turned the pages slowly, lingering on pictures of her childhood at the farm, and her father, Dziadzia, tenderly sweeping her fingers across the photos as if reaching out and touching him. "Julie—this is beautiful."

Dad stood behind Mom and looked on with her. "Where did you get all these pictures?"

"It was a group effort. Some you brought down from the attic. Others Mom found here and there in closets and drawers. I scanned them and made copies so I wouldn't have to use the originals."

"That must've taken a lot of time," Dad remarked.

"Sure did. I got a lot done at the scrapbook weekend and finished the rest here and there." I pulled up a chair and joined them at the coffee table. I pointed out a picture of them that had been taken shortly after they started dating. "*When* did you say you guys got married?" I asked sarcastically.

Dad laughed. "Well, you already found out the truth on that one."

I gave him The Eyebrow. "Yep. Ancestry.com doesn't lie. I was nearly three-years-old."

Mom slowly flipped the pages and when she reached the ones of Louise, she gently fanned through the rest of the book noticing that I even included pictures of her great-grandchildren. "You have pictures of *everyone* in here."

I smiled. There was no old-family/new-family distinction in this book. It was just *our* family.

"Can I finish looking at this later? We have to go to Putnam and to Angela's house for Mother's Day brunch."

"Sure. No problem."

She closed the book and put it back into the bag.

I was puzzled. She didn't seem to realize the scrapbook was a gift. "Mom, the book is for you—well, you and Dad really—you can look at it whenever you want." I paused. "Just don't hide it up in the attic."

"No. I won't. I'm trying to clean out the clutter. Yesterday I was going through some of the boxes in Little Mary's room."

Little Mary's room? Wow. I hadn't heard her call it that except once by mistake shortly after Mary died. Mom wasn't cleaning out Little Mary's things—those were long gone. Nevertheless, simply hearing *her* say Mary's name was precious. It was a sweet sound I rarely heard since she died—it rang a tiny bell in my soul.

* * *

With final grades posted, I planned to celebrate the beginning of summer freedom with a day paddling in the Long Island Sound. As I lugged an overstuffed armful of kayaking gear from the basement, my phone chimed with a new text message from Eric.

FYI a copy of the police report was sent to headquarters but is not ready to be released yet.

Not *ready*? What did *that* mean? I went into the living room, set the kayaking gear on the floor, and called him.

Eric explained that the report had to be "prepared for civilian use."

I was confused at first. "It doesn't matter that I'm her sister?"

"No. You're a civilian. The report isn't being requested for official police business."

"That's ridiculous. I have a right to know what any stranger with a badge and a uniform knows." Just like when I was a child, it seemed someone else was deciding how much of the truth should be revealed.

"The report was held back to redact names and protect privacy."

I realized I sounded ungrateful. I took a breath. "Okay. That's fair."

"...And so that crime scene photos could be removed."

"Oh. Okay." Another breath. I suddenly felt embarrassed for being angry. I hadn't even thought about *that* part of the report. Thankfully, some stranger with a badge and a uniform did.

I ended the call and sank my spine into the soft cushions of the sofa. Fingers interlaced behind my head, eyes searching the blurred horizon separating sky and ocean, I contemplated the sharp change in density and composition. On one side of that line you breathe freely, on the other, you drown if you remain too long. The police report that chronicled my sister's murder would be released to me in about two weeks. When I read it, would I be crossing a threshold from which I could not return? Either way, I needed to know. It was time to finish what I had begun nearly three years ago with my search for Mary. It was time to reconcile the past—all of it.

Gusty winds from an approaching cold front rattled the house and broke the Sound into a chaotic chop. Towering clouds stretched tall and dark, grumbled and threatened. The kayak would remain in the backyard that day as I retreated to my writing desk.

I thumbed through the photo album of newspaper articles that Robyn had assembled years back. Articles about when Louise went missing. The search. When she was found. All the court drama including the arrest, court continuances, and finally the sentencing.

Grandma had clipped the articles from the *Telegram and Gazette*, the *Norwich Bulletin*, and the *Webster Times*. Day after day, month after month, and into the following year. Our family had to relive details of Louise's death over and over; a heartless pummeling by the same relentless facts. Like watching a tragedy unfold over and over on the news as you foolishly hope for a fairy-tale ending; I read and re-read the articles hoping that something new would be revealed—something that would make it all make sense, a hint of justice, of hope. But there was nothing new.

I thought back to the magazine article from the mid-80s that included a prison interview with Louise's murderer. The predator insisted that he never meant to kill her. I was enraged, furious. He never *meant* to kill her? She wasn't an insect that was stepped on by accident. She was a loving 16-year-old child.

I wanted to kill *him*. I even imagined that his murder would be a public service to prevent future violence. I felt guilty knowing that it was my choice to allow him to live. That I didn't hunt him down and choke the life out of him. An eye for an eye. I should have sought vengeance. But then I would have been like *him*. Or is that just something I tell myself to quell my guilt? In any case, he's dead. Yet, he's the reason I struggle with this memoir. Even from the grave, he continues to hurt my family. He's the reason my mother worries that her firstborn daughter suffered.

Fists and jaw clenched, temples pounding, part of my anger stemmed from my own regret, not facing him when he got out of jail—maybe to kill him, definitely to let him know I was not afraid of him. The rest of my anger was rooted in resentment toward everyone else who also failed to act on Louise's behalf. The killer's parents who failed to notice the signs of a predator. Friends who didn't warn her. The local media who rehashed details every time the killer went to court. And Mom who just needed it all to end. Not contesting a plea bargain in order to avoid a jury trial and get an immediate sentencing. I understood it. I was still angry. He spent twelve years in jail. And then he was free to live his life as if he never destroyed ours.

A slanted rain began drumming on the window-panes, rinsing a salty film from the glass. The immutable facts remained unchanged. So much anger. So many questions of my own. And then there was Mom's question that needed to be answered most of all: Did Louise suffer?

* * *

On the anniversary of Louise's murder, June 17, 2017, Mom took the photo blanket I gave her last May out of the bedroom closet. She unzipped the plastic storage bag and spread it on the bed. "I'm only going to use it on certain occasions," she said.

I ran my palms over the soft fleece, smoothing out the deep creases. "Use it whenever you like. I have the layout saved. If it gets ruined, I'll order you another one."

Mom treated the blanket in the same way she treated her emotions about Louise, mostly keeping them folded up and stowed away. Within a week, I would come to understand this in a deeper and more compassionate way.

* * *

The following Sunday I tucked my journal and some nail polish into a duffle bag, a few last-minute things before picking up my nieces for the annual sleepover at The Ocean House. Eric stood in the bedroom doorway and tapped the edge of a thick legal-sized manila envelope against the palm of his hand.

"What's that?" I asked as I grazed past him to grab my jacket from the hall.

He was tentative, somber. "I'm sorry for what you will be reading. I'm sorry this happened."

I turned around slowly. My heart felt as if it sank to the floor. The report. "When did they release it?"

On the verge of tears, he looked away and set the police report on the night table—then immediately picked it up again. "Maybe you should leave this here while you're spending time with the girls this weekend."

"Actually, I think that'd be the best time to dig into it. When I'm *not* alone. And when it gets too heavy, I can put it away and focus on my nieces."

"It's been on my desk for almost a week. I kept forgetting to bring it home."

I knew it was more about avoidance and worry than absentmindedness.

He opened the envelope and nervously flipped through the pages of the report. "I skimmed it—didn't read it all. This should fill in a lot of gaps for you. Names you've heard. Places." He set down the report, held my shoulders, and looked into my eyes. "When it gets too much, or when you're thinking about it, promise you'll let me know."

I forced a smile. "I think Louise will be there with me when I read it." The wavering of my voice gave away my fear. I only hoped that would be true.

He nodded, straightened up, and cleared his throat, as if getting into cop mode. "There are statements from your sister Tammy in here. From many people. He was a sick individual. A girl named Debbie, I think her last name was —"

I interrupted him. "Adams. I called her my other *big* sister. She was one of Louise and Tammy's best friends."

"He assaulted other women on several different occasions."

I shook my head. "So. He had a history. I knew it. This never should have happened." I needed to move. To drive. To think. To read.

Eric pulled me close. "I know you're strong, but—"

"I'll be fine. I'd better get going." I tucked the envelope in my duffle bag, gave Eric another hug, and headed out the door with the paper time machine.

I thought about my nieces, the sleepover. Renee's daughter Isabella, and Robyn's daughter Genny are in their mid-teens. Nicole's daughters, Lauren and Sophia, are a few years younger. When they are in my charge, I never let them out of my sight. There are predators out there.

Rage simmered on the backburner in my heart. Sometimes I wanted to smash everything in sight. Sometimes I wanted to hug my family together and seal us into an impenetrable shell. I missed my family. I missed my sister. I was angry at her. I was angry with myself. I had a seething hatred for her killer.

I worried about that offshore storm. I wanted the truth, and I was willing to travel back in time to get it. I hoped it wouldn't drag me back to the past and drown me.

Chapter 29:

Soul on Fire

June 25, 2017

Two states and three towns later, my little Honda CR-V was crammed with an assortment of eight bags, two guitars, four girls, one aunt, and a pet hedgehog—all headed to The Ocean House. I would need this abundance of commotion and youthful innocence to buoy me as I explored life's dark, sinister side. We pulled into the driveway just after noontime. The girls lugged all their bags inside and commenced their takeover of the living room. While they unpacked, I went upstairs, set my laptop on the desk, and tucked the police report in a bureau drawer out of sight.

Footsteps on the stairs. Lauren's voice. "Auntie? Can we go down to the beach?"

"Sure. We have a few hours. Tell everyone to put on sunblock and fill their water bottles." They probably didn't need the reminders at their ages—10, 12, 15, and 16. But I've been close to them since they were babies and tend to deny that they are growing up. In my experience, a happy and peaceful childhood was not guaranteed, and I wanted them to bask in it for as long as possible.

After four hours of soccer, shelling, and swimming, we headed back up the hill to take showers. We planned to attend a fire ceremony that evening. My artist-friend Kwadwo (KWAY-joh) was hosting it for his two sons Kwabena (KWAY-beh-nah) 13 and Kwasi (KWAY-see) 12.

Kwadwo's family is from Northern Ghana, where the fire festival is an annual event. It is rooted in a tale of liberation. The story goes that a chief's son had gone missing and after sunset a massive torch-wielding search ensued. After some time, they found the boy asleep at the base of a large tree. The tribe believed that the tree was evil and must have cast a spell on the boy, so they set it on fire. The idea was not to kill the tree, but to rid it of the evil, allowing forgiveness and renewal.

For Kwabena and Kwasi, part of the ceremony was an "unbaptism" to free them of their religious affiliation. For me it was about the hope of forgiveness, liberation, and renewal—as the police report loomed unread.

* * *

We arrived at Kwadwo's house before sunset and both sides of the road were lined with cars. The yard was a lush green escape nestled among a stand of mature pines and hardwoods. A teepee of boards stood, waiting to be lit, within a stone circle near the middle of the lawn. Guests were milling about and chatting in small clusters. I could hear Kwadwo's laugh. He was stationed at the grill, flipping veggie burgers and tending to a big pot of chili. As soon as he spotted me, Kwadwo wiped his hands on his apron and stretched his arms wide. "Julie! I'm so glad you came!"

"Thanks for the invitation. I brought my nieces along. They're staying with me for the week." I pointed them out. "Genny, Isabella, Lauren, and Sophia. Girls, this is Kwadwo."

They exchanged hellos. "Genny is interested in art. She's considering Montserrat College," I said.

Kwadwo turned to Genny. "Montserrat? Good school. What's your medium? Mine is oil."

Genny fidgeted with the hem on her shirt. "I'm not sure yet. I like everything."

He patted her shoulder. "You've got plenty of time to figure that out. It's nice to meet all of you. Please, wander around. Grab some food and make yourselves at home. I'll start the bonfire a little later."

As the girls and I walked around, I recognized several guests, including Khushi, who led the India retreat, her mom, two of my mentors from the yoga studio, and several others I had met at a backyard barbeque at Khushi's house earlier in May. They were all part of the intricate and strong matrix of support I had built along this journey of reconnection.

After making the social rounds and sampling the pasta salad and vegan chili, the girls and I explored the property. We walked down a grassy slope toward the banks of a trickling brook, shaded by arms of oaks and maples. We made a zigzag path as we hopped from stone to stone upstream. We competed to see who could pluck the smoothest piece of quartz from the glittering grey pebbles that lined the stream bed. It seemed an idyllic setting, until I noticed that the bark on the trees appeared to be shifting, wavering, and crawling.

I bent toward a trunk to inspect. The entire thing was blanketed in an endless army of gypsy moth caterpillars, part of an outbreak that affected large parts of New England. The trees in Thompson had been decimated, but the ones in West Haven were untouched. So I was surprised to see this thick infestation in Bethany, only 20 minutes away. We retreated to the yard where Kwadwo was stuffing the wooden teepee with paper, preparing to light the fire.

As the sun set, he struck at least a dozen matches without success. The girls and I gathered some dry twigs for him and that seemed to help. Before long, the fire was a blazing, snapping, popping ceremonial symbol of cleansing energy. The guests gathered around the perimeter of the fire pit. There were about thirty of us hemmed into the yard, with fireflies and stars overhead, all connected in a circle of support.

Kwadwo passed around a wooden bowl filled with dried flowers, and a basket containing pens and small squares of handmade paper. "Please take a flower and a piece of paper, and write down an intention. Something you'd like to clear away. A bad habit, a worry, a grudge." What did I want to be rid of like the evil in the tree? What did I hope to transform? Or renew?

As people pondered and scribbled, Kwadwo disappeared into the house and returned accompanied by his sons and carrying one of his most prized paintings. He addressed the guests and spoke candidly about his mistakes as a father, and then in more general terms about human faults, hurting others, being hurt, and forgiving.

After the speech, he led a 20-minute guided meditation, during which I kept peeking out of one eye to see how the girls were reacting. They sat still and were respectful of the ceremony. The meditation was followed by a long period of silent contemplation. Kwadwo stood beside the fire, staring at the flames, holding onto an oil painting with both hands. All at once, he straightened his arms and dropped it on the fire. There was a collective gasp from my edge of the circle. I knew that painting was special. It had gotten him into NYU. As we watched the canvas burn, he explained that NYU wasn't a path of *his* choosing. It was one dictated to him, and he wanted to be free of it.

Wow. He may eventually need to have another ceremony to forgive himself for burning that painting.

Following his lead, thirty people stepped up one by one and tossed their intentions and dried flowers into the flames. In the meantime, with all our deep breathing, the mosquitos had found us. And they were hungry.

Kwadwo made his way around the entire circle, hugging and talking with each person, thanking them for being a part of the ceremony. We gathered our things, folded our blanket, and left.

During the 20-minute drive back to The Ocean House, the girls were dozing off and I thought about my intention. I had written down the date of Louise's death. I wanted to understand as much as I possibly could about June 17, 1973, and then burn the evil out of that day. Thich Nhat Hanh said, "If we want to understand someone, we put ourselves into his [or her] skin. The only way to understand fully is to become the object of our understanding." I wanted to understand Louise and the choices she made that led to her death. I had no interest in trying to understand the killer. But could I forgive?

I pondered the definition, trying to find a feasible angle of approach. Forgiveness means to stop feeling anger toward someone or to stop feeling anger about something that happened.

I needed to forgive Louise. I needed to forgive the day. I needed to forgive myself.

* * *

We got back from Kwadwo's house after eleven. "Pajama and toothbrush time," I announced. Groans filtered through the living room, which looked like a yard sale of clothes, shoes, books, and toiletries. "Come on. I'll help you set up the beds first."

They giggled and whacked each other with the couch cushions as they pulled out the sofa bed. While the other girls gathered blankets and pillows from the closet, Genny rummaged through the DVDs on the bookshelf. "Auntie, can we watch a movie?"

"Hmmm. I thought you guys were tired?"

She gave me a world-class pout.

"Make sure it's PG-13." I'm such a pushover.

She clapped her hands together, turned to the other girls, and waved a DVD over her head. "Okay, ladies, how about *Ratatouille*? It's Disney."

Whoop-whoops all around. Sophia stood near the cot, brushing her hair. "Can we have popcorn too?" A chorus of begging, "Oh-please-please-please. With extra butter?"

I smiled and shook my head. "A spoiled quartet. Let me dig out the hot air popper."

While the kernels were popping, I melted some butter in the microwave. When I removed the dish and set it on the counter, it spontaneously shattered in a spray of butter and glass fragments. I jumped back in surprise, confused at what made it explode. Engrossed in the movie, the girls didn't notice. I wiped up the butter, swept the floor and plucked ceramic splinters from the fibers of the rug.

As I took a step to empty the dustpan, I winced and grabbed my ankle, lifting the sole of my foot to see blood oozing out around a shard lodged in my left heel. I grabbed a pair of salad tongs and quickly tugged. A bright red trickle formed drops that fell and splattered on the hardwood floor. I wrapped my foot in a towel, washed my hands and hobbled into the living room with two large bowls of popcorn. "If you guys want butter, you're on your own. Just don't use glass in the microwave."

They barely looked away from the TV but gave a collective round of "Thank you."

I stepped gingerly up the stairs and pulled open the drawer to get my pajamas. The police report was sitting on top of my clothes. Stamped at the bottom of the cover page was the date it was retrieved from storage. I hadn't noticed before—May 17, 2017—my birthday.

I filled the foot spa with warm, soapy water, submerged my wounded foot, and sat down to read. The 248-page case file began with a 26-page summary of the most relevant witness interviews and events leading to Louise's death and the killer's arrest.

It began with the killer's cowardly, partial confession where he stated that he and Louise had left a party together. I knew that. He also stated they had drinks at a bar. And a waitress saw them leave arm in arm. *That* I did *not* know. Why did Louise trust him?

The summary continued with witness statements from Mom and Dad. Details of conversations between them and the killer. How Dad identified Louise at the hospital because Mom wasn't sure. The girl didn't look like Louise. But there was the cut on the bottom of the girl's foot, exactly like the one Louise got just days before she went missing. Mom had described it to me on one of our boat rides around the lake. "She cut it on a piece of glass, swimming at the towers. It was a nasty cut. She soaked it in warm water and put peroxide on it."

I swirled my foot in the basin of water. Louise—are you trying to get my attention? Trying to let me know that you're here with me as I read this?

* * *

That night, I managed to get through the first 26 pages and flipped through the rest to get an idea of how it was structured. The remainder of the case file consisted of individual daily reports from each officer and detective that worked on the case. Much of it seemed repetitive, disorganized, and overwhelming. I would need to take it bit by bit.

For the next few nights, when my nieces were settled into the safety of a dead-bolted, curtain-drawn sleep, I planned to sequester myself upstairs by the privacy of my desk lamp and read subsequent sections of the case file. I wanted to understand Louise's death, to make some kind of peace with her choices. I knew I would have to read about the killer. I knew my hatred would surface. I also knew that as much as I would be taking care of my nieces that week, they would also be helping me to find my way back to the light, after disappearing into the darkness of those pages.

To burn the evil without killing the tree. That was my task. I had to find a way to burn the anger within me and not destroy myself in the process.

Chapter 30:

Two Hundred and Forty-Eight Pages of Truth

There is nothing that my hometown of Thompson is famous for. Most people, unless from the area or familiar with the 70s NASCAR circuit, have never heard of it. Our little town was so peaceful and still that at night, unless there was a race at the speedway, the only sounds were the spring peepers and the cows as they swished their tails. Crime was rare in our small town. But that year, 1973, violence, both natural and man-made, seemed to close in on us; an invasion of monsters that could reach down from the sky with their inescapable wringing grasp, splintering lives and homes.

In any given year, Connecticut might experience one tornado. The year that Louise was killed, there were eight. Tornadoes have the highest wind speeds of any natural hazard, and the destruction they cause is unmistakable, cutting a precise path as if consciously selecting, planning, and executing. These killers have no conscience or compassion. They have no remorse or regret. There was a ninth tornado that year, but it wasn't recorded by the National Weather Service. It was a heartless monster with a history of violence toward women.

* * *

Arthur Richard Taylor. Each night, as I turned the pages of the report, I read about this abomination of a man. Originally, I imagined the investigation would be mostly about Louise, but it was focused on the main suspect, Taylor. I combined details in the report with what I already gleaned from Mom, Dad, Tammy, and officers who had worked Louise's case. And what I learned made me sick.

He grew up in the quiet corner of Northeast Connecticut and graduated from Tourtellotte Memorial High School in the mid-60s. The same high school Louise would have graduated from in 1974, if he hadn't murdered her.

After graduation, Taylor joined the military and fought two tours in the Vietnam War. He volunteered for a third tour, but by then, the Army knew better and refused to send him back. Taylor went AWOL, landing in Tampa, Florida. He married a woman named Annette in 1969, and they had a son.

During the first year of their marriage, he revealed a violent and bizarre disdain for female hitchhikers. Taylor repeated a story to several people about a female friend of his who was picked up hitchhiking and later found dead, with her throat cut. The tale implied that he was either a witness or the one wielding the knife. In either case, when Taylor moved back to Connecticut in 1970, there was a monster among us.

His spree of violence in Thompson began in September of 1971 when Taylor picked up a 21-year-old acquaintance, Donna, who was hitchhiking. She smiled and thanked him for stopping. He ranted that she should know better, threatened her with a knife, bound her hands and feet, and drove around with her in the trunk of his car "to teach her a lesson." Taylor told Donna that the last hitchhiker he picked up he had hung from a tree until she was almost dead.

Three months later, his violence and perversion escalated when he picked up an 18-year-old hitchhiker. As with Donna, Taylor held a knife to her throat and tied her hands, but this time he brought the girl to a secluded area in Thompson and raped her. The 18-year-old did not know Taylor. She reported the attack but could not identify him to police at the time.

In 1972 he was arrested for unlawful restraint from the September '71 incident with Donna. His wife Annette left him. Several times throughout their three-year marriage, she urged Taylor to see a psychiatrist, but he refused. To save the marriage, he finally agreed, and Annette moved back in. One evening about two weeks later, Taylor had been drinking and flew into a rage when she refused to have sex with him. He grabbed her by the neck and tried to strangle her. Luckily, Taylor's sister, Debby, was staying at the house, heard Annette's screams, and ran into the bedroom to physically pry his hands from Annette's throat.

After the assault, they divorced, and Taylor lived with a woman named Linda for three months. His cold-hearted and violent nature quickly became evident as he bragged to Linda about the assault on Donna, referring to it as "teaching her a lesson for hitchhiking." While with Linda, he intentionally shot himself through the hand "just to see if it would hurt." Apparently, Taylor reacted with a smirk and claimed it "didn't hurt at all."

Linda left him after an incident that took place outside a local bar. They had been inside drinking for a few hours, and Linda was chatting with a male friend she had known for years. Taylor was unusually quiet. As soon as they walked out, he pushed her against a wall and threatened that if she "ever did that again she would never see her twenty-first birthday."

During the same time period, he also started hanging around at the Butts farm in Woodstock, where Tammy and Louise met him. Many of their friends who hung around at the farm regarded Taylor as "a little strange," but others were hoodwinked. He told elaborate tales about the war and about living in Florida—experiences and places that captured the small-town, teenage imagination.

In the fall of 1972, the 25-year-old Taylor dated one of Louise and Tammy's best friends, the 15-year-old girl I knew as *my other big sister,*

Debbie. After they broke up, he found perverse delight in terrorizing her. Taylor shot at Debbie and her friend Karen with a pellet gun and threatened to hang them from a tree. They were afraid to say anything; they thought no one would believe them. It was still a dark time for women's equality, and this sleepy northeast section of Connecticut called "the quiet corner," has certainly never been a bellwether for political activism.

Taylor had no permanent place to live, squatting at a shack near the farm in exchange for work, crashing at his parents' house, or trespassing at a camp trailer in the East Thompson woods on Quaddick Lake. The camp was in a densely wooded section of the state forest, and the only access in or out was through a narrow, winding hidden drive. It looked and smelled forgotten, air heavy with the mold of a leaky roof and vines clinging to the soffits. The owner lived in Rhode Island and hadn't used the trailer in years. If you were predisposed to evil, it was the perfect place to hide sin.

The following April, Taylor met a 17-year-old girl at a party in Dudley, Massachusetts. She was there to celebrate her aunt's engagement. Taylor didn't know the aunt; he crashed the party and convinced the girl to leave with him. Once he had her alone, Taylor took the girl to the camp trailer, tied her up, and raped her. Before letting her go, he shoved her against the wall, pressed a piece of rawhide to her throat, and threatened to kill her.

She went with her parents to the Dudley police station the following day to report the crime. But she didn't know the rapist's name and didn't know which town the camp trailer was located in.

It may seem inconceivable that he was roaming around, free to prey on naïve teenage girls. But at that time, there was less communication between police departments, and fewer resources at their disposal. This was the early seventies—thirteen years before DNA testing and twenty-one years before Connecticut created its first sex offender registry. It wasn't until 2008 that the Violent Criminal Apprehension Program

(ViCAP) made its database available to all law enforcement agencies, allowing them to access and update cases.

This was 1973. And Taylor's latest victim, the 17-year-old he took away from the party, was from out of state. She didn't know where she had been taken and didn't know the identity of her attacker. Police would not connect Taylor with this crime until they investigated Louise's death, less than two months later.

* * *

Sunday June 17, 1973

It was a typical Sunday at The Compound, except that it was Father's Day. Mom had made pancakes, Dad's favorite. My step-brothers were visiting from Webster, and we had to squeeze nine kids, aged 4 to 16 years, and two parents around the table. The energy we generated from the commotion—arguing, laughing, tattling, goading, and jabbing—could have powered a small country. Louise and Tammy, the oldest two of our clan, usually trailed the rest, but the scent of coffee and bacon effectively stirred them from their nightly teenage hibernation.

That Sunday morning, neither of them was interested in lingering at breakfast, and Louise got right to the point. "Hey, Mom, can me and Tammy go to the Butts farm today? They're having a pig roast."

Mom looked around the table. "Who has dish duty?"

Shane grumbled and slid his chair backward. "Ugh. I do."

Mom turned to Louise. "Make sure you're both home by eleven. You have school tomorrow."

"Okay." She grinned, grabbed two strips of bacon, and ran back up to her room. Tammy followed.

Louise had her license and a car, and in only a week, she would have finished her junior year of high school. Her honor society induction certificate hung on the wall, next to the one for perfect attendance. Situated on her bureau, just below the awards, an incense burner sat ready to mask the stench of an occasional joint. Despite being an introvert, Louise had a busy life. When she wasn't at work or school, she spent time with her sibs or among her large group of friends. That Sunday in June was no exception.

Louise put on a comfy pair of patched, hip-hugger bell-bottom jeans, and a flower-print sleeveless blouse. She brushed her shoulder length, straight blonde hair, sliced a perfect middle part, and tucked each side behind her ears. Propping her left foot on the laundry hamper, she pulled the Band-Aid from her heel and inspected the cut. The hydrogen peroxide fizzed, foamed, and stung a bit as she tipped the bottle. *Drip, drip, drip*, on the cut. She put on a fresh Band-Aid and slid her feet under the red, buckled straps of her Dr. Scholl's sandals.

It was just before noon when our pretty, petite, 16-year-old climbed into her pea-green '64 Nash Rambler with her younger sister Tammy. They were ready for an afternoon of teenage life in the 70s: peace, love, and good vibes. I hope I said goodbye. I hope I told her I loved her. But I don't remember. I was busy with my 4-year-old Evel Knievel antics, riding my big wheel in the driveway, trying to spin out in the gravel like the commercials on TV. It seemed like any other day. "Happy Father's Day!" Louise called out as she and Tammy drove off.

Louise and Tammy picked up Debbie and their friend Karen and met a few others at Stratton's Spa, a popular hangout in town. A mini-caravan of teens with fake IDs drove to Webster to buy beer, Boone's Farm apple wine, and a dime-bag of pot. When all the people and paraphernalia were gathered, they headed to the Butts farm.

The roads are like kiddie-coasters in Woodstock. They cut through large, low mounds of rolling farmland, where the population of cows is greater than people. A large plume of smoke was like a beacon, visible at least a quarter-mile away. Nothing the Butts family does is subtle. As they passed the farmhouse and the barn, the smell of cow manure, cigarettes, and roast pig greeted them. Parking was haphazard along the stone wall at one end of the hay field, and there were a dozen cars and pickup trucks there when Louise and Tammy and their friends arrived.

Nearly fifty people had already gathered around the glowing fire pit in rowdy clusters spanning three generations: Grandfather Butts, Mother and Father Butts, and six of their ten children. Each age group had invited friends as well. There were people sitting on coolers, in lawn chairs, or on tree stumps, wavering in various states of inebriation, swearing, arguing, and laughing. Distorted Jimi Hendrix, Black Sabbath, and Led Zeppelin blared from the 8-track player of a pickup truck parked near the fire. It was a mash of farm boots, hand-drawn tattoos, pony tails, patched jeans, and black leather vests with rawhide stitching, decorated with Hell's Angels or Vigilante insignia. The guest of honor was the whole pig, skewered and tended by Father Butts as he turned the spit occasionally, in between swigs of beer.

The nearby woods were a welcomed escape from the fireside frenzy, where teens could pare away from the adults into smaller groups. They shared marijuana or sometimes acid or speed which their older friends bought and encouraged them to experiment with. Tammy was hanging around with Debbie and Karen, giggling about different boys at the party. Louise went for a walk along a narrow cow path into the woods with one of her friends, Roy Wonoski, who had a crush on her.

Louise had also spent a lot of time talking with Chris Butts and his friend, Taylor, around the fire and in the woods. Taylor was building rapport, consciously selecting, planning, and executing. Getting Louise to trust him. A couple hours into the party, he had convinced Louise that they should leave and go build a campfire.

Around 7:00 pm, the party imploded in typical Butts fashion as Mother and Father Butts and their friends were staggering drunk and on the verge of a melee. The younger kids knew well enough to leave before they were kicked out. It was Louise's friend Donald's birthday, and a few of them boarded an old blue school bus to continue the celebration elsewhere. Warren, who owned the bus, turned to Taylor. "We'll meet you at the bar at King's Inn."

Taylor followed Louise as she walked toward the parked cars in the open field. Tammy stopped him. "Where are you going?"

He took a drag from his cigarette. "We're going out in the woods to build a campfire," he replied, not mentioning the King's Inn.

Tammy watched them walk away.

A chill descended with the setting sun. Debbie approached Louise who was talking with Chris Butts and Taylor near the Rambler and tapped her on the shoulder. "Hey, can I get my coat from your car?"

Debbie followed Louise around to the driver's side as Taylor got in the passenger seat. Louise reached for the coat and handed it to Debbie.

"Thanks," Debbie said, backing up as Louise got into the Rambler. Clutching the coat with both hands, she crouched down and asked, "Where are you guys going?"

Taylor didn't respond. Louise repeated what Taylor had told Tammy. "We're going to make a campfire."

Louise pulled out of the field and headed to the King's Inn to meet Warren and her friends. She was unaware they had changed plans and decided to go to the Slovak Club in Webster instead.

* * *

Louise sat at the King's Inn bar with Taylor, sipped on a Coffee Sombrero, and waited almost two hours for the blue bus to arrive. It was dark out when they left the King's Inn arm-in-arm.

Still wondering why her friends hadn't shown up, Louise and Taylor stopped by the towers around 11:00 pm to see if Warren might have taken the other kids to hang out there. As they left the towers, still under the guise of building a campfire, Taylor was behind the wheel. He drove down Quaddick Town Farm Road, past the state park and turned left onto Baker Road, a narrow, dirt road that cut into the dense forest and around Quaddick Lake.

While Taylor drove Louise further into isolation, Mom was rushing Little Mary to the emergency room at Day Kimball Hospital with an asthma attack. Mom's worry was focused on Little Mary. She had no reason to think that *Louise* might be in danger.

Shortly after Mom reached the ER, Tammy arrived home from the Butts' party, alone.

"Where's Louise?" Dad asked.

"I don't know. She left before me."

Sometime around 11:30 pm, Taylor brought Louise to the camp trailer. Louise sat on the grass near the water, by the bright light of a waning gibbous moon that had been full just two days before. She gazed out at the moonlight reflecting off the water, alone at a trailer deep in the woods, not knowing that a serial rapist sat beside her. Not knowing this was the same trailer where he had assaulted a 17-year-old girl, just two months earlier.

Monday morning around 1:00am, Mom brought Little Mary home from the ER. Louise's Rambler was not in the yard, and Mom's worry returned, now focused on Louise.

* * *

The sun rose at 5:16 am and Tammy had hardly slept. She waited until 6:00 am and called Louise's best friend, Liz. "Louise didn't come home last night. Do you know where she could be? The last time I saw her was when she left the Butts farm with Taylor."

"I dunno. Haven't heard from her."

"I'm going to look for her after school. Can you help?"

"Sure."

After Tammy left for school, Mom called the police barracks. "My daughter is missing. She went out last night and hasn't come home yet."

"How old is your daughter?" the dispatcher asked.

"She's sixteen."

"When did you last see her?"

"My other daughter Tammy saw her around seven last night."

"Has she ever run away before?"

Mom tried to remain calm. "She didn't run away. She went to a pig roast and didn't come home."

"We typically don't start searching until she's been missing for twenty-four hours. If she doesn't come home this afternoon, you can come to the police barracks and fill out a missing person's report."

Mom hung up. She brought me and Little Mary to Grandma and Dziadzia's house, and then went out looking for Louise.

* * *

Tammy had gotten home from school at 12:30 pm. Still no Louise. She started calling all their friends. Everyone who had a car picked up a couple of other kids and drove around Thompson and the surrounding towns looking, asking, hoping.

At 4:00 pm, Taylor called Tammy, claiming that he and Louise left the party and headed to a bar in Oxford, but she was drunk and had been driving recklessly. He claimed he asked her to pull over and let him out, and in the early morning hours, he walked about 15 miles back to the shack in Woodstock.

Something about the story was off. Tammy questioned his timing. "You left the party around seven. Oxford is only a fifteen-minute drive. Why didn't you get out of the car until early morning?"

He quickly changed his story. "Oh yeah, it was around nine-thirty or ten."

Tammy had a bad feeling.

* * *

At 5:30 pm, Dad got home from work to find Louise still wasn't home. Tammy relayed the story Taylor had told her about last seeing Louise in Oxford, Massachusetts. There was no AMBER alert program in 1973. Mom and Dad drove to the local police departments near Oxford to let them know that Louise was missing. After 24-hours, they went to the state police barracks in Danielson and filed a missing person's report. Police officially joined the search.

After Mom and Dad returned home Monday evening, a few of Louise's friends stopped over to see if there was any news. Cars in and out of the driveway, each time headlights glared through the living room window, they held their breath—was it Louise?

Liz picked up Taylor, his sister, and another friend, and they had searched around Oxford, Auburn, and Worcester. Taylor was the only one who knew they were looking in the wrong places. At 9:00 pm they stopped at The Compound. Taylor sat at the kitchen table across from Mom and Dad, looked them in the face and said, "Louise will come home."

Tammy knew he was lying about something. After Liz and Taylor left, Tammy sat down with Dad and revealed every hangout and party spot in town. They spent the entire next day, Tuesday, scouring each of those locations for some trace of Louise.

✳ ✳ ✳

By 9:00 am on Wednesday, Dad, Tammy, and her friend Karen were already combing the Douglas State Forest in Massachusetts.

Shortly after 11:00 am, while they were still in Douglas, a botanist from the University of Rhode Island was walking in the woods off Wakefield Pond Road in East Thompson, looking for wild orchids. He found the body of a teenage girl.

The state police tracked Mom down at the dentist office where she had taken me, Mary, Kevin, and Shane. Officers asked Mom to meet them in the parking lot of Grant's department store; they had some news about the case. They needed her to identify the young girl found among the wildflowers.

While we were transported in the police cruiser to the hospital morgue, troopers picked up Taylor at his parent's house and brought him to the barracks for questioning.

Before Mom went in the room to attempt an ID, an officer had told her the girl was wearing a high school class ring and he mistakenly said the initials inside were LRT instead of LAT.

"Those aren't her initials," Mom replied. "Her middle name is Anne."

I remember spinning around the support columns in the basement of the hospital, like they were maypoles. One of the detectives shouted to a security guard at the hospital, "Hey, watch those kids!" Shane picked me up and scolded me, but I had no idea what was happening.

While I gleefully circled the maypole, Mom was in the morgue trying to force her eyes to focus on a sight that no parent should ever have to see. She stared at a cut on the girl's left foot. It looked exactly like the one Louise had gotten. "I'm not sure. That's not her. I don't think that person is my daughter."

At 5:00 pm, Dad arrived at the hospital, talked quietly with Mom, and agreed to view the girl's body in an attempt to identify her. Yes. The girl was our Louise. Any trace of hope obliterated.

* * *

On Thursday, a cold, numb silence descended on The Compound and took the place of warm pancakes, commotion, and raucous laughter. It wasn't long before jarring headlines stared up at us from the permanent black ink of all the local papers: "Thompson Girl Found Slain," "Thompson Girl Murder Victim," and there were others. The headlines were different, but the articles parroted the same cold, immutable facts that refused to let us be. Grating on my family's nerves like my incessant

4-year-old curiosity driving me to ask the same question probably thousands of times—where's Louise?

In the late morning, someone from Woodstock reported an abandoned car on a dirt path near their home. It was Louise's Rambler, with her red Dr. Scholl's still patiently waiting on the floor of the passenger side, just where she had left them.

The day after Louise was found, hours after her car was recovered, Mom had to starch her dress, don her heels, and attend Shane's eighth-grade graduation. Whispers about the mother of the murdered girl, distance, avoidance, no eye contact. As if she had a contagious disease. Time and life and people can all be so heartless. Events are compressed together, crashing into each other, a senseless jumble of tragedy and celebration, without precedent or etiquette.

When I was younger, I remember wishing that Mom was softer, more vulnerable. Now I understand why that was not possible. She would have completely fallen to pieces.

The days that followed generated new headlines, most of which referred to our honor student with perfect attendance, warm-hearted sister, and firstborn daughter as *the murdered girl*—"Autopsy of Murdered Girl," "Funeral Saturday for Murdered Girl." Only one headline referred to her by name—"Sweet Sixteen and Louise is Buried." It was written by a woman.

* * *

Amidst an already unimaginable experience, the case file revealed a storm of confusion. Crime dramas on TV present neat linear facts and unambiguous evidence, but real life is messy. People make mistakes, lie, keep dangerous secrets, and trust when they shouldn't.

A Thompson resident had mistakenly reported seeing Louise hitchhiking the day after she went missing. Someone else claimed that

Louise's car was parked in a friend's driveway the morning after the party at the Butts farm. That was a mistake too.

When interviewed, several of Taylor's acquaintances said they had seen him in both Rhode Island and Massachusetts bars the night of Louise's death. He had been at none of those places.

There was also a fatal hit-and-run accident in the area, the same night of Louise's death. Once her body was found, townspeople made wild speculations that Taylor had caused the accident and then tried to cover it up by murdering the witness. Police quickly ruled out any connection, but the rumors lived on.

Despite the misinformation that muddied and slowed the investigation, there were also a few key discoveries that helped police make significant progress on the case.

Thursday, June 21st, during a police interview, an acquaintance of Taylor told police that Taylor had bragged about a rape that occurred in April, two months before Louise's death. They contacted the girl, and since they had a picture to show her, she was able to identify Taylor as the rapist who assaulted her. With additional details from Taylor's acquaintance, she also confirmed that the camp trailer in East Thompson was the scene of the crime.

Police searched the trailer and directed fireman to pump out an open well on the property. They recovered Louise's purse and a grey plaid flannel shirt belonging to Taylor. Investigators concluded it was both the scene of the rape in April, and Louise's murder in June.

But by the time police went to arrest Taylor, he had fled the state, with help from his sister. They sent a be-on-the-lookout (BOLO) message over the teletype to all state and local agencies requesting assistance in apprehending the fugitive.

* * *

Louise's wake was Friday evening from 7:00 to 9:00 pm on June 22nd and her funeral was held on Saturday morning. The line of people stretched down the sidewalk, around the building, and into the parking lot. Louise's friends from Thompson, Woodstock, Putnam, and Webster, her classmates, teachers, family, and friends of the family filed into St. Joseph's church, as six of her closest male friends carried her casket. They gathered to say goodbye to Louise, who liked to read *Seventeen* magazine, hang out with her friends, and buy pretty clothes. Louise who had a part-time job at Bates Shoe Factory after school to pay for her own car. Louise who would remain sweet sixteen forever.

On June 24 at 8:30 pm, the New York State Police arrested Taylor hitchhiking on the NY state thruway at exit 45 near Canandaigua. Considering his disdain for hitchhikers, it was ironic that he was picked up while hitchhiking. Police cuffed him and now he would be the one held against his will. The following day he was extradited to Connecticut.

The judge denied bail, and on June 26, after speaking with a priest, Taylor finally gave a partial confession and was charged with Louise's murder. In the newspaper photo he looked worse than a rabid animal. A cowardly parasite with his head lowered, hiding behind a dark curtain of hair and a bushy beard.

The case was continued several times. Initially, a public defender was not available and later they had to wait for a court-ordered mental examination. Each continuance brought new rounds of headlines and articles rife with the same sharp details that cut over and over. As the case dragged on, with each day and each delay our family had to re-live the murder of our Louise. We were victims of the public's right to know.

The whole experience was so awful that when the killer accepted a plea bargain, my family was relieved. Because even though it meant a reduced sentence, at least we could escape the humiliating magnifying glass of a widely publicized jury trial.

On April 5, 1974, the following spring, Taylor was sentenced to 10-20 years in state prison on a charge of manslaughter in the first degree, in Windham County Superior Court. The state's attorney, in his summation of facts, described the killer as "a cold, heartless individual who gets his sexual kicks forcing himself upon young girls." He added that Louise "made the mistake of resisting."

* * *

The shock of Louise's death never subsided. It seeped into our bones and became part of all of us. Later, and for decades after—there were triggers. For Tammy, they included an intense fear of being alone. She moved to the Butts farm three weeks after Louise's body was found. She couldn't stand all the empty space at The Compound.

A few months after the sentencing, Mom ran into Taylor's parents at the grocery store. Slowly, they pushed their shopping cart alongside hers and waited for her to notice. "We are so sorry about your daughter," Mrs. Taylor said quietly.

Mom glanced up at the dark beady eyes that met hers. She recognized Mrs. Taylor, but all she could think of were those eyes – staring at her from across her kitchen table and the voice that said, "Louise will come home." Mom nodded.

"We didn't raise him to be that way," Mr. Taylor added.

"I know. Thank you for saying that," Mom said as she nodded again and looked away. She pushed her cart around the next corner into June of 1973, left her groceries, and walked out.

After reading the case file, I understood those triggers more deeply and gained a sense of how many there were. They rippled out far from the epicenter of June 17th, to the first hint of summer's approach. Father's Day, a high school class ring, a cut on the foot, an article about child abduction or murder, dark thoughts that filter into the mind when someone is late, or a TV crime drama episode about a serial rapist.

And never again would I look at certain things the same. A plaid flannel shirt on the man sitting across from me on the train is now like the one Taylor wore. The one that was retrieved from the well. Seeing Dr. Scholl's sandals used to make me smile and think of my sister wearing them. Now I see my niece admiring them in the thrift shop and stop short of convincing her not to buy them as they remind Mom, Tammy, and me of the last pair of shoes that Louise wore. The pair that was found as she left them, on the passenger side floor of her car, hours before her death, when she perhaps slipped them off to check the cut on the bottom of her foot. The one that would never have a chance to heal.

Now I know where Mom goes when she stares off into space, and I know why she goes there alone. A wise person once said, "We grow up thinking that our parents will never understand our struggles, but the truth is that they invest much time making sure that we never feel theirs. "

The strength, grace, and composure Mom and Dad exhibited throughout the ordeal was profound. To read the depth and detail in their statements, how they responded to impossible questions, how they searched for Louise, how *everyone* searched for her. It made me realize that people *did* step up on Louise's behalf to try to get justice for her. They helped her keep the last promise she made: "You're not gonna get away with this." They helped her save countless other potential victims.

But justice was short-lived. Taylor was discharged from prison after twelve years, on September 20, 1985. The reason for his release was "sentence time served." He moved back to the area right after I began my junior year of high school. Sweet sixteen. The same age Louise was when she was murdered.

Within a year, Taylor was arrested for drunk driving and leaving the scene of an accident. In 1989, he was arrested again and sent back to jail for possession of a firearm. Shortly after completing that jail stint, he moved to Florida, claiming he was a victim of police harassment. Right. *He* was the victim.

On July 14, 1991, Taylor finally had the decency to die. Although *how* that happened remains unclear. As I sat at my writing desk biting my fingernails, I read and re-read his obituary countless times. It stated that he died "unexpectedly at home," but like much of the obituary, that was probably bullshit. It portrayed him as a regular honest person—a war hero, and a fisherman for the past two-and-a-half years, leaving behind parents, sisters, and a son.

A war hero? What an insult to all dignified servicemen and women. The army recognized what he was. He didn't fight for a cause. He fought for the pleasure he took in hurting and killing others. He wasn't a fisherman either. He was a drug-dealing, psychopathic serial rapist and murderer who preyed on teenage girls.

Initially, I was fuming. But in reviewing the obituary more carefully, I noticed a detached quality in the writing. Like the case file, it was a *just-the-facts* type of report, even though there were few "facts" in it. One bit of truth could be inferred by what was *left out*. There was no mention of a *loving* family or any single person on earth who would miss him. It was just a standard obligatory notice.

Still, that didn't negate the fact that when he was released from prison, he had a new chance at life. A chance that he stole from Louise. How was *that* justice? Many people posed that same question, and a few may have personally tried to tip the scales.

Uncle Bruce had threatened to kill Taylor several times. After the sentencing, Bruce intentionally got arrested and sent to jail for the sole purpose of beating him up. And he succeeded. When Taylor was discharged, Bruce kept track of his whereabouts and stopped Taylor as he was about to go into the department store where I worked. "If I ever see you here again, I'll break both your legs." On his death bed last year, Bruce called my brother Shane saying he wanted to make a confession. But he never got the chance.

And then there was Roy Wonoski. He had a crush on Louise, had taken her out on several occasions, and spent precious time with her at the party before she left with Taylor. He also had an anger management problem. Taylor had claimed that after Louise's body was found, Roy came to his parent's house and threatened to cut his throat.

I wonder where Bruce and Roy were when Taylor took his last undeserved breath. Did either of them visit Tallahassee in the summer of 1991?

When news reached Connecticut that Taylor was dead, rumors began circulating. Mom said someone told her that Taylor was found on the floor of a grimy trailer, stabbed to death. His throat was cut, and he was left to die—the supposed fate of his hitchhiker friend in Florida in 1970.

There were so many questions, so much uncertainty. I wanted to reach out to one of the detectives who had worked on the case, but I was too riddled with anxiety to do it. And by amazing chance, as if someone deliberately crossed our paths, I ran into him at the grocery store as I was first writing this chapter. I wanted to know how the monster died, where he was buried. The detective offered to help get whatever information he could. I had forgotten to give him my phone number, so he stopped by Mom's house to get it. She called me after he left.

"Julie, Detective Guillot stopped by here. What did you want to know about Louise? You could have asked me, you know."

I thought she was mad at me for snooping around. "I wanted to know how the piece of filth died. I wanted to know if he really got his throat cut."

Mom was silent for a moment, then responded. "Did he?"

"It didn't seem so, but he was pretty beat up when they found him." The entire truth may never be known, as his death was not investigated, but I relayed to her everything I had found out. The official cause listed on his death certificate was a massive heart attack, but that seemed impossible for a heartless monster. Through public records, reports, statements, and conversations with detectives, I pieced together the day humanity was scrubbed clean of his existence.

After his move to Tallahassee in '89, Taylor had continued his parasitic, drug-ridden life in a rural tumbledown trailer park. His nickname was "moccasin," and he spent his days "hanging out" with other unsavory characters who vanished immediately after his death. He hid behind the alias of Charles Michael McGregor, and when he spoke to young girls on his street, they ran.

The last time Taylor was seen alive, he had been walking along Joe Thomas Road, away from the trailer park. Two men who lived in the area, Will and Jerry, were at Will's house, working on a lawn tractor and noticed Taylor walk by around 10 am. They didn't speak to him. Will's granddaughter, Christy, had also seen Taylor walking along the road. Around 11:30 am, she was playing in the yard at a friend's house down the street when Taylor stopped and said "hi" to her. She ran to her grandfather Will's house a few blocks away.

An hour later, Will and Jerry drove toward town to get a part for the tractor, when Jerry spotted a body in the woods, not far from Will's driveway, about 75 feet off the road. Jerry pointed to the woods. "Look—do you see it? "

Will stopped the car. The body was face down in the dirt and its shirt was hiked up like it had been dragged there. "Wait to see if it moves," Will said. It did not.

"Hey. Is he dead?" Jerry asked.

Will turned around and went back to his house to notify the police. They returned to the scene and waited. EMTs and fire personnel arrived first and rolled the body over. The ID on the body was that of Charles Michael McGregor. There was a bloody gash on his forehead and blood on his hands.

The cause of death was clearly more involved than a simple heart attack. What prompted it? How did he get the cut on his head? And who dragged his body? Was it an altercation followed by a drug overdose? Was someone teaching him a lesson? Exacting justice? Charles Michael McGregor, AKA Arthur Richard Taylor, was attempting to hide his lewd and violent past. But the stink of his own rotten heart finally betrayed him.

His landlord knew his true identity and approached police after Taylor's death to enlighten them. Who else knew Taylor's criminal history as a child predator, rapist, and murderer? Did Will know? Why did Will's granddaughter Christy run away from Taylor? Had he approached Christy before?

Maybe there was some justice after all.

* * *

In the early morning hours of June 30, 2017, the fifth and final day of the sleepover, long after my nieces were dreaming of unicorns and rainbows, I finished reading the report of my sister's murder.

The final pages consisted of possessed property forms—lists of catalogued items that belonged to Louise or Taylor that had been seized as evidence. After the case was closed, the property was released back to the families upon their signing a receipt form.

The first of the forms had Taylor's father's signature and listed the items he picked up: a large folding knife, a five-foot length of rawhide, a twelve-foot length of rope, a blanket, a plaid flannel shirt, an army rifle, and a sawed-off shotgun.

The last several pages listed items that belonged to Louise: her high school class ring, a blue plastic peace symbol, an address book, a hairbrush, a round compact of Yardley cheek gloss, notes about operating a machine for her job at the shoe factory, and a brown leather change purse. I stared at Dad's signature at the bottom of the receipt, imagining the emotional burden of his task—driving to the police station to pick up the ghostly remnants of Louise's life—blonde strands still wound around the bristles of her hairbrush.

I recognized some of the same lonely items I had felt drawn to decades before. Items that were stowed away for years at The Compound, old memories out of sight, alongside Great-Grandma's old porcelain dolls with the demonic teeth, and Mary's jewelry box with the twirling ballerina, all tucked side by side within the cedar chest.

I thumbed through the final pages of property forms over and over. That was it? I flipped back and forth through the report several times, and finally went downstairs to make a cup of tea. As the tea kettle whined and hummed, I leaned against the archway between the kitchen and living room and watched my four not-so-little angels sleeping peacefully, safely.

I had stayed up each night until about two am, for the better part of a week, mining each sentence in the case file. I flagged paragraphs, highlighted key interviews, and typed out a painstakingly detailed timeline. I knew I would eventually reach the end, but it still hit me hard. Because it was such an abrupt end—to both Louise and to being immersed in her world.

I recalled names and smiles, bedtime stories, incense, and mini-bike rides that went along with them. People whom I loved and who loved me. The report helped me understand why I felt so disconnected in the present. I had lost that family, I missed them terribly, and until recently, I had denied the depth of that pain.

Denial sustained the contract of silence, the saddest wall that can ever be built. After 44 years, I had finally taken steps to dismantle that contract. I never expected that the police report would be a catalyst to grief. And there was something else I hadn't expected. I still had questions.

The case file covered the *facts* of Louise's death, and the unrelenting effort to catch a heartless killer. It did not and could not bring me into

Louise's inner thoughts and explain *why* someone like her, so smart and independent, would take such a tremendous risk to be alone with Taylor.

Most importantly, because he didn't give a full confession, it also did not answer Mom's question—did she suffer?

But the report reminded me that I had an extended family of *other* big sisters out there. People who loved me and would probably be willing to help. Louise and I had some friends in common. It was about time I reached out to them.

PART FIVE

Transcendence

"The most authentic thing about us is our capacity
to create, to overcome, to endure, to transform,
to love, and to be greater than our suffering."

—Ben Okri.

Chapter 31:

The Reclamation

July, 2017

Fingers poised on the keys, I signed on to Facebook to send a private message to my other big sister, Debbie. What would I say to someone I knew when I was 4 years-old? As I alternately typed and deleted one drawn-out sentence after another, the empty text box and blinking cursor convinced me that simple was best.

Me: *Hi Debbie. Do you have any time this week to meet up and chat for a few minutes? I'd like to talk with you about Louise.*

I also called Louise's best friend, Liz Smith, and left her a message. "If you are the Liz who was friends with Louise Tefft, can you please call me back? I'm Louise's little sister Julie, and I'd like to talk with you about her."

After a surprisingly short few minutes, I heard a ping from the messenger app on my phone. It was Debbie, responding to my PM about meeting up.

Debbie: *Hi Julie, well I work second shift, so it would have to be before 2pm.*

Me: *That's good. How about Friday? Do you drink coffee?*

Debbie: *Why yes, I do.*

Me: *How about if I buy you a cup of coffee—you name the place and time—and I'll be there.*

Debbie: *How about Thompson Dunkin' Donuts around say 1:15pm?*

Me: *Sounds good. Thanks. I really appreciate this.*

Debbie: *No problem kid.*

* * *

That Friday morning, I swept, mopped, dusted, scrubbed, and polished the main floor, basement, and the loft. When I caught myself alphabetizing the bookcase, I grabbed my journal and flumped into a lounger on the deck.

In just thirty minutes, I had to leave the lake house to meet Debbie. I was both thrilled at the prospect of seeing her and increasingly anxious. What would I ask her? What if she didn't remember or didn't want to talk? My hands trembled as I brushed away salty tears that trickled down my cheeks into the corners of my mouth. Fear of disappointment. Fear of treading into uncharted waters. I sniffled and wiped my face. I hadn't talked with her since I was 4; I'd never spoken with her about Louise.

The surface of the lake churned in broad, swirling currents. Kids squealed and giggled on the opposite shore. An engine revved. A breeze rustled the oak leaves and mussed the feathers of songbirds at the feeder. I glanced south, past the old Quaddick Cemetery where Tammy and I did gravestone rubbings, all the way to the far end where the towers used to be, where Louise swam with Debbie and me in the summers. The last place Louise stopped before she went to the camp trailer.

Why did they hang around with him? Why did they trust him? A strong breeze chilled my bare arms as I jotted down questions that I hoped Debbie could answer.

* * *

A light blue Pontiac sedan was the only car in front of the coffee shop when I arrived. As soon as I pulled into the adjacent space, I recognized Debbie. Her hair was short, but still light blonde—with a little help—and her smile lit up the entire block. She stepped out of the car dressed in mauve scrubs, grinned, and opened her arms wide. "Oh, honey."

We wrapped our arms around each other, and I swallowed hard. When she called me *honey,* the sound of her voice unearthed something ancient. The pure, unconditional love I had for her, and for my sister Louise.

We made small talk—*Where are you living? What are you doing for work?*—ordered iced coffee and found a small table in the corner.

Debbie secured the lid and swirled the plastic cup. "So, you want to know about Louise. What did you want to ask me?"

"I was so young. I remember bits and pieces. What was she like?"

She wiped her brow dramatically. "Whew. Okay." She chuckled. "*That's* a relief."

I took the lid off my cup and stirred my coffee with the straw. "What did you *think* I was going to ask?"

"I thought you might be mad. Like, why did I let Louise leave with Taylor?"

"Oh. No. I don't blame you, Debbie." My heart felt the misplaced guilt she had clearly been holding on to all these years. I reached across the table and held her hand. "I know enough about Louise to know she was stubborn like the rest of my family."

She tilted her head from side to side. "Still, I wonder. What if I'd have made a bigger deal of it? I mean, I asked her where they were going, but it wasn't like I told her *not* to go."

I nodded. I knew survivor's guilt well. The what-ifs, the *why did I survive and not them.* "I just don't understand. She was so smart. Why did she trust him?"

"He was older but still just part of the group. We *all* hung around together. All different ages, alcohol made us friends—we all partied together."

"You dated him, right?"

Debbie looked down, nodded, and took a sip of coffee. "Yeh. He was mean after we broke up. But I never thought he could do *that*."

"I believe you."

She continued to explain that a bunch of stuff had come out during the investigation. None of their friends realized how dangerous he was. "He hung around at the Butts farm and worked with two of the Butts kids at another farm in Woodstock. The Spaulding farm. He was different. A little crazy. Some of the younger guys looked up to him." She set down her cup, clearly not comfortable talking about Taylor. "But you asked about Louise."

I smiled. "What's your favorite memory?"

"Well, we had some crazy times. But one that really stands out is smoking pot with her behind St. Joe's church."

I shook my head and replied sarcastically, "I knew she was a rebel, but behind the *church*? Nice." "Well, yep. We were kinda crazy."

"I have good memories of you. And hanging around with everyone."

She leaned back and waved a hand through the air. "We used to take you *ev-er-ee-where*! You'd be standing up on the front seat or in the back of the car laughing, smiling, blabbing away. You loved it. You were so cute. We took you to the West Thompson dam, the towers, the state park, Coach's Corner for ice cream, everywhere."

I grabbed a napkin from the dispenser and dabbed my eyes. I realized why I felt abandoned. From camaraderie, car trips, and swimming—to silence, stuckness, and disconnection. I realized why I had been drawn to befriend women Louise and Debbie's age all my life. I had been trying to fill the unfillable emptiness of death.

We talked for over an hour about anything and everything, just like sisters who hadn't seen each other for a long while. We hardly drank any of our iced coffee. I knew she had to go to work at the nursing home. "I don't want to make you late," I said.

We walked out together. "You should come over to the lake sometime for a boat ride," I said.

She smiled. "We should get together soon. You're so cute! You're *exactly* the same as I remember you. A little taller, but not much!" We laughed.

I hugged her so tight I didn't want to let her go. I was holding a part of my life that existed when Louise was alive. In so many ways, being with her was like spending time with Louise.

"Love you," she said.

"Love you too," I replied, feeling the powerful and instant recall of a bond unfazed by tragedy or time.

Something else Debbie said was particularly satisfying. "*You're exactly the same as I remember you.*" Somewhere within those words was anchored a profound truth, fixed and permanent. I hadn't *lost* Louise. Abiding by the contract of silence, I had blocked everything out. Including my feeling of connection. As I drove home crying wet, blubbery, pull-over-so-you-can-catch-your-breath kind of tears, I knew exactly *why* I had blocked it out. It hurt like hell.

* * *

A couple of months passed without a return call from Liz. I accepted that I either had the wrong person, or she just didn't want to go back to that time and place. It was one week into the fall semester, and both floors of the library at Gateway Community College in New Haven were congested with students learning how to do research, slogging through the stacks, and struggling with MLA format at the computer stations. I sat in a cubicle on the ground floor in the quiet zone, getting ready for class. As I clicked through lecture slides, my cell phone lit up with a Massachusetts number. I assumed it was my sister Robyn calling from work. I returned a few student emails and noticed I had a new voice message.

I held the phone between my ear and left shoulder, half listening until I heard a gentle voice say the phrase "Louise's best friend." Every atom in the universe hung suspended in time. Instantly it was just me and the voice.

The message continued. "You called me in July, but I couldn't understand the message. I never use that number. I only check it about once a month. It's always telemarketers. I played the messages just today and heard yours. I could barely make it out. I was your sister Louise's best friend." I dried the corners of my eyes with my sleeve. *Collect yourself. You're in the library at work.*

Liz left her cell phone number and an offer for me to call her back. I scanned the room, feeling like everyone was staring at me, waiting to see what I would do next.

In that moment I was tangled in a knot of disbelief, joy, and sadness. Just hearing those three words, *Louise's best friend*, made me want to rest my head on the desk and sob. I hadn't expected this. Without warning, 1973 had called. And I had to pull myself together and give a geology lecture on plate boundaries? I stuffed my laptop in my bag and climbed the tall, center staircase of the library.

I walked out into a long corridor that stretched the entire length of the community college building. The large windows and cathedral ceiling gave a sense of limitless potential. Inspirational quotes covered the walls. One by Martin Luther King Jr. caught my eye that day. "Hate cannot drive out hate. Only love can do that." For decades I had been silently supporting my family by harboring hate and anger toward Taylor. But that would never bring me closer to Louise.

I climbed two more flights toward my fourth-floor classroom in a mental struggle to pack forty years of accumulated emotions neatly away for the next hour and fifteen minutes. My heart beat faster. *Maybe I'm out of shape. Lots of stairs. Wipe your eyes, fix your collar. Breathe.*

I proceeded to give a lecture about convergence, stress and the occurrence of earthquakes and volcanoes at plate boundaries. Unpredictable, deadly events with the power to heave, crush, and bend continental slabs of rock, transforming life and landscape. The solid earth was a welcomed and much needed distraction. At the end of the class period, the students asked a few questions and filed out. I collected my papers into a messy pile and crammed them into my bag. I wanted to listen to the voicemail again.

I sat in the driver's seat of my car, alone in the cement cave of the parking garage basement. I played Liz's message three times, memorizing her voice, her words. The sound of her speaking Louise's name.

I arrived home, made dinner, and gathered the courage to call Liz.

"Hi, Julie, yes—I remember you! Louise's little sister. Tiny, little Julie. Bright blonde hair, three-years-old. So adorable!" She chuckled. "You're probably a little bigger now."

I laughed and wanted to cry at the same time.

Liz continued. "I am—I was—Louise's best friend."

I liked that she used present tense first by mistake. "Yes. Thanks for calling me back."

She apologized once again for taking so long to get back to me. Her words spilled out quickly. "What questions do you have? I can tell you anything. She was a shy girl. We were both virgins. She was very shy and kept to herself, but she wasn't afraid to speak her mind."

"Mmhmm. Okay." I was taken aback by her candor, but the characterization sounded familiar. Dad had described Louise as an introvert, hard to get close to. Her guidance counselor at school had said she was known to press a point on occasion.

"What questions do you have about Louise?"

I didn't waste any time. "Why did she go with Taylor? Why was she alone with him?"

A brief pause, as if she might have been expecting me to ask about Louise's favorite food. "We wanted to be popular but didn't fit in. I had dyslexia and wasn't good at school. Louise was really smart, but she was shy. We hung around with the wrong class of people."

"Uh-huh." I listened intently, jotting down some of what she was saying so I could reflect later.

"In high school, people who wanted to fit in but weren't good at anything joined gangs or did drugs for attention. We didn't do drugs, but we liked to drink." She chuckled in reverie. "Boone's Farm apple wine. It was 99 cents a bottle."

I recalled what Tammy had said—that Louise could be reckless with drugs. And that Debbie's favorite memory was smoking pot with Louise behind the church. I thought about how some people are like gems, showing different facets of themselves to others.

Liz continued. "Louise liked to hang around the Butts Farm. She liked Chris Butts, he was Taylor's best friend. Taylor liked me. He was— well—strange, but I *never* thought he was like *that*." She was quiet for a moment. "I had to identify her clothes. I was a mess afterward. I kept seeing Louise in my dreams at night." Another pause. "Spent three years in counseling." Her voice trailed off. "Couldn't get over it."

I felt guilty. I could sense her anguish over the phone. I never knew she was asked about Louise's clothes. I had been processing this for a while, but for Liz, it must have been jarring. "If you can't or don't want to talk about this I understand," I said.

"No, I'm fine now. I can talk about it. I just have another call coming in. Let me take this. It's my granddaughter. I'm driving. Can I call you back in a couple of hours?"

"Sure. Yes, of course." The call ended and I was lying on the couch in 2017, staring at the ceiling. I couldn't believe I had just spoken to Louise's best friend.

There was so much more I wanted to ask her, but between her and Debbie's responses, I had begun to accept the reality that I would never have all the answers I sought. That there was *no* person who could explain Louise's choices on the evening of June 17, 1973. She decided to go with him. She thought it would be fun. She didn't think she was in danger; none of them did. Some people had fragments of truth, but no one knew enough about the monster to warn her, except for Taylor himself. Maybe in some ways I was still searching for someone to blame. Some bit of new information that would finally make sense of all this. But my journey confirmed the sentiment in DeVita-Raeburn's book on sibling loss--that sometimes the only sense you can make of something is that it doesn't make any sense at all. Maybe, finally, that will be enough.

I stepped out onto the front porch at The Ocean House and watched a band of dark clouds approach. Gusty winds tinged with the smell of rain whipped sand and dry leaves in a chaotic frenzy. The sky crackled and boomed with electricity as a band of severe thunderstorms rolled through West Haven. It was tornado weather.

I decided to go to the gym while I waited for Liz to call me back. My cell phone always within sight, I did the circuit, glancing at the screen after every set. Nope. No call yet.

Around 9:00 pm I arrived home, flopped onto the bed and dozed off, phone in hand.

* * *

Liz never called back, and I wasn't really surprised. Perhaps she feared returning to a place that she and her sanity had barely escaped. I was grateful that she was able to speak with me at all. Both she and Debbie helped me to realize that from my 4-year-old perspective I had thought of them as big girls, but they were just innocent kids unaware that a killer lurked among them.

After talking with Debbie and Liz, I used their stories to link the tattered memories in my head and the feelings in my heart. I had circled back to the seventies and gotten to know Louise again. Reclaiming her rightful place in my heart, and in the parts of my personality that she and my extended family helped to shape, in the four short years we were together.

I had a clearer understanding of her choices. I could stop blaming her for leaving me. She was just 16, trying to find her identity, trying to connect. Exploring people and places, taking foolish, immature risks, not thinking of consequences. She was being a teenager.

I can't change the past. I can't physically get Louise back any more than I could get my 4-year-old self back. But this journey was never about living in the past. It was about learning, understanding, and connecting. It was about reclaiming the memory of my sister, finding my way past the saddest wall ever built, and taking my family with me.

I miss Louise every day. I am deeply indebted to those who were willing to share feelings, memories, laughs, tears, and regrets. I learned and remembered so much about the intelligent, independent, self-righteous, young woman that Louise was. Thank you, Debbie and Liz, for giving me the confidence to reclaim the memories of my sister. They do not belong in the pages of a police report. They belong in our family scrapbook. Where she is alive and well and living her life.

Chapter 32:
Leo's Service

On August 4th, 2017, Louise would have turned 61. I ran my Swiss Army knife along the edges of her gravestone, brushed off the clippings, and placed a bouquet of roadside daisies on the lichen-splotched granite. I sat down on the lush, green carpet, slid off my sandals and pressed my bare feet into the cool grass. A fleecy brown bunny with a white puff of cotton on its rump hopped among the gravestones. It nibbled on clover and occasionally paused to sniff the air. It was just me, Louise, and the bunny as I talked to my sister.

"I think of you and miss you, Louise. Happy Birthday. I got together with Debbie in June. We talked about our amazing adventures. It made me happy but sad at the same time. I'm sorry for the way you were taken away from us. I'm sorry you had to go through that. We'll never forget you." I sat quietly for a few minutes and watched the rabbit disappear among the wetland ferns at the edge of the cemetery.

As I drove out past the church where Louise and Debbie had smoked pot, the sound of the church bell startled me. *Clang. Clang. Clang.* Three jolting rings. I glanced down at the clock on the dashboard. It was only 2:57. I shook my head and smiled. Was it Louise saying thank you? *You're welcome Louise. I guess you liked the flowers.*

On the way home I stopped by the grocery store, bought a small ice cream cake, and stashed it in the freezer at The Lake House. The sun was starting its afternoon dip toward the horizon as I walked down to the dock with my life jacket and launched my kayak. I paddled across the lake, admiring the glossy green foliage that had completely recovered from the gypsy-moth-caterpillar assault last summer. With each stroke, the blade of my paddle created a wake of tiny eddies in the amber-colored water, stained like tea from the tannic acid of the oak and maple leaves.

I leaned back, doing an aquatic version of the limbo, and floated under the Brandy Hill Road Bridge, through a meager passage too low for motorboats. My face about two feet from the girders, I glanced up at intricate webs with brown spiders the size of quarters, lying in wait. The pungent smell of petroleum from the creosote-soaked boards dissipated, as I returned to daylight on the other side of the bridge. Once into the larger and deeper section of the upper lake, the beige sand of the state park beach was visible in the distance, beyond the white and red swimming buoys that looked like floating propane tanks. Several families enjoyed the afternoon sun, as they picnicked, swam, and built sandcastles. The park limits were demarcated by newish, large homes, some three stories tall, crowded together along the shore.

Gently wriggling free from people and progress, the arms of nature drew me closer. After another mile of paddling, the lake became a shallow soup, thick with milfoil and pond lilies that bloomed in satiny petals of pastel yellow and pink. I crossed under the narrow bridge on Baker Road where my brother Kevin and I used to go fishing. Where I used to swim until the day I had seen a hefty, black water snake the size of my arm, coiled and soaking up the afternoon sun on a hot, flat rock.

The undeveloped shoreline along this section of the lake called Stump Pond was guarded by an army of mountain laurel, swamp azalea, and high-bush blueberry. It was where more than four decades ago, Dad used to back his boat trailer down a hidden, grassy drive and launch his Jon boat. He sat on one of the bench seats, casting for bass and pickerel, while I leaned over the low gunwale, swept my tiny hand into the water, and trolled for lily pads. Just beyond the launch to our left was the site of the lone camp trailer with the screened-in porch, perched on a hill in the pine forest.

Forty-four years later, I was at the same spot, carving through a skin of lily pads, scanning the land for a clearing among the trees, or perhaps the raised cement cover from the old well—looking for traces of the last place Louise went. The trailer was long gone, having been taken away some time after the summer of 1973. The abandoned shoreline was overgrown with weeds and a dense barrier of woody brush. Perhaps nature's attempt to heal the land from sin and sorrow.

My kayak drifted into the weeds where sticky webs clung to the bow, and my forearm. I dug my paddle into the soft sediment and pushed off, back into deeper water. A flash of bright white tail feathers caught my attention. One of the resident pair of eagles who nest at that end of the lake circled and glided silently overhead. With its six-foot wingspan, the bird of prey soared above the tops of hundred-foot white pines as I leaned back, admiring its freedom and fearlessness.

On the long paddle back to the lake house, I thought about how good it felt to recognize Louise's birthday. After 44 years, I made the decision to celebrate her life, rather than recoil at her death. And I wanted to set a new precedent.

* * *

I lashed the kayak onto the storage rack, grabbed the cake from the freezer and drove to The Compound. Eric and Dad were up on staging, replacing clapboards at one end of the house. As daylight was ending, we put away the tools and went inside. Mom washed her hands while Eric heated water for coffee. I set the shopping bag on the table and slid out the cake. "Mom, can you get me a knife to cut this?"

"What are we celebrating?" Dad asked.

"Mom knows," I said.

She turned toward me, wiping her hands on a dish towel, her eyes searching my face.

I helped her out. "It's Louise's birthday."

"Oh. Yes, it is." Mom seemed pleased as she handed me the knife. She never forgot June 17th each year, but this would be our first celebration of Louise's birthday since she turned forever sweet 16.

I opened the cabinet and grabbed four dishes. "I think Louise wants us to celebrate." They gathered at the table as I doled out the cake. "I brought her some daisies today."

Mom handed a mug of coffee to Dad. "Louise loved daisies— Debbie picked a huge bouquet of daisies the day of the funeral and put them on Louise's casket."

"There was a cute brown bunny hopping around the gravestones. Just like the pet rabbits we had," I said.

"Really? Dad and I were at a cookout earlier, and I saw a brown bunny nibbling on some grass not far from the lawn chairs. It didn't seem afraid at all."

I shrugged, and we exchanged a smirk. Beautiful fleecy brown coincidences. Precious connections.

Dad opened the fridge to get milk for his coffee. "I'm almost done replacing the clapboards on the back. Then I'll start on the far end near the road." He returned to his seat at the table.

I passed him a fork. "Clapboards there as well?"

"Yep. And a downspout for the gutters." Dad grabbed the word jumble he had cut out from the newspaper and playfully flung it my way. "Whaddya make of this?"

I flashed him the eyebrow and scanned the riddle.

"There's a memorial service tomorrow for Leo Butts," Mom said. Leo was Tammy's ex-husband and had just succumbed to a lengthy illness.

I glanced up, cake balanced on my fork. Mom doesn't go to wakes or funerals. "Really? Where is it?"

"It says in the paper. I have it right here." She shuffled through a stack of sale flyers on the table, unfolded a newspaper, and handed it to me.

I read aloud. "A burial service will be held at noon at The Coman Family Cemetery, Brickyard Road Thompson." I folded the paper and looked at Mom. "Did you want to go? I can pick you up."

No hesitation. "Okay. That would be good."

What?

"It will? Okay. You want to go. Okay."

While we finished our cake, Dad and Eric discussed the virtues of composite versus wood siding. I ruminated on the significance of Mom going to a burial—and her lightning-fast response. I always knew she liked Leo, but this unprecedented decision would take more than simple fondness.

* * *

Tammy had first met Leo at the party at the Butts' farm the night of June 17, 1973. "I thought he was *so* cute," she told me. "He had a girlfriend, but I didn't care. I flirted with him anyway."

She saw him again the next day. Louise hadn't come home the night before and hadn't gone to school that day. Tammy knew something was wrong. After school she walked to Stratton's spa and past St. Joseph's church. She stood on a bridge over the French River, leaned against the guardrail, and ran down a mental list of possible places to look.

Tammy barely noticed cars as they passed behind her or the lingering idle of the one that had stopped. A male voice startled her.

"What are you doing here?" he asked.

She turned around. It was Leo, the handsome dark-haired boy with the kind eyes from the Butts' party.

"You shouldn't be here by yourself," he said. "There's a girl missing."

"I know. She's my sister." Tammy turned back to the river and stared at the rushing water.

That day, Leo helped her search for Louise. Three weeks after Louise's body was found, Tammy moved into the Butts' farm. She and Leo eventually married and had three children. Leo was not perfect, but during those first few weeks and months after the murder, he, and the craziness of the Butts' farm, filled a gaping hole in Tammy's life. He helped Tammy survive the death of her sister. Perhaps that was the root of Mom's decision to attend Leo's service. A sense of profound gratitude.

I remember being fond of Leo myself. He was a gentle soul, one of the few soft-spoken members of the Butts family. His brown eyes, dark, curly hair, and olive skin all exuded warmth and kindness. He was part of the reason I liked to visit the Butts farm. Tammy wasn't the only one with a crush on him. I thought he was cute too. Sadly, many in the Butts family struggled with alcoholism, and despite how hard Leo fought, it eventually destroyed his and Tammy's marriage.

* * *

The following day I arrived at The Compound around 11:30 and walked into the kitchen. Angela was sitting at the table, lecturing Mom about her garden. "You should have planted rosemary this year."

Mom wore a sour expression. Before I had a chance to ask if she still wanted to go to the burial, Mom zipped her purse, grabbed her jacket from the back of the chair, and turned to me. "Are you ready to go?" She didn't appreciate advice on her garden. "I don't know where the Coman cemetery is," she said, walking past me toward the door.

I glanced back at Angela and shrugged. "I don't either, but I hope we can find it."

Mom sat in the passenger seat, brown leather purse clutched in her lap, as I drove across town and into Woodstock. In the absence of road signs, I found what I thought was Brickyard Road. Motoring slowly along, we noticed several cars turning onto a private dirt drive that led into the woods. "Do you think that's it?" I asked, more to myself than Mom. "I bet it is."

After another half mile, the winding gravel gave way to a one-lane grassy path with a line of cars parked on the right. Around the next corner we reached a wide clearing occupied by several mud-splattered pickup trucks with big knobby tires. Bottles of Jack Daniel's and Wild Turkey adorned the hoods. "Looks like we're here." I parked beside one of the trucks.

We walked toward a white canopy set up just outside the stone-walled cemetery. A stew of people milled about, smoking cigarettes and tipping back brown bottles of Budweiser. It was as if we had driven through a time warp and arrived in the 70s, with most everyone still wearing their bandanas, ponytails, and center parts. But they were four decades older, slumped by life and today by grief. Their hair overtaken with gray or gone. Their arms covered with faded green and blue hand-drawn tattoos on skin creased by many years of working in the hayfields.

We said hello to Maverick Butts, one of Leo's 14 siblings. Six-foot three, full beard, and cigarette hanging from one corner of his mouth, he set down his bottle of Bud, bent over and hugged Mom. "How's retirement treatin' ya'?" he asked.

She responded by telling her tale about her escape from Day Kimball Hospital, referring to her stay as "the time they tried to kill her."

Mom also recognized Dave Butts, Leo's cousin. People still called him Pee Wee. All the Butts kids still had their nicknames earned in adolescence, as if 15 names weren't *enough* to remember. Leo's was Skunk.

Mom stopped to say hello to a couple of people she knew from her days working at Cumberland Farms. I noticed Chris Butts leaning against the front fender of his car, sidled up to a bottle of liquor. He had been friendly with Taylor before the arrest. Statements from the police report filtered into my mind. Chris had searched for Louise. He told police that

Taylor had been acting strange and confirmed that he had seen Taylor wearing the flannel shirt that was pulled from the well at the trailer.

Louise had had a crush on Chris, and he knew it. But he liked Debbie. It was typical innocent teenage drama. They *should* have grown up together.

A familiar voice broke my thoughts. "Hey! How have you been, Ma? Remember me?" It was Kellie, an old high school friend of my sister Nicole. She rushed over and gave Mom a hug.

"Hi," Mom said. "*Of course* I know you. You used to sleep over all the time."

Kellie laughed and turned to me. "Yeah. There was this one time Nicole and I snuck out to smoke with our friends. We thought we got away with it, but when I was leaving next morning Mom asked us: *Where'd you girls go last night?*"

I glanced at Mom and nodded.

Kellie continued. "We tried to deny it and play stupid, but she snapped at us: *Why are your shoes all wet then?*"

"Yep. I could never lie to her either," I said. "She always knows."

We all laughed, but it was true. Mom noticed every detail and it used to drive me crazy, but at that moment, her unusually sharp instincts finally made sense. It was hypervigilance. Always searching for anything that didn't belong. Things that might indicate potential danger. I espoused her strict attention to detail. Despite its tragic roots, it makes for a great scientist.

We found a seat, but most people remained standing. Leo's sister, Wendy Butts, was a preacher and gave the sermon without notes. Tammy and Leo's daughter, Jessica, gave a brief, heartfelt speech about her father. Two other women also said a few words about Leo's life, and the Butts men walked around slapping each other on the back and toasting Leo. They were gruff farmers and bikers with little use for sentiment. They loved each other and didn't need to spew a bunch of fancy words to show it. Mom and I signed the guest book, took a prayer card, and lit a candle for Leo. Divorce or not, he was part of our family too.

I turned to one of his brothers. "Will his ashes be buried here in the cemetery?"

"No. We're probly gonna take 'em to the middle of the fourteen-acre field, light 'em up wid black powder and blow 'em sky high. Skunk woulda liked that."

I smiled and nodded. "Right."

It was a Butts event through and through. No airs. This was the way they lived and the way they honored the dead. We said our goodbyes and got in the car. Mom helped navigate as I backed up and turned around amidst a sea of people and pickup trucks.

"I'm glad we went," she said.

"Me too. It's good to pay respects to people."

She fidgeted with the strap on her purse. "We should have called Shane. He might have wanted to come to this. I should have called Tammy last night."

We reached the pavement of Brickyard Road within a couple of minutes. I searched for a station on the radio. "Do you want the air conditioner?"

"No. It's fine." Mom tucked Leo's prayer card into her purse and set it on the floor. "You know, Tammy testified against Taylor in court."

I shut the radio off. Tammy had mentioned this to me before. "I can't imagine. She was only fifteen."

"She was afraid to look at him. She glanced up just long enough to point him out to the judge. To say that he's the one Louise left the party with. That was when she noticed his purple shirt. She said she'd never forget the cold feeling in the courtroom or the sight of that purple shirt."

The car was quiet for a few minutes. Purple was the color Dicky painted Louise's room after she died. Did it remind Mom or Tammy of the shirt? I exhaled, trying to unwind myself from that thought.

"The Butts' never change, huh?" Mom said.

"They are characters."

She nodded. "I always liked Leo. He used to call me *Ma*. Even after the divorce."

We talked more about Tammy and Leo and the colorful memories we each had of the Butts farm. I dropped Mom off at The Compound and went to the lake. She called me an hour later.

"I just got off the phone with Tammy. She was so glad we went to the service. She was on her way, but when she got to Fairlee, she got nervous and turned around. She didn't think anyone from our family was going."

"Oh, that's too bad." I surmised her anxiety was similar to Mom's. Louise's funeral did a number on her too. "Well, I'm sure she understands. I should have called her. I bet she's really happy we went."

"Yes. And I told her that we had cake for Louise's birthday yesterday, and she thought that was a *great* idea."

I smiled and looked out across the lake. It felt good to keep my promise.

"She wants us to come up and visit her soon."

"I would love to. We should definitely do that."

* * *

A few days after Leo's service, I walked into the kitchen at The Compound and Mom was baking. "It smells amazing in here!" Louise, Tammy, Mary, and I all loved to bake with Mom. It's a tradition that the new family shared as well.

Mom shuffled over to the counter and grabbed a knife from the butcher block. "I made peanut butter and jelly cake." She cut a big piece and handed it to me. "Do you know who found that recipe?"

I shook my head, mouth full of cake, licking jam off the ends of my fingers.

"Louise did. She copied it down from a *Ladies' Home Journal*."

Mom hadn't made it in decades, yet the flavor and texture were instantly familiar to me. This was Mom's little way of sharing something so meaningful to her. It's her way of saying *I do remember Louise. I do think of her.*

Louise had loved to bake, and she copied the recipe from a magazine onto a 3-by-5-inch card. Mom tucked it into the little tin Keebler recipe box. The top of the box was painted to resemble a red-tiled roof and the front of the box showed a kitchen scene of three Keebler elves gathered around a table, baking in their kitchen. Mom sent off for it through the mail with 99 cents and three box tops from saltine crackers; the ones Tammy and Louise dared Shane to eat while sitting under a blanket over the heat register in the floor. No water, and as many saltines as you could eat.

I hadn't seen that recipe box since I was a kid. I thumbed through the cards and pulled out the recipe for the PB&J cake. Flour, eggs, peanut butter, strawberry jam. It wasn't the ingredients that held my interest, but the shape of the letters linked together into words. It was Louise's handwriting. I pressed the card between my palms and smiled.

"There's one in there for a wheat germ drink. You wrote that one," Mom said.

Although it seemed we were separated into discrete little corners of her life, Louise, Tammy, Mary, and I could all be found nestled together in the 3-by-5 cards of that little tin box. It was a reminder that Bardys have a titanium exterior, but they *are* vulnerable. They just don't see the point in broadcasting it.

Recipe for PB&J cake:

2 ¼ cups flour

3 tsp baking powder

½ tsp baking soda

½ cup shortening or butter

2 eggs

½ cup sugar

1 tsp vanilla extract

½ cup milk

½ cup creamy peanut butter

¾ cup strawberry jam

Pre-heat oven to 350 degrees; grease 9" x 13" cake pan. In a large bowl, sift together dry ingredients, set aside. In a medium bowl, whisk/beat shortening (or butter), eggs, sugar, vanilla, milk, and peanut butter. Add to dry ingredients. Stir in Jam. Spread batter into pan and bake for 20 to 30 minutes, until toothpick inserted in center comes out clean.

Chapter 33:

From the Ashes

September, 2017

Eric took the helm as Mom, Dad, and my niece Genny stepped from the dock onto the pontoon boat. We'd invited them over for a late summer tour of the lake. Genny's cell phone rang as I threw off the dock lines.

"Auntie, can we pick up my grandma Joyce? She's at a picnic across the lake."

I swept a hand toward Eric. "Ask the captain."

"The more the merrier," Eric said. "Tell her to be ready."

He punched the throttle, and the boat lurched forward, squashing us together. He chuckled. At that speed, it took less than a minute to cross the lake.

Joyce waved and hurried to the floating dock. As she stepped onto the boat, she joked, "I have a noontime reservation for the deluxe lake tour." Joyce radiates kindness in all directions and is well-versed in the concept of bent but not broken.

"This tour includes the bird-watching package," Eric announced. I pushed away from the dock and we cruised slowly, on the lookout for herons, swallows, mallards, and Canadian geese.

Once we were underway, Joyce turned to me. "Oh Julie, I went to the cemetery in Webster and saw your sister's stone. It's beautiful."

I beamed. "Thank you, Joyce." It warmed my heart to think that others could and perhaps would visit Mary too.

Joyce continued. "I remember little Mary. She was in the ER with your Mom for an asthma attack and I had brought my son Drew in for the croup. He was just a baby. Mary was so sick herself but came up to us before she left and said *I hope your baby feels better soon.* She was such a sweet little girl."

I could feel Mom's attention on both of us. I smiled. "Mary always thought of others. Thanks for sharing that memory," I said.

Mom swung her feet back and forth, her petite frame allowing them to clear the deck. "My father is buried there too."

"Is your mother with him?" Joyce asked.

"No. I have her ashes in the living room, but I should probably bury them before she gets *really* mad."

Everyone chuckled. But it was true. Grandma's ashes had sat, wrapped in plastic and sealed in a blue chipboard box on the entertainment center since 1996. And no, I imagine she was not happy about it.

Grandma's name had been carved into the beautiful monument of Barre granite, along with Dziadzia and Little Mary's before the stone was set in the cemetery. The burial was only awaiting Mom's decision. And after 21 years, it seemed as though she was finally considering it.

Eric stood up from his captain's seat and pointed. "Look. At the far end of the cove. A pterodactyl."

A wave of laughter. I shook my head and gave him the eyebrow. "It's a *heron. A great—blue—heron.*"

* * *

It took more than four decades, but I finally figured out that no Bardy will ever be pressured into a decision. I called Mom the day after the boat ride. "I'm not going to bug you about it, but whenever you're ready to bury Grandma, just let me know."

"Who do we need to contact? And how much will it cost?"

"Valerie said we should contact the funeral home."

"But we didn't have a service for Grandma."

"That's right. I guess it would be Paul, the caretaker, then."

I called Valerie, but Paul was on vacation until the second week of September.

"Can you call back mid-week that week? That will give me a chance to talk with him," she said.

"Sure. No problem."

"Oh—I have to tell you—your determination about your sister inspired me to get a memorial stone for my father. He died over thirty years ago. I feel so much better."

I smiled as I felt my eyes fill. "It's important to honor the people we love. It sets something free in the world—for me it was something I didn't even know I was holding on to. I'm sure your father is happy to be remembered."

In a small way it was my action that had brought Valerie to get the stone for her father. But on a deeper level of course the credit belonged to Mary. Because her little heart was so powerful, the love she brought into the world was *still* working magic to help others.

✳ ✳ ✳

Grandma's burial was set for 10:00 am on Friday, September 22nd. The plan was to meet first at The Compound. Eric and I took separate vehicles so he could run errands after the service. Mom, Dad and Robyn were talking in the front yard when we arrived.

Mom picked up her purse and sweater from the stone wall. "Okay. Let's go." She marched toward the car.

Eric waved his arm toward Dad. "C'mon Bob, you can jump in with me. Let the women go with Julie."

"I'm taking my own car. I have to go back to work," Robyn said.

When I got into the car, Mom had her seat belt buckled, purse on the floor, and sweater folded neatly in her lap. "Do you have Grandma?" she asked.

"She's in the bag behind my seat."

We left the yard and headed to the cemetery. Mom smoothed the folds of her sweater. "What will the hole look like? How deep will it be? Will I have to see Dziadzia's casket?"

"Paul told me it would be a small, rectangular hole about two feet deep. It won't be as deep as Dziadzia's casket." I turned on the radio and searched for a news station.

Our caravan of three vehicles parked one after another in a neat row near the St. Peter's section. Dad, Eric, and Robyn walked ahead, gathering at the family plot. I grabbed the bag with the urn. As Mom and I approached the gravestone, she paused and turned to me. "You can't see the casket, can you?"

I walked ahead a few steps and then turned back to her. "No. It's not that deep."

We joined Eric, Dad, and Robyn who were standing around the grave engaged in typical banter, as if we were at the kitchen table at The Compound. Mom was quiet.

How was this supposed to go? I had never been to a burial with my parents. I had only been to church three times that year. I couldn't rattle off prayers from memory. Anyway, I didn't want to take over. This was Mom's call.

"Hey." Robyn turned her attention to me. "Remember decorating the Charlie Brown tree at Christmas time?"

"Of course I do. I was scrubbing sap off my hands for a week after. What about black coffee and fried baloney? What kids have *that*?" I added. We stood around reminiscing. None of us had planned any formal agenda, except for Mom.

She let us continue for a minute, and then called us to attention. "I have some prayers that I want to recite." She peered at each of us in turn. Robyn and I glanced at each other, then clasped our hands and bowed our heads.

Mom's voice was soft but clear. "Auntie and I used to kneel by our beds and say these prayers with Grandma when we were kids." A tug at my heart. I imagined her at the house, in moments of solitude, perhaps walking up to the horse barn to feed Miss Lilly, thinking about which prayers would be best.

She recited The Lord's Prayer, Hail Mary, and Glory Be. We joined in as best we could as she prayed with her mom one last time. A few birds chimed in from nearby branches. We shared a moment of silence after the prayers. Having the chance to say goodbye surrounded by family was comforting. I hoped Mom found comfort and peace in being able to honor her mother's life.

"Oh, I almost forgot," I said as I reached into my bag. "I brought photos to share." I passed around some pictures of Grandma at different stages of her life: her and Dziadzia's wedding; standing near the garden at the farm; baking with Mom and Auntie; visiting with uncle Frank; and a photo of her rocking in the chair by the wood stove at The Compound, when Mom and Dad were taking care of her. Mom lingered on each of the photos, fingers pressing the curled edges. She smiled at the one of her, Auntie, and Grandma in the kitchen, hands and aprons dusted with baking flour.

After glancing up at the overcast sky, Eric lifted Grandma's urn out of the bag. "Let's give Grandma a goodbye kiss." I glanced at Mom, curious if she would buy into such a display. She reached out without hesitation, held the urn in both hands and pressed it to her lips. I recalled the way we would line up in front of the rocker each time we left Grandma's house. One at a time she would hug us and hold our head with both hands and kiss us on the cheek. Another tug at my heart. That experience, that day, I felt the full force of the mother-daughter-sister bond.

We drew closer and watched as Eric carefully placed Grandma into the tiny rectangular grave, resting a few feet above the love of her life. The man whom tea leaves had predicted she'd marry. Mom reached into her purse and took out a Ziploc bag. It looked like dirt. It *was* dirt.

"I brought this from the garden at the farm," she said, sprinkling the clumps of the rich brown soil into the grave. Such a simple act yet imbued with so much love. Mom had taken time to go to the farm and scoop some soil from the garden, bringing her parents a piece of the land they loved so much. Land that had been a source of physical and emotional strength. She was full of surprises. A deeply sentimental woman whose stoicism was a thin, stiff veneer over her true nature—able to fold like soft chocolate. Bent but not broken.

Chapter 34:

Fearless.

June, 2018 (four years after the coffee shop conversation with Dad about Mary's grave)

I gravitated toward that place. Like the inescapable pull at the boundary of a black hole, so intense that no light can escape. It was Sunday June 17, 2018. And it was Father's Day. The anniversary of Louise's murder. A *Perfect Storm* of triggers sucked me into the dark funnel of the grief loop. My thoughts were consumed with justice for Louise. I felt compelled to go to the site of the camp trailer. I wanted to take back every last thread of her memory, and I needed to make peace with that place in order to do it. I had reclaimed her memory from the police report, and now I wanted to take it from the scene of the crime.

The old path to the camp trailer was barricaded with boulders and hadn't been used in decades. I pulled off the road as far as I could, passenger door scraping against the bushes. My heart drummed inside my chest. As I stepped out of the car and scanned the surroundings, a dead silence left me feeling exposed and vulnerable like a field mouse. I locked my car and began threading my way down the overgrown path, deeper and deeper into the woods. It would be getting dark soon, but whatever force compelled me was stronger than fear. We *needed* to go—Louise and me—back to that place and time when she was still alive.

Thorns scratched at my ankles as I stepped over fallen branches, through woody brush and witchgrass thick with spider webs that clung to my arms and face. The smell of pine sap tinged the summer air. My feet followed what used to be a gravel drive, two parallel ruts with an eroded central berm, overtaken by thorns and vines.

After a few hundred yards, I reached a familiar fork in the path where Kevin and I had veered left over a sand barricade with his Honda-100 dirt bike. With me on the back, he rode down an embankment and around the cracked and sunken pavement of the old, abandoned racetrack. I leaned to one side and looked over his shoulder as we whizzed along the straight-away until it dead-ended in a swamp. I imagined fans cheering and shouting from the dry-rotted and half-collapsed wooden-plank grandstands. We weren't supposed to go there. Mom had forbidden it.

I moved past the fork, keeping to the right. Dry leaves and pine needles crunchy and slick underfoot. Overgrown branches of wild raspberry thorns scratched and lodged into my forearms. I paused every few yards, peeled them from my shirt and trudged on.

As I neared the crest of a small hill, the brush thinned, and splotches of light from the sinking sun filtered through the canopy of white pines. A sudden, strong breeze sent a wave of goosebumps up my forearms. The shoreline was in sight. That was the place.

Shadows shifted in shape and color. A contorted, haunting play on light. The rustle of leaves. The sound of crunching in the space behind me. I spun around, froze in place, and held my breath. What was there? A chipmunk? A bird? The call of crows shrieking from somewhere in the nearby woods shredded my last bit of courage, but I wasn't leaving there without her.

I wanted to do what I wished Louise had done. She sat on that grassy slope by the water, unsuspecting—if only she had turned around and run for her life, for her family. We needed her to live. She was just a kid.

In my mind, I grabbed her hand tightly, turned back, and ran--racing to get beyond the shadows, beyond the strange noises, beyond the feeling that evil was crawling on my skin. Away from the spot where the camp trailer sat in 1973, back toward the road, back in time before Louise made the decision to be alone with him. Wishing she had realized the pull of the black hole before it was too late.

Time was lost. Everywhere and nowhere. Running for her life, for my life, for the sake of honoring our family. Poison ivy slapped my feet and ankles, bugs swarmed my head, branches snagged my exposed legs and arms, flip flops nearly flew off, snapping against the soles of my feet, heart racing, head pounding, chest and face sweaty, sticky, left hand clutching my keys. Where was my phone? A flash of panic—had I dropped it? Oh. I was holding it. I just ended a call with Mom. I slowed down to get my bearings.

She had called me just as I had turned away from the vacant site, overgrown with rhododendrons and mountain laurel, shaded by towering white pines nearly seven decades old. The camp trailer was gone, but that was the place.

"Where are you?" Mom had asked. Her voice sounded suspicious. Did she know where I was?

"I'm headed back—to the lake house," I huffed, rushing to escape. But the sound of her voice was an instant comfort. I slowed my pace from frantic to hurried. "Just went for a walk in the woods."

She had told me what she made for dinner, and suggested Eric and I stop by. Her presence gave me courage. It felt serendipitous that she had called. There we were, Mom, me, and Louise at that camp. As the light of day faded, I wanted to get us the hell out of there, leaving the tragedy behind. Taking Louise's memory out of that place so we could remember how much we loved her, without being consumed by the crushing pain of losing her.

"You sound a little out of breath," Mom said.

"I'm rushing to the car—before it gets dark. I'll call—when I get back to the lake."

The clamor of crickets and spring peepers grated against my eardrums and up into my temples. Mosquitoes with pointed siphons buzzed and swarmed, an army of blood-sucking memories. I gripped my phone, my keys. I ran. Toward the car. Faster. Out of that forgotten place where people had dumped old toys, tires, and mattresses. No part of Louise's life belonged there.

The clearing was just ahead. It was getting hard to see. I didn't want to be there in the dark on that day. Especially that day. I ran toward the last few degrees of twilight. I ran for Louise. Moss covered road, two old tire paths, and rusty orange sand shifting beneath my feet. Predator and prey. The end of the innocence. I cried loud, soaking, angry tears. Come with me Louise. I'm taking you out of this place.

We drove back along Quaddick Town Farm Road, past the state park, took a right on Quaddick Road and drove past the dirt road to the towers. I imagined the hands of time moving counterclockwise as I travelled opposite the route she took in 1973, *out* of the Thompson woods. It was another ten minutes to the King's Inn near the highway overpass, where she had her last drink. Then back further, a final ten minutes traversing hummocky farmlands, to the 14-acre field at the Butts Farm in Woodstock, where the party had been. I sat in my car by the stone wall for a moment, imagining Louise near the light of the glowing fire pit saying: *No, I'm not leaving the party with you. I'll stay with Tammy and Debbie.*

If only it were that simple. If only a car ride of her last fateful trip could reverse the events of that night. I thought about how difficult murder is to understand. If Louise had been killed in an accident, or by an illness, would it be easier to accept? Thinking about the deliberate way she was ripped away from us made me so angry. He had no right. I forgave the day, I forgave the place, and I forgave Louise. As much as I try to forgive Taylor, my anger toward him rages like an unchecked wildfire. Yet I know he is dead and is burning in hell.

I never expected closure. In my experience, it's a term used by those who've not been mauled by loss. So what did this journey bring to me and my family then?

It has become clear that as much as I want to help Mom and Dad, it can't be done in the way I imagined. I can't speed the process of grief, take away their sadness, or reach into their brains and replace traumatic memories with peaceful ones. Triggers will remain. And every spring Mom will begin her descent into the grief loop. On June 17th she will be devastated all over again. Every year Dad will remember when Louise wished him a happy Father's Day and drove out of the driveway for the last time. My promise to do whatever I could to help them was a promise I will need to honor for the rest of our lives.

The compelling need to answer Mom's soul-wrenching question, *"Did she suffer?"*, took me to unforeseen places. It gave me the confidence to reach out and connect with a life that I felt exiled from. In the end, the answer wasn't spelled out in the 248-page police report as I had expected. Instead, it came from conversations with state police, local detectives, with Dad, Tammy, my half-brothers, Louise's best friend Liz, my other big sister Debbie, and with Mom herself. It materialized when I found the courage to reach out and get to know my sister Louise.

I realized her strong will and conviction would never allow her to be a *victim*. She didn't bargain or beg for her life by making desperate promises to cover up his crime. Louise sacrificed her life to preserve her dignity and uphold her belief in right and wrong. Her fearlessness protected other teenage girls from a deadly serial predator. My sister Louise was a fiercely bright and uncommonly brave teenager. And after reading 248 pages of what my family went through during this whole ordeal, I'm sure I know where she got her strength. From Mom and Dad.

Louise made two promises: that she would tell the police, and that the killer would not get away with it. Although she was not physically here, she managed to keep both.

Louise did not suffer. Suffering implies passivity to some degree, and passive she was not.

I know that, because I *know* her. I *am* her.

We share the unbreakable mother-daughter-sister bond, and more importantly, we are Bardys. With that, I bang my fist on the table and say out loud just like Grandma: *My mother wasn't afraid of anybody, her mother wasn't afraid of anybody, and I'm not afraid of anybody.*

I know that we have all suffered for Louise and perhaps sometimes and in some ways we always will. But I am finally ready to embrace my Bardy inheritance. It has taken 45 years, but I am ready to say that I am much closer to fearless now than I ever was.

And it all began with Little Mary. My journey to honor her put me on a path of reconnection, where I learned about the indomitable nature of that name and all that it means to my family. From Little Mary to Mom, to great-great grandma Mary, the tea leaf reader, in all these Marys, as I examined the tapestry of my heritage, I traced back threads of myself and gathered the strength to reclaim buried memories.

In the end I needed to find Mary so that she could fulfill her last unfinished task as my big sister. To help me find her grave, question the contract of silence, and most important of all, to help me, Mom, and Dad grieve—for her *and* for Louise. I hope this journey has brought some healing to Mom and Dad.

As a wise person once wrote, *We remember them so that there is not death.*

They remain a part of us when we reclaim their rightful place in our family.

They must not be forgotten.

They will be remembered.

Acknowledgments

This book was made possible with the support of the following beautiful souls: Mom and Dad for helping me understand and sharing their memories with me; my sister Tammy, my other-big-sister Debbie, and Louise's best friend Liz, for helping to gather information and sharing difficult memories; Kristen Orr, for her enthusiasm; and my husband Eric, who read countless revisions and cried with me, because he understands the pain of sibling loss.

I sincerely appreciate the beta readers (Melissa, Pete, and Dan) who volunteered their time to read and comment on an early draft, and my writing groups for their encouragement and thoughtful feedback: The New Haven Intrepid Women Writers, The Worcester chapter of Soul Sisters Writing group, Hank Herman and the participants of the Mark Twain and Trinity writing workshops. The Brooklyn-NYC writing/social club, and my friend Erin, who invited me to write with her in Arizona and who inspires me to continue writing. Thank you to my editor, Rachel whose skillful suggestions helped me tighten the manuscript considerably.

Many thanks to the Rose Reading Room at the New York Public Library, The Mark Twain House, The Wisdom House in Litchfield, Kripalu in Lenox MA, the Apple Tree Inn in Lenox MA, The White Mountains National Forest, The New Haven Free Library, The Branford Library, The Milford Library, The West Haven Library, Barnes and Noble in Worcester and Milbury, and Starbucks on Sawmill Road in West haven, for providing space to write and revise. Many thanks to the Breathing Room Yoga Studio in New Haven and The Abode of the Message in New Lebanon NY, for helping me stay grounded and focused as I wrote.

My entire family is eternally grateful to Frank Griffin, Paul Guillot, and the Connecticut State Police, who worked tirelessly to get justice for Louise, looked out for my family for decades after, and never forgot my sister's name. Finally, to retired detective Larry Guillot, thank you for setting aside your own grief to selflessly help resolve mine.